Yoga inVision 4

mental lifting force

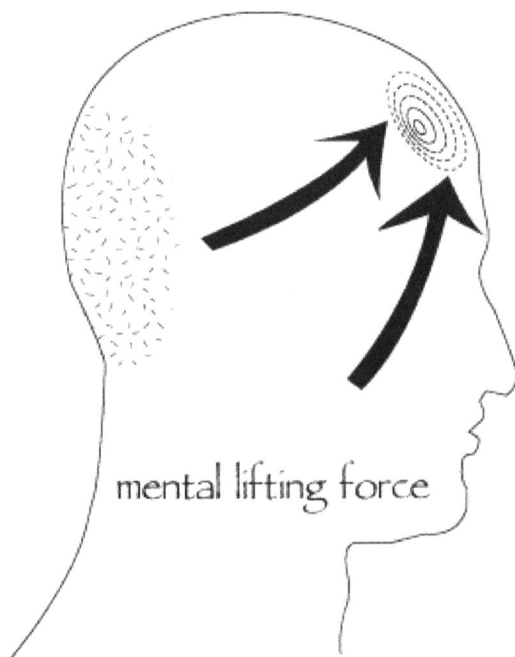

Michael Beloved

Shiva Art:	Sir Paul Castagna
Illustrations:	Author
Correspondence:	

Michael Beloved
19311 SW 30th Street
Miramar FL 33029
USA

Email: axisnexus@gmail.com
             michaelbelovedbooks@gmail.com

Paperback ISBN: 9781942887140
EBook ISBN: 9781942887157
LCCN: 2017902016

Table of Contents

INTRODUCTION

This is the fourth of the Yoga inVision series. These give beginners ideas of the physical, psychological and spiritual experiences one may have when doing asana postures, breath-infusion breath methods and pratyahar sensual energy withdrawal. Beyond that is higher yoga, which Patanjali named the *Samyama* procedures. *Samyama* was defined by him as a combination of dharana deliberate focus, dhyana spontaneous focus and samadhi continuous spontaneous focus since during practice, these progress one into the other. If you are expert at pratyahar sensual energy withdrawal, you will find that you graduate to dharana which is deliberate focus of your attention to a higher concentration force or person. As soon as you are mastering the dharana you may slip naturally into dhyana which is an effortless focus on a higher concentration force or person. Once you practice dhyana, samadhi happens as the continuous effortless focus on a higher concentration force or person.

Many persons who take to spiritual life feel that they can construct a path as they advance. This idea denotes failure. After all, if the supernatural and spiritual environment, is not already there, no one will create it now. It is either there or it is not there. For instance, if you are moving to a different country, then of course you will fail if the country intended does not exist. It has to be there already. Similarly what you are aiming at in spiritual life, must be there already, or you will find that your idea of it is incorrect. This is why I speak of a concentration force or person. I could have said concentration person or divine person, or God. I did not because I do not know how your spiritual path will develop.

You may leave an island in the safest boat and still the vessel may sink. Therefore you have to keep your mind open and be willing to work along with providence. In spiritual development, there is providence too. What you desire to have you may not get. What you wish to see may never appear to you.

These Yoga inVision journals show how sporadic my course of yoga was. This is after years of practice. It gives some idea of what to expect. Once you get through the lower yoga practice, you will see advancement in a more stable way but it will be incremental, adding up little by little, with bright flashes here and there, now and again.

Part 1

On this day I had a tantric sexual experience. While doing yoga in the astral world, a man came to me. He was with his wife. After a while, the man left. Both of them were doing yoga for celibate purposes, but the woman had no success because her sexual appetite was voracious. The man was frustrated because he could not get her body to give up its huge sexual need. The man went away in disgust, instructing the woman to stay with me for instructions.

Looking over her subtle form, I saw that she could not attain celibacy as rapidly as he desired. In any case, suddenly, the woman's subtle form overpowered mine. She then sat on my face. The tongue of my subtle body entered her vaginal passage and then one of my hands also entered, because her vaginal passage was extended, all the way within her body up to her head.

This woman had such a sexual craving that in that parallel world, her body was constructed with such an extra-long sexual opening.

Remark:

This experience is shocking, if not downright revolting and outrageous. One may wonder:

How could such actions be part of anybody's spiritual life?

The answer is this:

There are different kinds of bodies, all depending on the particular dimension in which the form exist. Each body has particular tendencies. After some time with that woman, I was switched out of that dimension.

Muktananda

He said, "Do the uddhiyana bandha, the belly fly-up. Use the lotus posture. Do rapid breathing with the hands on the eyes, closing the ears. Then do uddhiyana bandha and arch over. The fingers should be on the knees, with the elbows out on a curve. Do the fly-up. Pull up the belly. For those ascetics who practiced for a long time, this works to lift kundalini

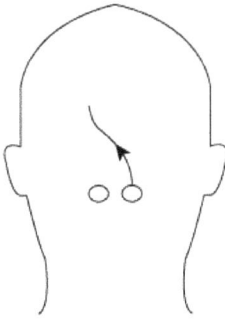

1 — left side in-breath

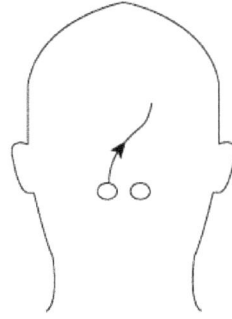

2 — right side out-breath

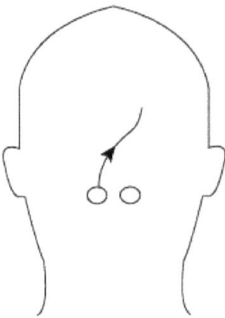

3 — right side in-breath

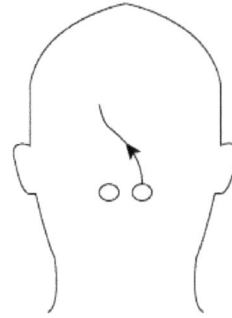

4 — left side out-breath

Arrow line shows movement of infused breath energy in brain

I did this breath-infusion practice for alternate breathing.

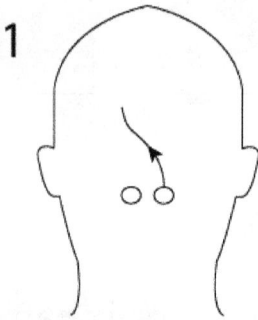

1   left side in-breath

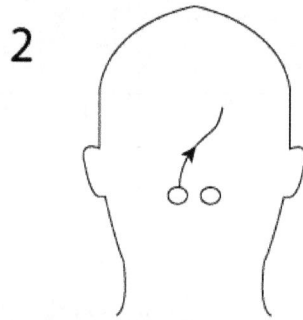

2   right side out-breath

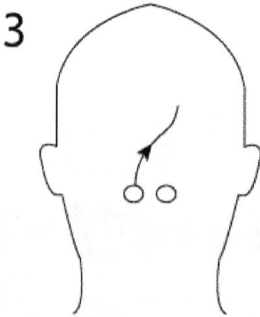

3   right side in-breath

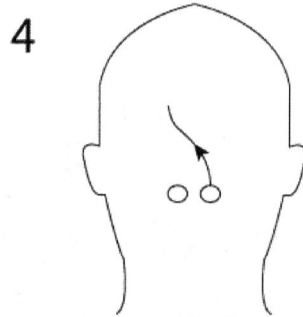

4   left side out-breath

Yogeshwarananda

He gave a woman-thigh stretch.

Muktananda

He gave this breath-infusion practice for alternate breathing.

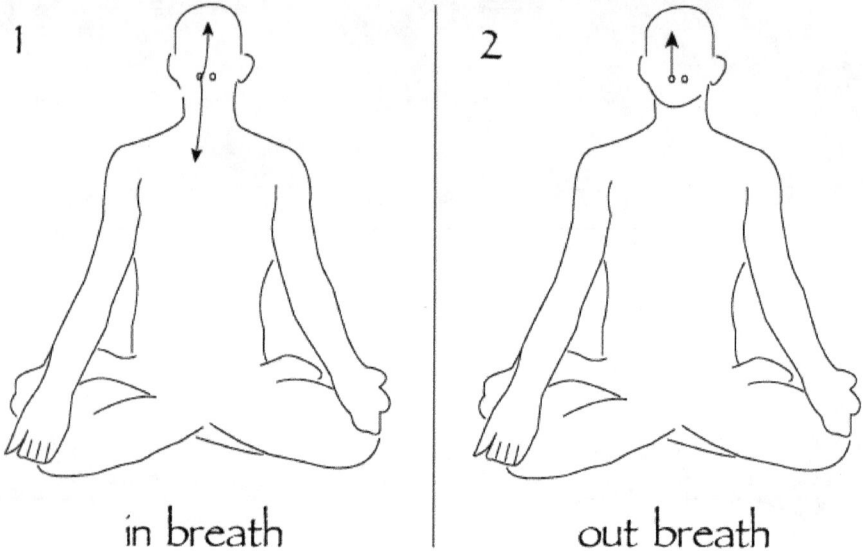

1

2

in breath

out breath

Muktananda

He made some points: He said, "Unless one does breath-infusion one cannot slow the intellect. One cannot control its thoughts, creations and receptions. One cannot reform it. There will be no supernatural vision."

Muktananda

He explained that sugar addiction begins with breast feeding, with milk and affection flowing through the subtle breast of the mother. This affection feels desirable. It is a combination of certain subtle energies. Later, one develops addiction to sugary preparations.

Muktananda

He said, "The subtle body's training is done effectively after the kanda is dissolved. That is when subtle sexual fluid is no longer stored in that body. Instead the energies are evenly diffused with no focusing for sexual purposes.

He gave some instructions for breath-infusion.

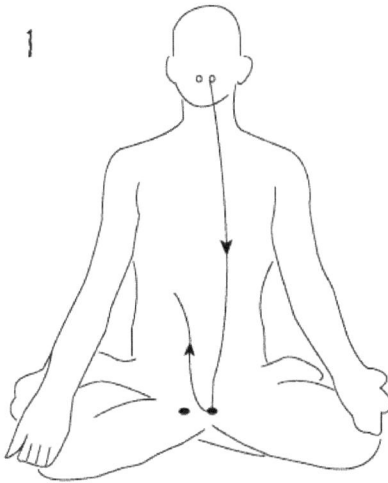

left in-breath   left out breath

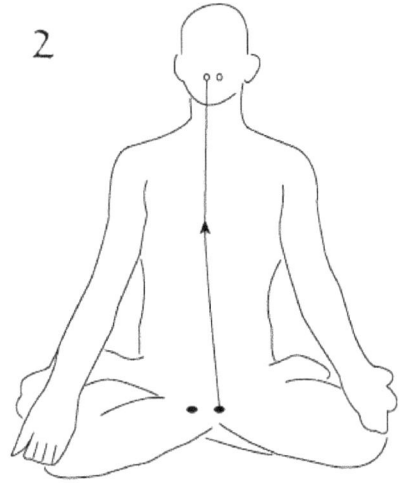

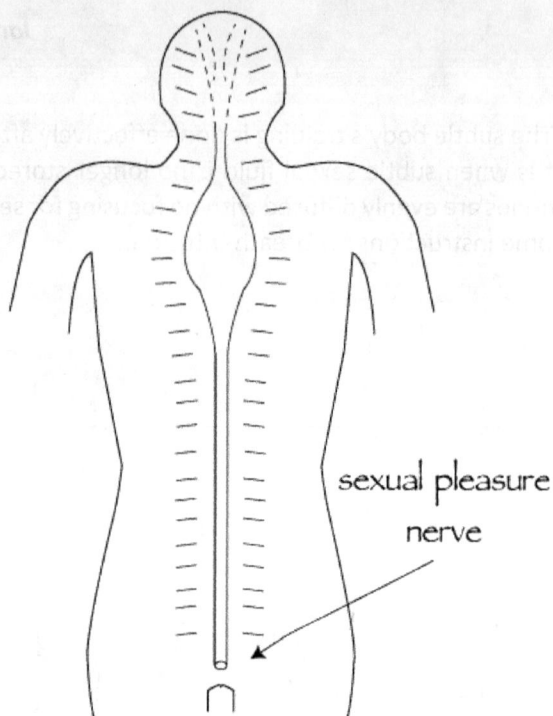

sexual pleasure
nerve

Muktananda

Rooster poses.

As you go down run hands down calves to the sex nerve at the back of the leg, the Achilles tendon. That passage is electrically the same as the spine.

Yogi Bhajan's hand grip

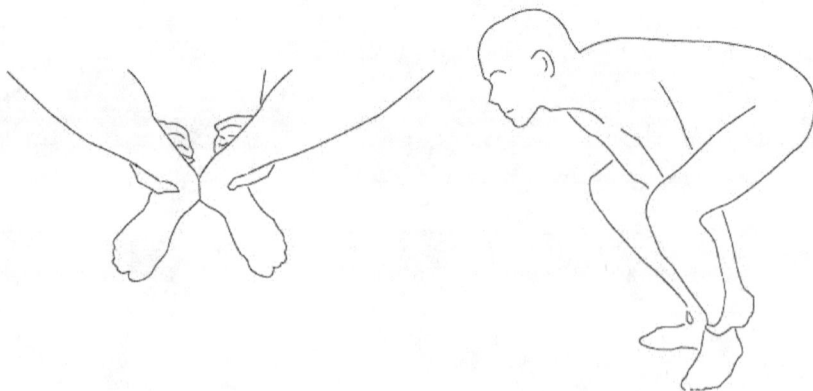

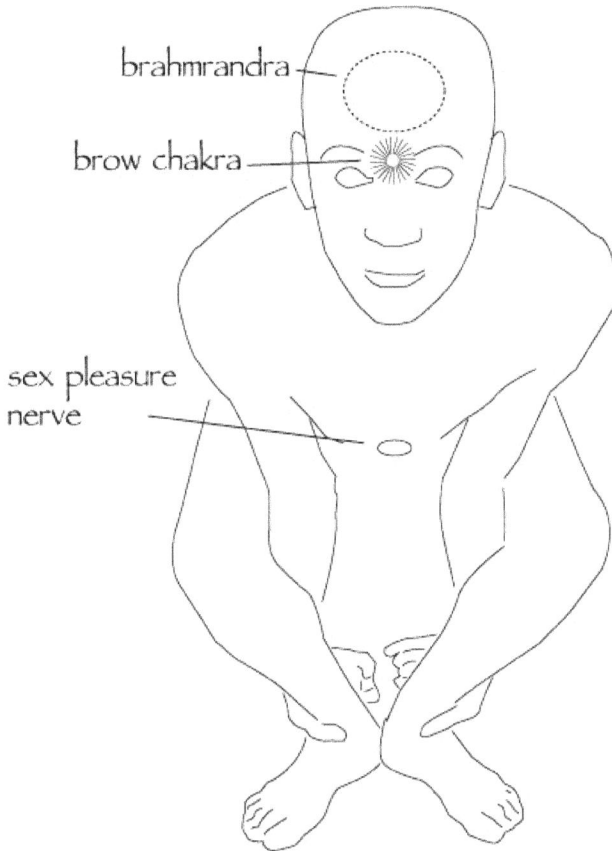

brahmrandra

brow chakra

sex pleasure
nerve

January 12, 2003

Muktananda

He said, "Full absorption focus means no disciples. Each yogi who attained it, did so when he had no disciples. Shivananda, for example, had many disciples who practiced for full absorption but he took these disciples after he passed the student stage. Allowing the intellect to contemplate the problems of disciples is prohibited."

January 13, 2003

Muktananda

He showed a white misty light in the intellect. This becomes manifest in the subtle form of those yogins who take only one meal per day and who do no late eating.

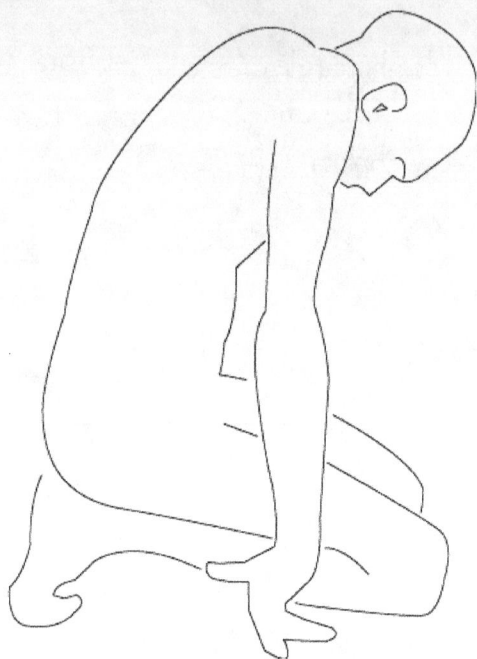

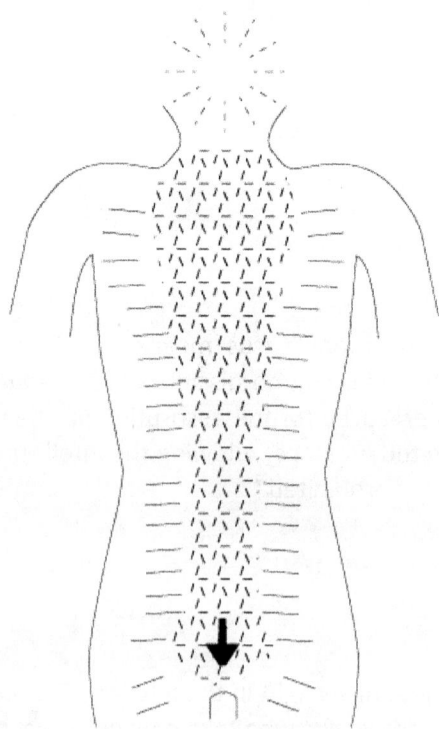

January 13, 2003

Muktananda / Yogeshwarananda

Muktananda said, "Track the small impulsive images and sounds. Sometimes a subjective picture is seen. Track to find its location. Then position the attention there. This positioning of the attention on the exact spot where it appeared, curbs the intellect's imaginings.

January 13, 2003

Yogi Bhajan

He gave a woman's procedure.

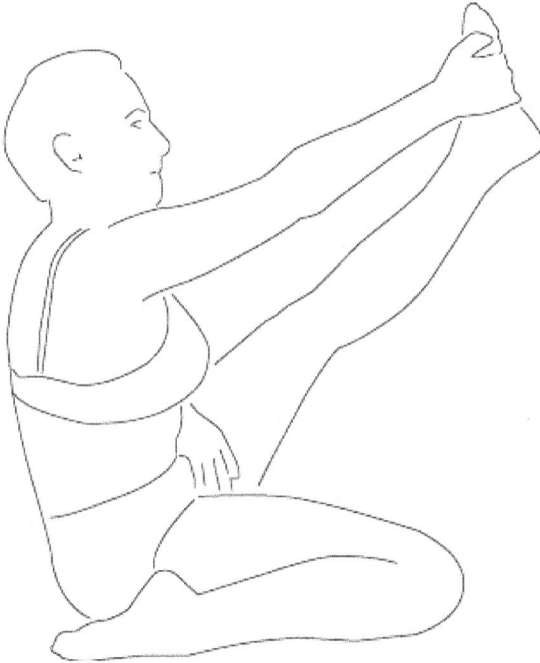

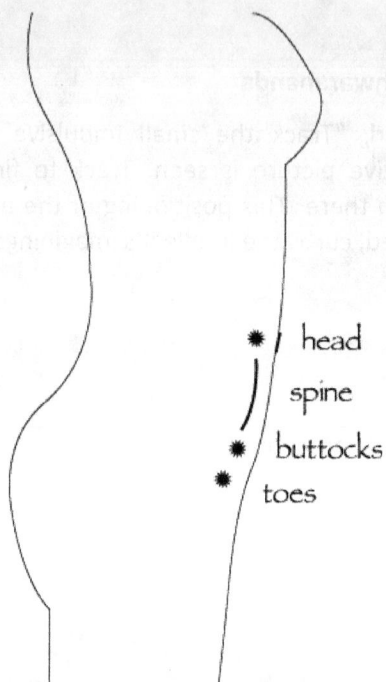

head
spine
buttocks
toes

touch points

January 13, 2003

Yogi Bhajan

He gave this woman's procedure. This is for menstrual discharge regulation. It clears the menstrual ducts and in the subtle form it eventually stops their secretion. One should do the preliminary bhastrika breath-infusion and then do these exercises while surcharging the body with fresh air.

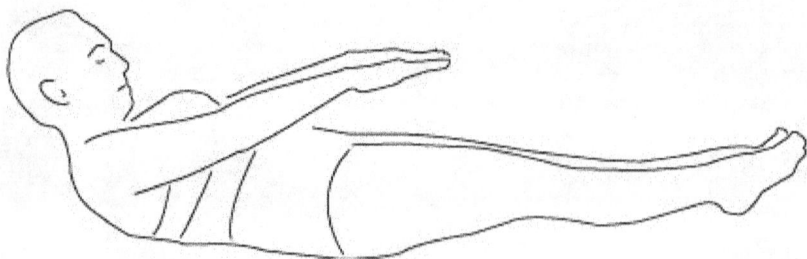

January 13, 2003

Muktananda

He assisted in an effort to restore the subtle body's state before I took birth. That consisted of moving the kundalini energy up above the navel, thus relocating the sexual urges of the body.

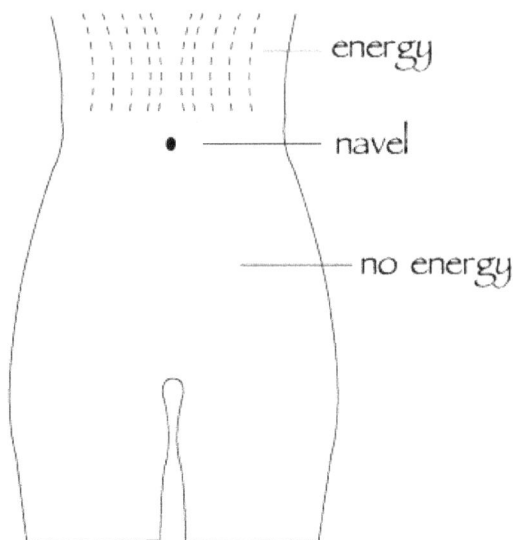

January 15, 2003

On this day, in association with Muktananda, I realized that the intellect's greed for images destroys the efforts for full transcendence absorption.

Muktananda made comments:

"A good session of bhastrika breath-infusion with cooperation from pranavayu, when the energy in the trunk of the body is clarified, is sufficient preparation for doing the dharana deliberate transcendence focus. When there is a thorough session of breath-infusion and much help from pranavayu, one does not have to do alternate breathing."

He showed a technique for seeing into and through the sky of consciousness. This is a focusing skill where one goes to the places in the mind environment where images arise. One stays at these mental locations, while holding the intellect in a stillness while giving it the freedom to visualize thoughts. I asked him if that was a secret process.

He replied, "I discovered how this operates. My guru, Nityananda, did not show this. Mostly in the tradition, each yogi figures out these things for himself."

January 16, 2003

A woman's in-thigh stretch.

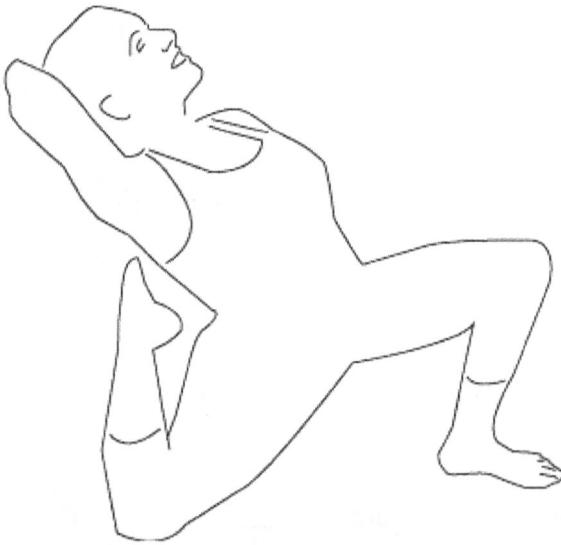

January 16, 2003

Muktananda

He said, "Study both sides of the imagination orb. Look at its reception of ideas. Consider its transmission or contemplation. Use what you observe for controlling the mechanism. Take detailed notations of how it operates. Track its tendencies and functions."

Muktananda

He said, "Do not get involved in the schemes of the intellect. Do not become bewitched. Simply observe how it functions. Note its operations, not its contents."

Remark:

This is an important instruction in the preliminary practice of the 6th stage of yoga practice, that of dharana. In that practice one changes the approach so that one observes the operations of the intellect and not its contents. Generally a human being is bewitched because he helplessly observes the contents of the intellect.

Durga Ma

This Goddess gave a vaginal pump-in-air procedure for females. It is done in the posture below.

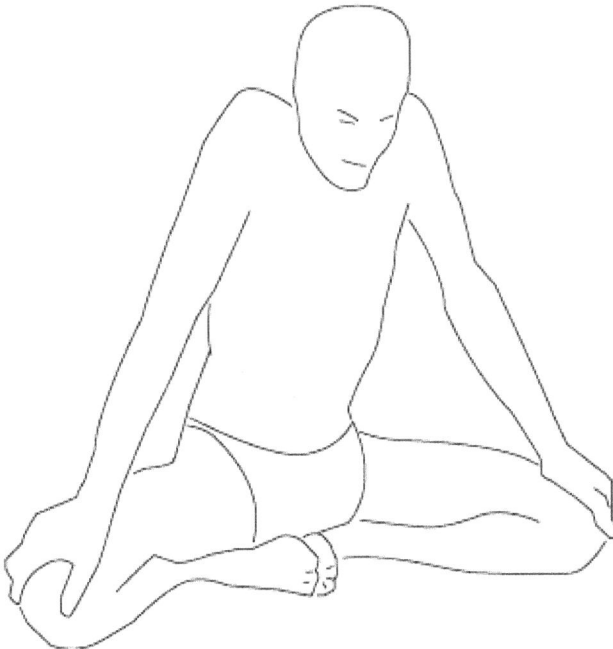

This is another one from the Goddess. This is for the hips of the female body. One should do the first posture shown below which is the cartwheel posture. Then, in the second posture, one should do breath-infusion focusing on the hips.

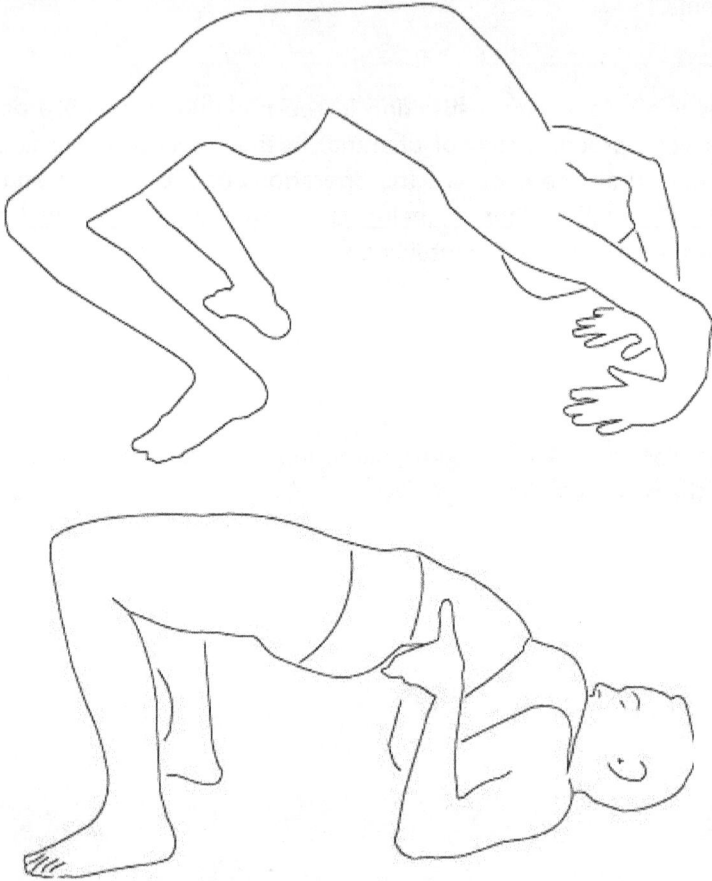

January 17, 2003

Yogeshwarananda

He gave this rooster pose to do with rapid breath-infusion. This works on the back just below the neck between the shoulders.

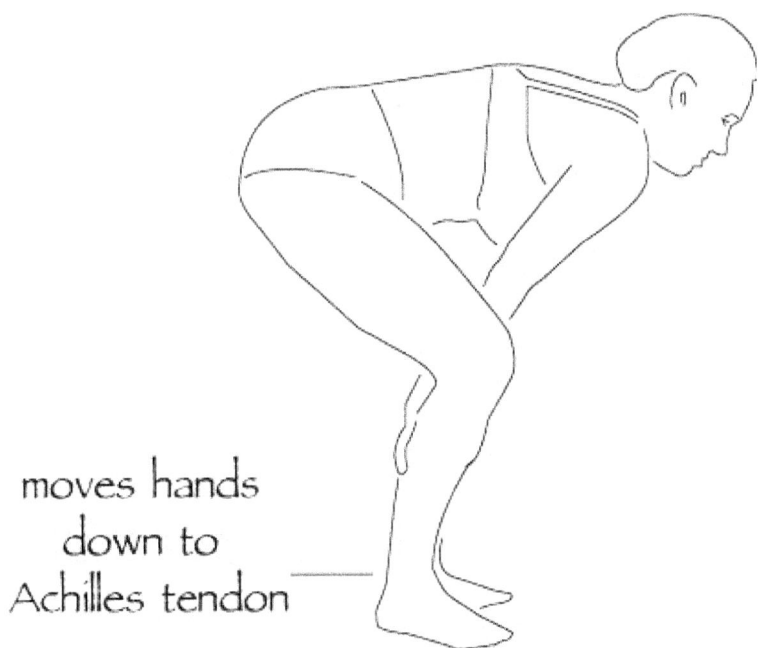

moves hands
down to
Achilles tendon

January 17, 2003

Yogi Bhajan

He gave this woman's kriya. This is for working on the thigh area at the vortex of the crotch.

raise one knee at a time

then raise both knees

Yogi Bhajan

He gave this breast kriya for women.

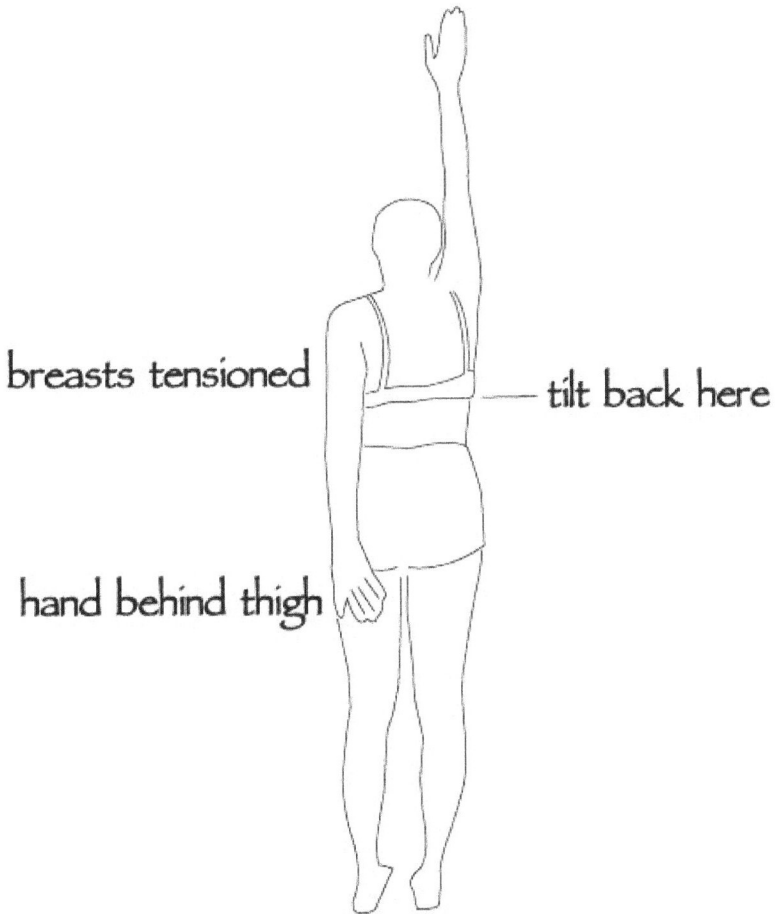

breasts tensioned — tilt back here

hand behind thigh

He also gave this up-under-the-knee and under-the-thighs technique for women.

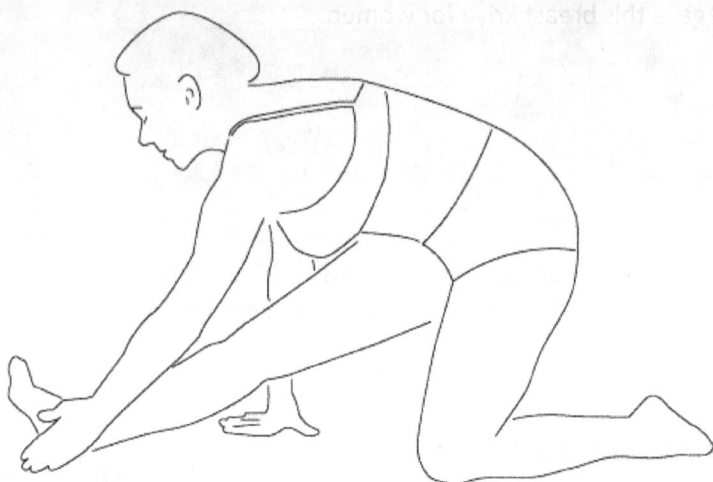

Muktananda

He said, "The intellect eats everything presented to it, even if something is presented that was not observed by the observing-self. It likes to gurgitate impressions received through the senses or recalled from the memory."

He gave a meditation for stretching the imagination orb.

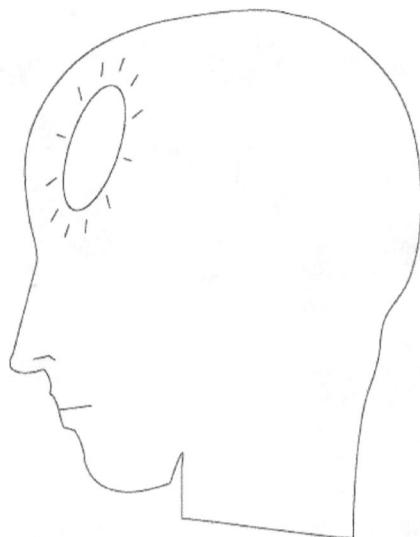

Muktananda

He requested some alternate breathing after I did a session of bhastrika rapid breathing. He said that I should pull up the front space which is a spinal coordinate. He instructed that I catch the intellect's operations and consider how those movements were taken in by the senses or created by the intellect's rearrangements in the imagination orb. He instructed that I stop the intellect from acting. And that I should talk to the intellect for its cooperation and subsequent reform.

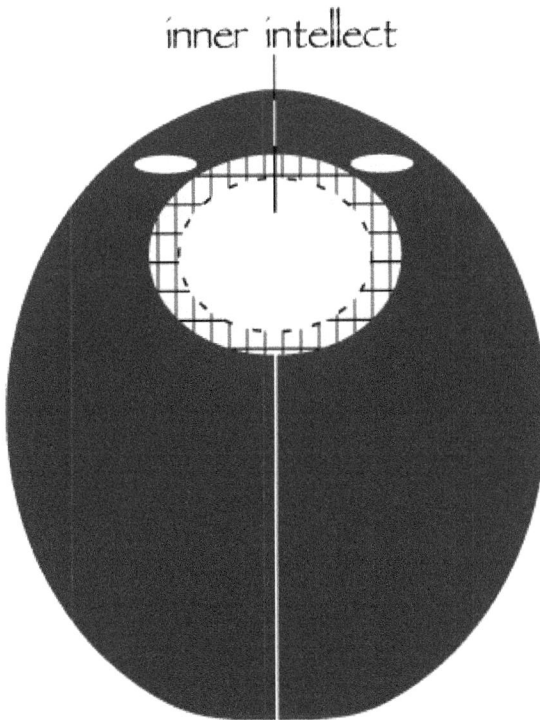

inner intellect

random thoughts,

ideas, images

and undisclosed memories

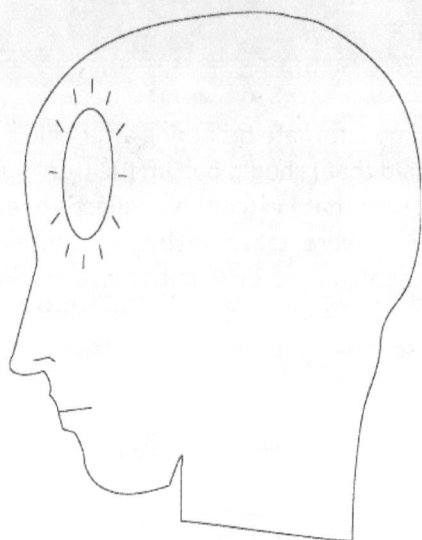

January 19, 2003

These are women's procedures.

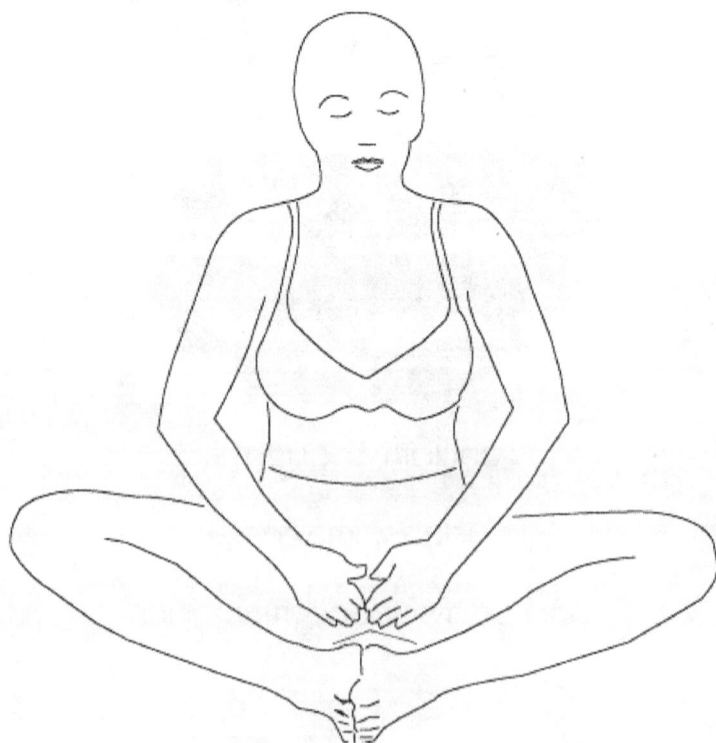

under thigh
vaginal clearance

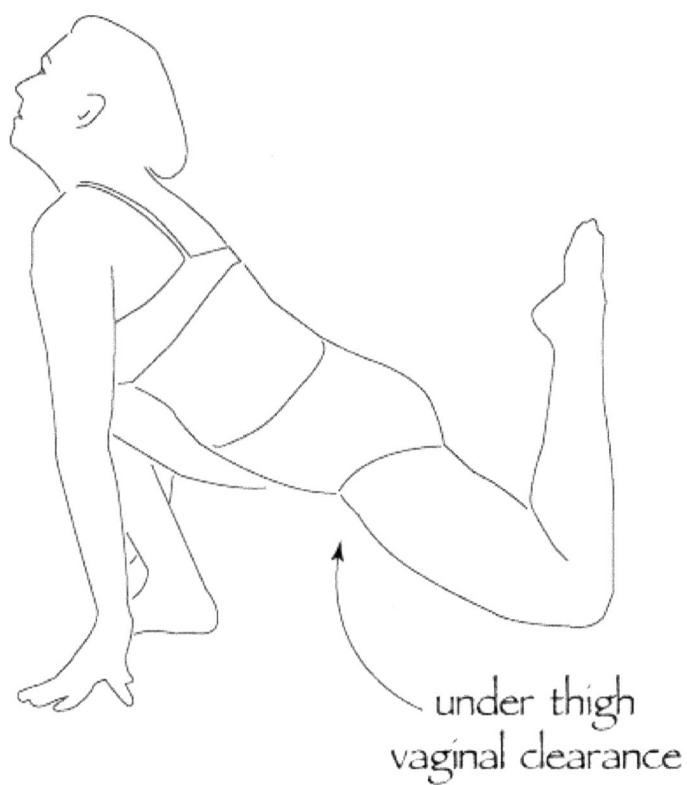

stretch breasts on ribcage

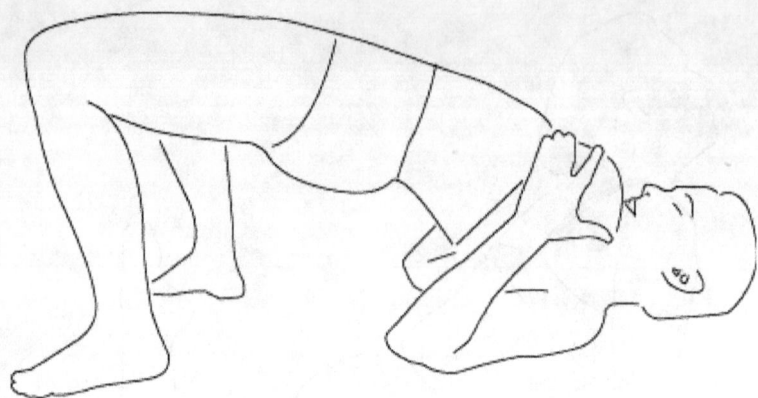

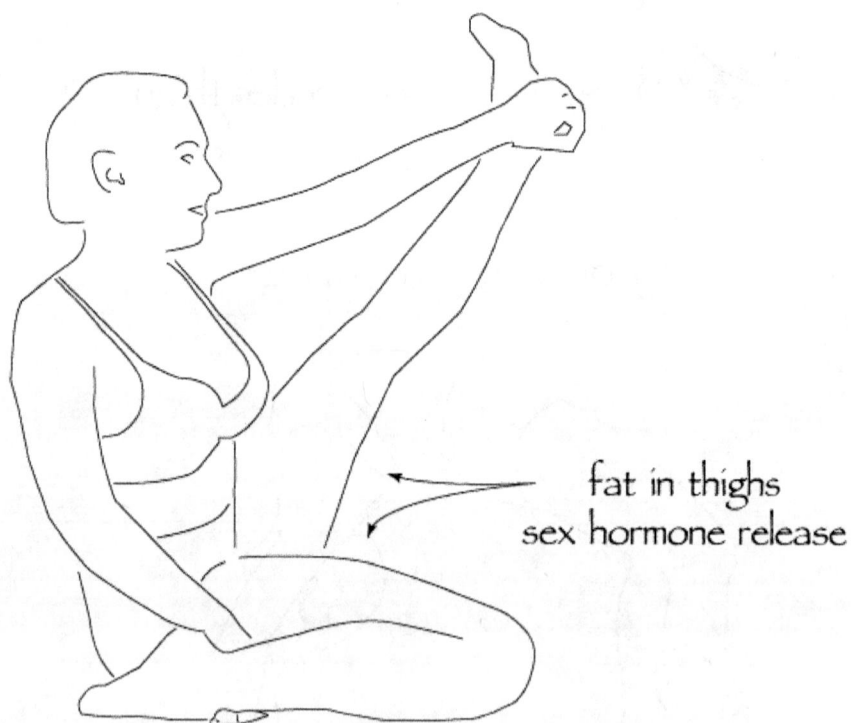

fat in thighs
sex hormone release

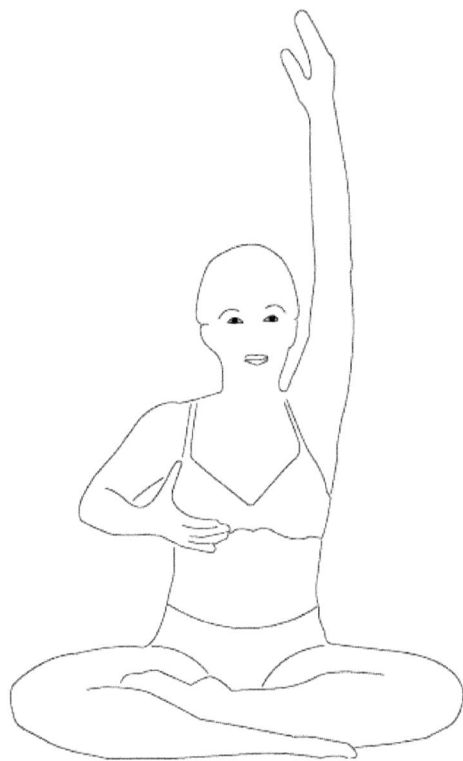

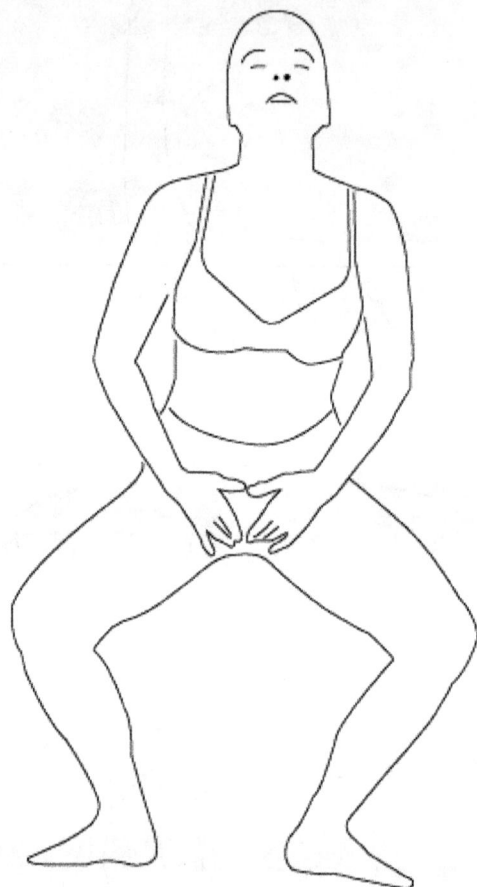

Part 2

January 20, 2003

More women's procedures.

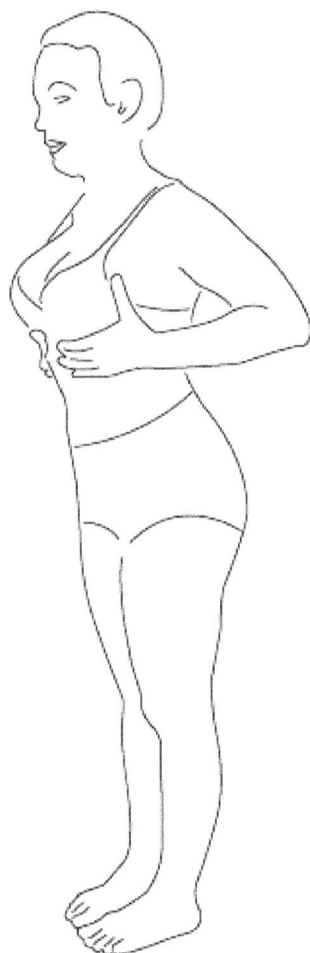

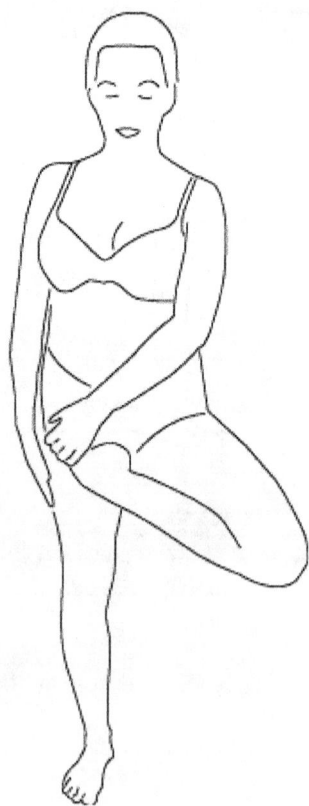

January 21, 2003

This is one for the womb pump-out for women.

This is an instruction for alternate breathing.

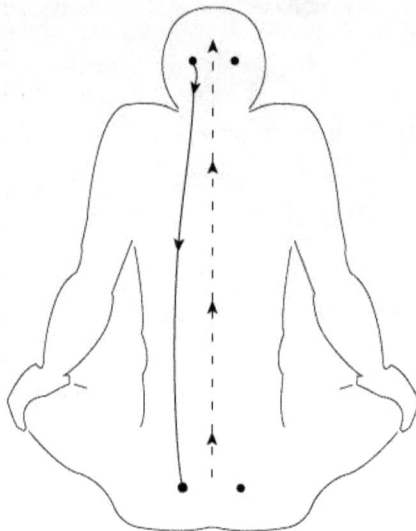

left side in-breath   left side out-breath

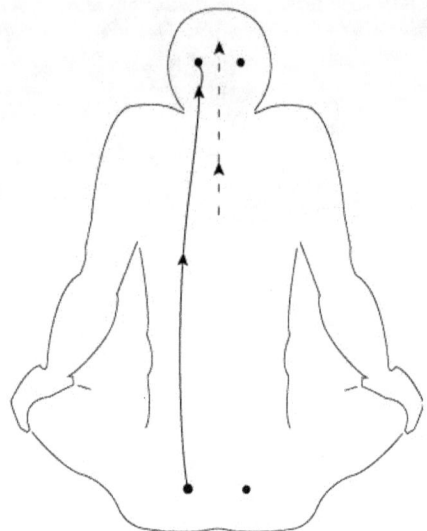

January 21, 2003

Muktananda

He said, "Be sure to time it. Keep track. Keep notations."

Remark:

This was during an afternoon meditation. I saw a warm red-orange ball in the frontal part of the subtle brain. Muktananda suggested that instead of alternate breathing I should do rapid breathing again. He wanted me to make some kumblak breath expulsions while I did the meditation.

My advice is that one should make it a habit to meditate after doing postures, locks and breath-infusion. Even though some very advanced yogis meditate without doing postures and breath-infusion, they get a different experience because their subtle forms are purified. Those who meditate without that purity, do not meditate in the proper way. Of course, if someone has a hectic schedule, he may not have sufficient time to do postures and breathing exercises. He may be satisfied just sitting or lying down and meditating. However, his meditation will rarely give him spiritual perception. It will calm him down and remove stress produced from a hectic lifestyle. That meditation is not the meditation done as a result of yoga practice. Technically speaking it is a form of mind resting or mind sleeping. It is not really meditation.

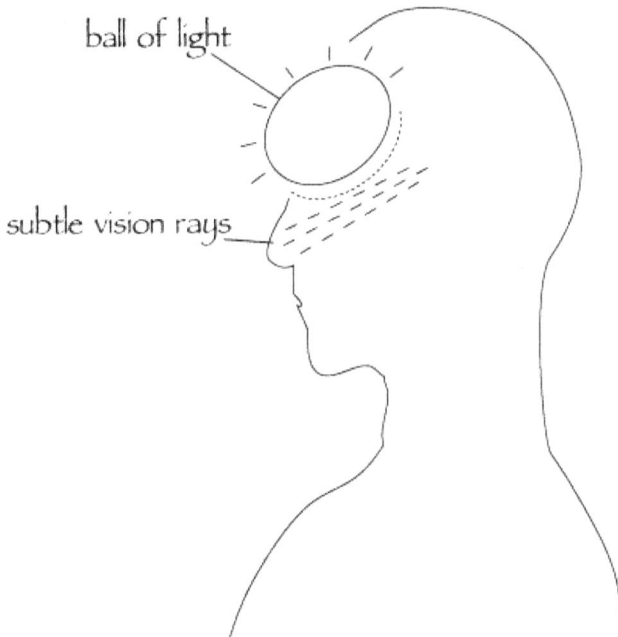

ball of light

subtle vision rays

January 22, 2003

This is a back-of-the-head clean-out

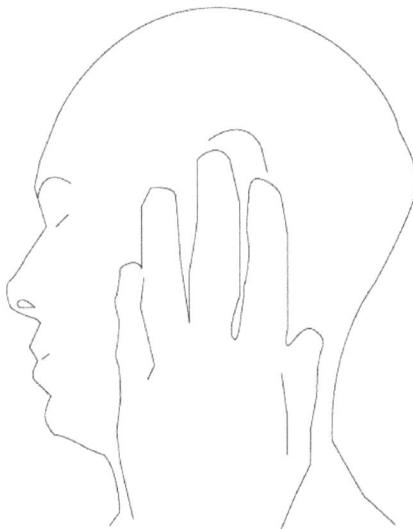

In the beginning of yoga practice, one can clear the easy-to-reach parts of the subtle body. After much practice, one is inspired or is shown how to do postures which effect the hard-to-reach areas. One realizes that a person cannot become purified overnight. It takes time. Each person should devote time to practice. Some students have more impurities. Some have less. Regardless, it requires individual practice.

January 23, 2003

Muktananda

A yogi must limit the diet otherwise there would be no fruitful meditation on a consistent basis. When one has a counterproductive diet, the lifeforce becomes preoccupied with digestion and excretion duties. It then decreases the interest in yoga practice. This affects the yogi adversely.

Muktananda gave this under-the-knee thigh exercise.

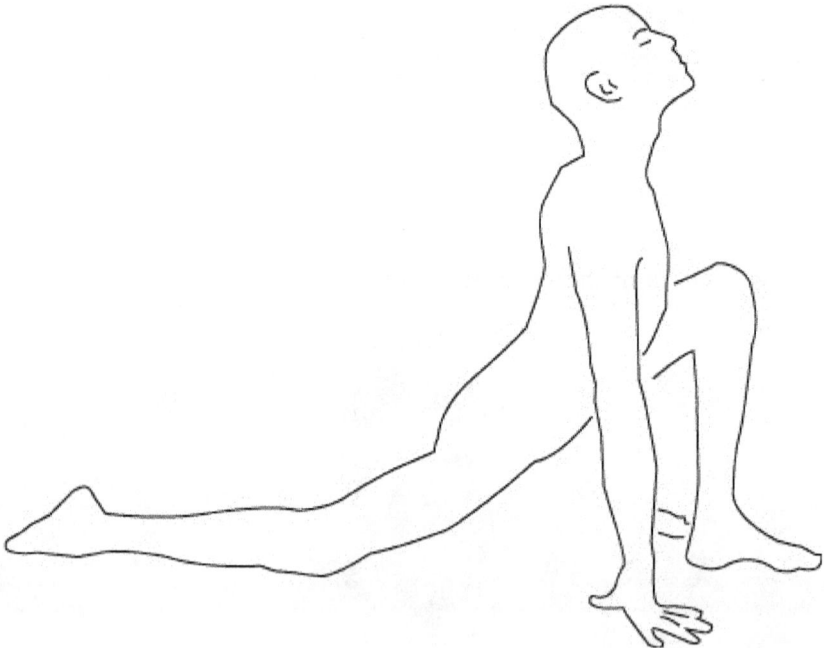

Muktananda

He said, "The imagination orb is different to the subtle eye and different to pranavision. It is different to the brow chakra vision. It forms into a tiny white light when imagining something.

"Go where it imagines each time you find it doing so. Be familiar with its operation, not its content. You used that imagination orb to see Padmanabha Vishnu, some years ago."

He gave this kriya for women. This one may be practiced by men as well.

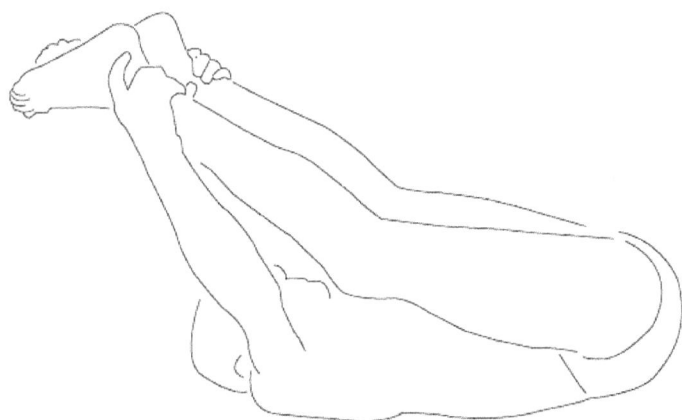

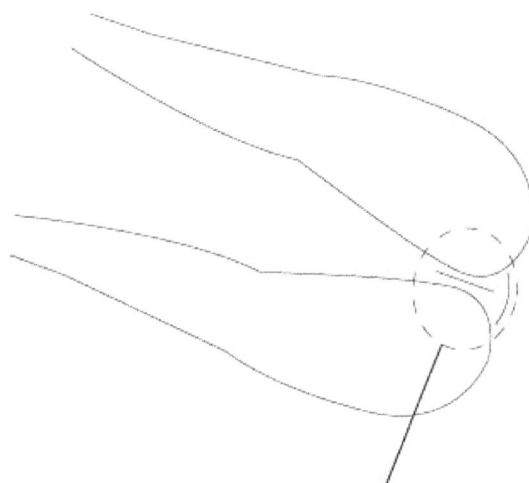

thighs-vagina-buttocks

region

January 25, 2003

Muktananda

He said, "The intellect's imagination orb can be traced by sound impressions just as well as by the images it creates."

He also informed that a woman can get extra benefits from the stretches which affect the abdomen area. A woman's sexual apparatus is within her body. It stretches automatically when abdomen flexes and other abdomen related stretches are done.

January 26, 2003

Muktananda

He gave a woman's anus-yoni region kriya. The yoni is the vaginal apparatus.

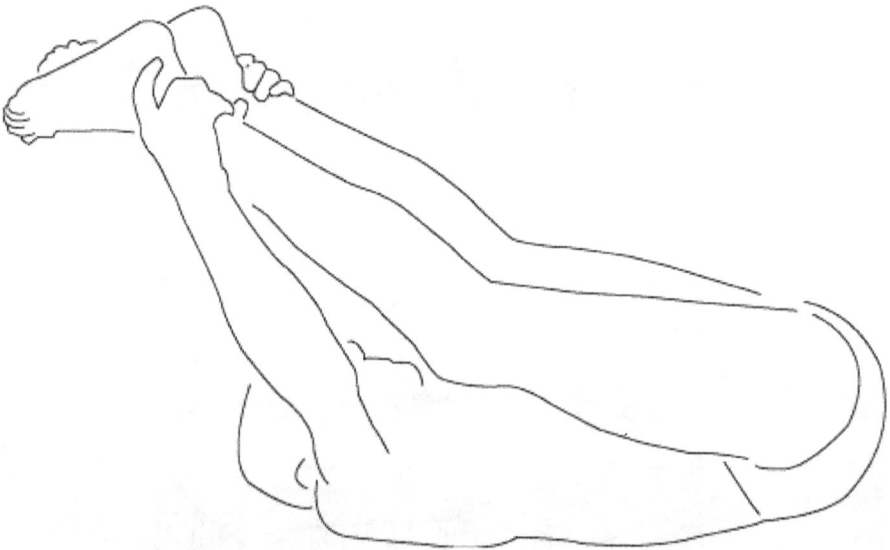

Muktananda glorified the lotus-front-over posture, saying that it helps to ease the body for sitting for long periods in lotus posture for experiencing the transcendence absorptions. It frees the sides where the thighs join into the body. It eases the lumbar region.

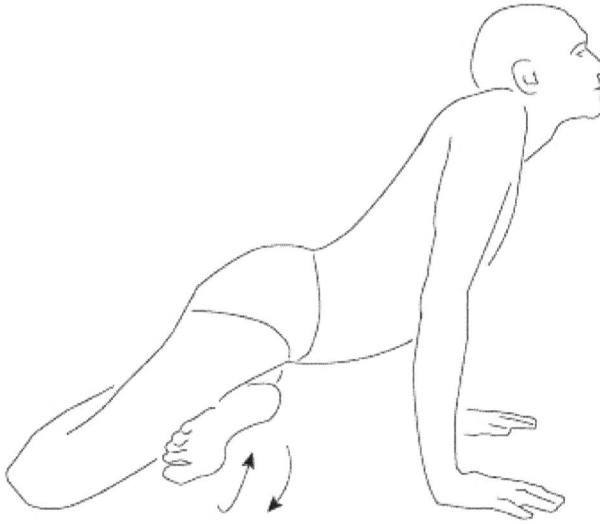

move body up and down

He again stressed the necessity for stopping the automatic functioning of the imagination orb. A yogi should guard the intellect from casual, whimsical and incidental intake of sensual data. If this is not done, one will not develop supernatural vision. Arjuna was awarded supernatural sight for seeing the Universal Form but most other yogis will have to work with the austerities to develop vision.

Muktananda gave this instruction, "Everything heard, seen or sensed must be processed at a later time. However, a yogi can use the incidental impressions to find the imagination orb and to continually curb it. It is the same with memory. What is stored in memory can be activated at any time to keep the yogi preoccupied for associative thinking and conceptualizing. These facets of the intellect were condemned by Patanjali in the Yoga sutras. If one does not stop the intellect from its natural way of pursuing and contemplating mundane objects, one will not experience supernatural vision. What Patanjali said about completely stopping the mental or emotional operations is absolutely correct. The idea that one can convert the mundane impressions into divine ones or into associative divine ones, is false. But one cannot realize this until one gets the experience of the intellect being changed into a supernatural eye."

Yogeshwarananda

He said, "Be blessed to follow my line of research. Complete some of what I described in brief."

Remark:

With his assistance, I used the orb lights to see the organs in the psyche. The vision was clear at time and indirect at other times. As it is with yoga, with long practice, this improves.

Yogesh showed the telepathy border in the mental terrain. This is the place at which the thoughts from others penetrate the mind. He instructed that this border be made resistant to penetration of lower thoughts which come from persons who are not yogis.

From in my crown chakra, he instructed. He said, "Come on this side (the left side of the subtle brain). Bring it over here. Focus on the horse that it created. Watch how it attaches itself to what it illustrates."

Remark:

The intellect impulsively conceived of a horse. This was a result of thinking of how to tame the intellect by indulging it in what it likes to imagine but observing its process while doing so. In the beginning of trying to curb it, one must do many such practices.

Yogeshwarananda showed another procedure on this day.

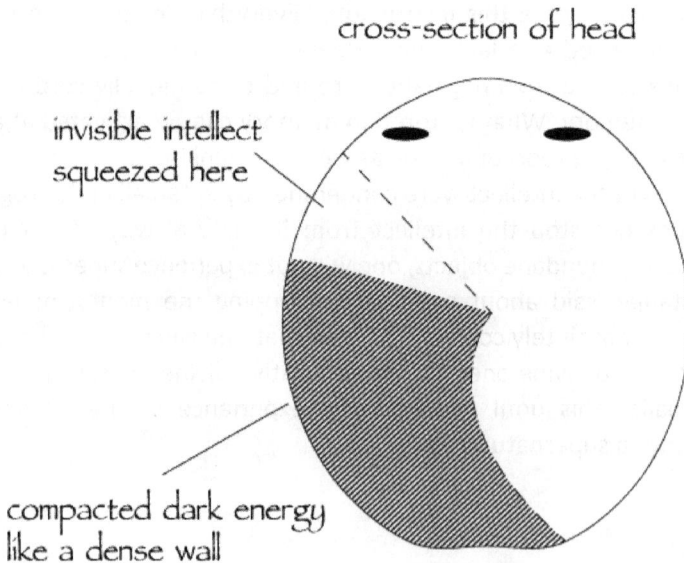

cross-section of head

invisible intellect squeezed here

compacted dark energy like a dense wall

Muktananda

He gave a female suck-up inside-thigh exercise. This draws the energy through the sexual organ up through the body into the brain. One should stand with the heels twisted inwards. Hands should be on the hips. One should do a slow down-draw breath, pulling hard on the inhale.

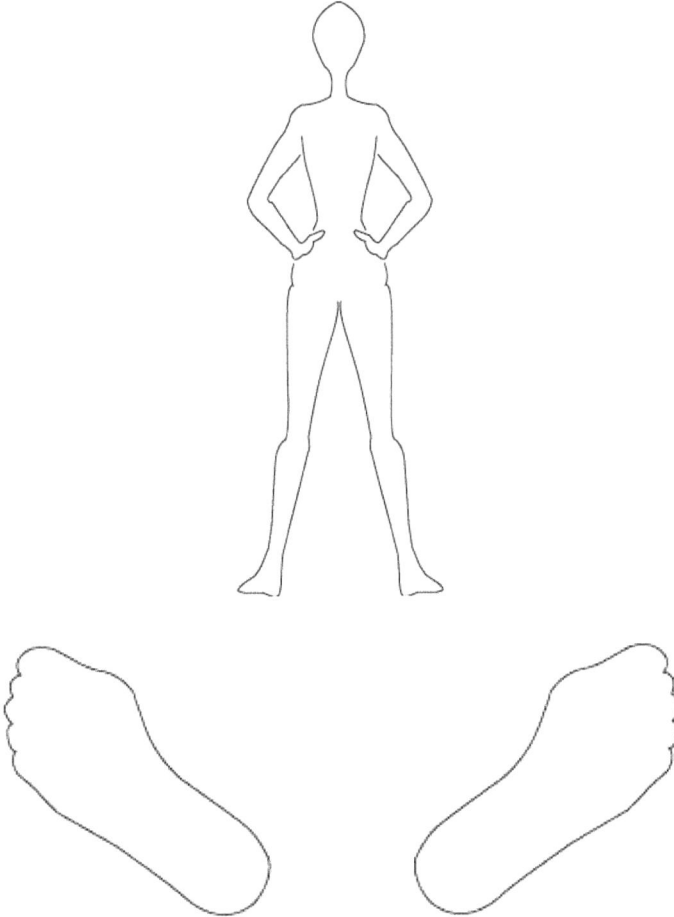

Yogesh said that dharana, the 6th stage of yoga, begins after the sense and sex objects are abandoned. This means getting a focus-controlling hold on the intellect. The intellect has a strong instinct for sensual pursuits. It will not desist unless it is forced to do so.

January 29, 2003

Yogi Bhajan

He said, "Use rapid breath-infusion during the spinal twist. Remember the swing spinal twist.

Remark:

That swing spinal is done in the way shown in this diagram.

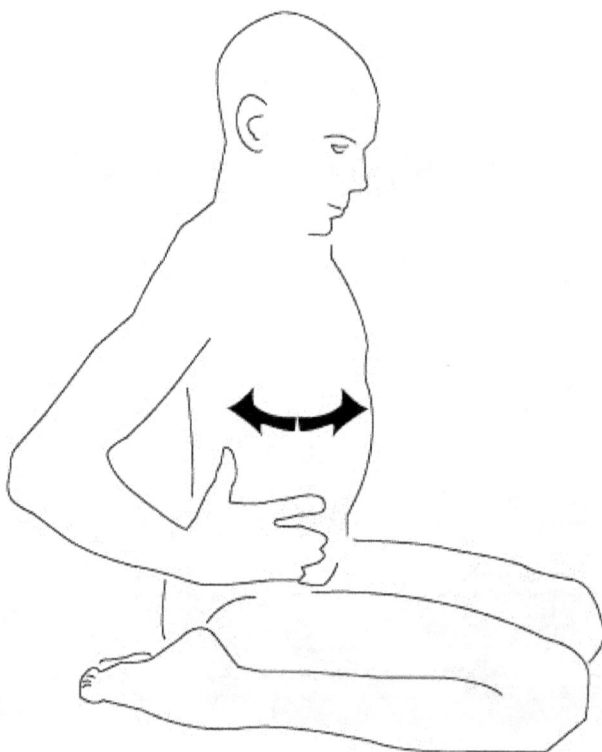

Yogeshwarananda said that I should control the excitement impulse. I should not allow it to scamper after bright subtle or supernatural lights.

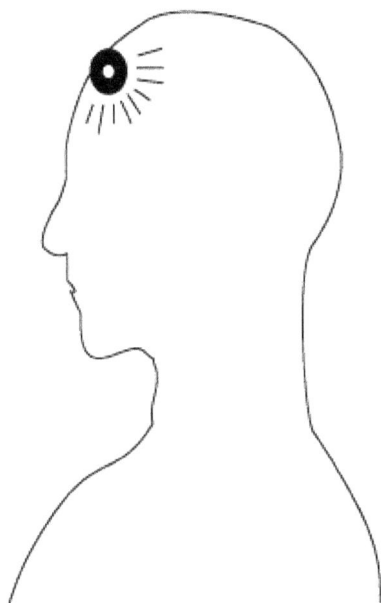

January 31, 2003

Muktananda

He gave a woman's procedure. This is for clearing subtle slime from the vaginal passage. It also serves to remove cheesy or crusted accumulations in the passage. These exercises are aimed at the subtle form, but they have an effect on the gross body as well.

Muktananda said that celibacy is completed when through the practice of asana postures, the belly cells no longer send energy and liquids to the genitals.

Remark:

As it is with these bodies, the cells are interested in contributing energy for reproduction. To change this, one should practice postures, breath-infusion and body contractions otherwise one will remain with a sex-prone demeanor.

January 31, 2003

Yogeshwarananda

He said, "Dharana begins after pratyahar is completed. Breath-infusion must be mastered too. By it, the mind's crazy thinking is curbed."

January 31, 2003

Ma Durga

She gave a woman's vaginal procedure.

This is done bending over with the fingers by the lips of the vaginal entrance in the side grooves which are between each thigh and each lip of the organ. The woman does breath-infusion as she assumes that posture while standing and bending over.

January 31, 2003

Yogeshwarananda

He instructed, "Suppress the excitement seeking part of the intellect. Although it is not seen, concentrate on the light.

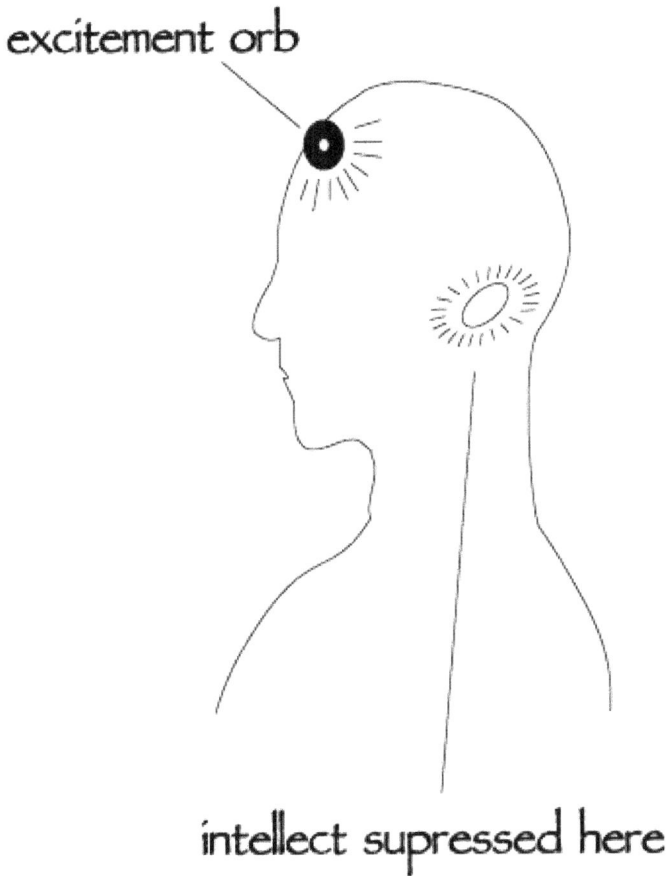

excitement orb

intellect supressed here

February 1, 2003

Yogeshwarananda

He showed a grace energy. This was not seen visually. This is a type of supernatural sensing vision. Yogesh stressed that a yogi should not neglect prana vision. Much is understood directly by pranavision which is not a visual eyesight. Pranavision is accurate nevertheless. Modern machines like the X-ray and other imaging technology, work by pranavision. A yogi develops that perception by doing the austerities consistently.

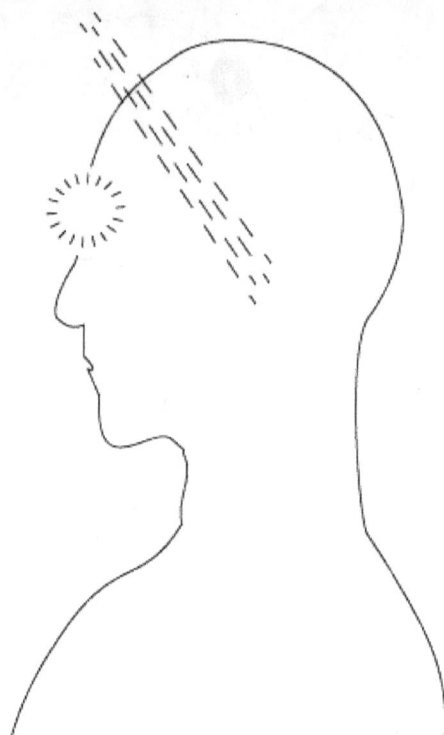

grace energy

February 1, 2003

Yogeshwarananda

He said, "Deliberate transcendence focus begins when thoughts stop. Notice how impossible it is to meditate when the thoughts develop and carry you away. You spend most of the time with displayed thoughts. They have the power to capture your attention."

He gave a procedure for seeing through the pin-size eyes in the knee area. This is a type of prana vision. Just as a fly has multiple eyes which form one large eye, so in the subtle body here and there, there are pin-sized eyes which grouped together form eyes. This was seen in the posture below.

pranavision through this knee

February 3, 2002

Yogi Bhajan

He gave a temple clearance process. This is done while assuming lotus or half lotus. One puts the fingers on the temple of the head as shown.

Here is a woman's vaginal air-out procedure. This is done after an intense session of breath-infusion. The woman stands and puts one foot out while her hands are on the hips. In that pose, the lips of the vaginal passage part away from each other. While doing bhastrika rapid breathing with eyelids closed and concentrating on the vaginal area, she does rapid breathing on one side then the other.

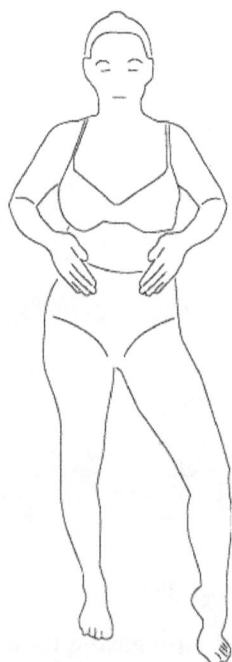

Here is another woman's procedure for pumping air through the vaginal area.

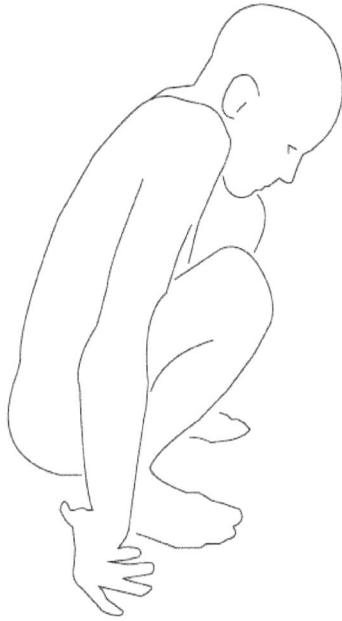

This is a process for pushing air through the Adam's apple in the throat. There is a nadi tube there that is one-fourth (¼) inch wide. In this hands are tensed flat on the floor.

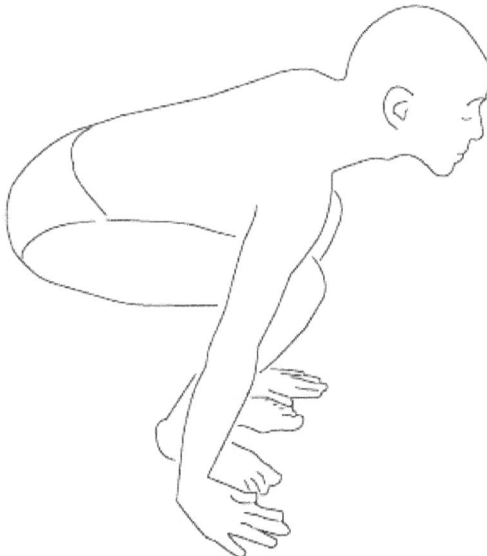

Yogesh gave a woman's womb-pull exercise. In this posture, the lady sits between the heels. She spreads her knees apart. She does abdomen flexes, especially in the extreme right and left corners.

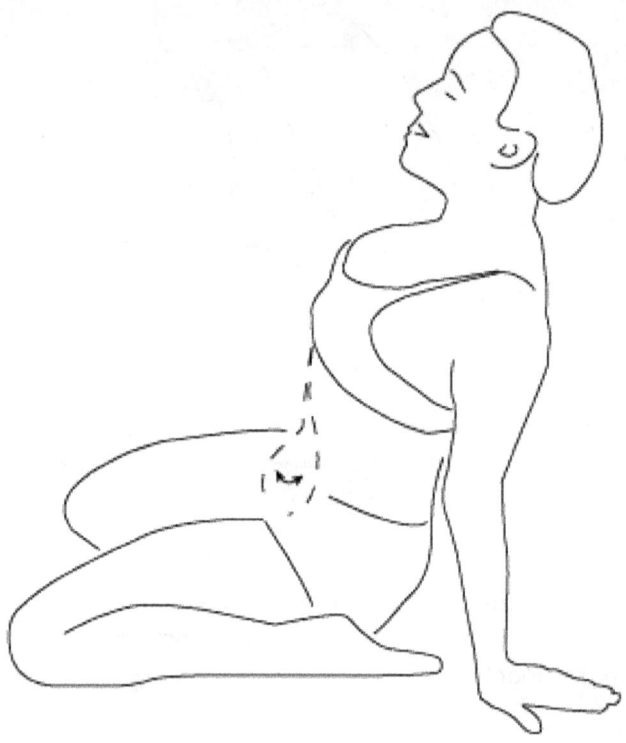

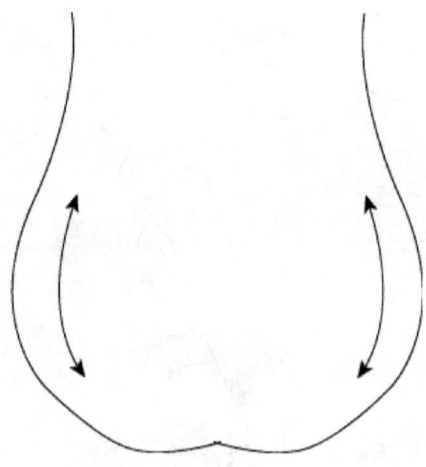

He gave another posture for women. This is for working on the lumbar area. This area is important to women due to the menstrual cycle. The palms of the hands push on the lumbar area with the fingers pointing up. The woman does rapid breathing with inner concentration.

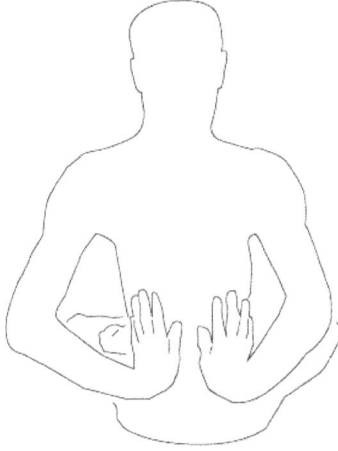

January 4, 2003

Yogeshwarananda

He gave what he called the first lessons of dharana practice.

This is when one cannot see the lights of the intellect organ but one can detect the orbs of sensing energy. One feels this as a warm subtle orb of energy somewhere in the head of the subtle body. One focuses on the orb but one does not use picture vision. One does not look up, nor down, nor to either side. One focuses on feeling its location.

use feelings
to perceive
the light

Bhumi Ma

She is the goddess of the earth, the Mother Earth personified. She is a supernatural being. She has parallel expansions. One such supernatural lady came to me. She was the patron deity of the country of Guyana, where I acquired the present body.

She said, "You took that body from us. Please return it promptly."

After this I noticed that the mother of my body who passed away in 1992, stood behind her. Once this lady, my mother, told me that the country of Guyana looks like a female body. If one looks at the map of that country, one will agree. The middle portion of the country has a narrowed area like a thin waist. The deity showed me that she was the patron of plantain trees. She handed me some subtle plantains to eat.

Yogeshwarananda

He said, "Deliberate transcendence focus is impossible when thoughts are present. Do whatever is necessary to bring on thoughtlessness. He gave this technique.

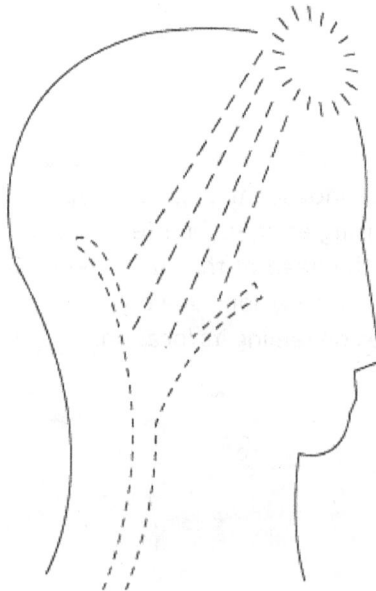

Yogeshwarananda

He showed the mouth of the kundalini in the neck. It was open as if it were a serpent eating the rays of light which emanated from the intellect.

February 7, 2003

Muktananda

He said, "A consistent kundalini awakening stays at the mouth of the sushumna below the brain, coming out at the neck. It is V-shape.

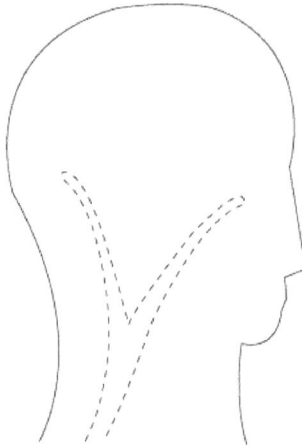

February 9, 2003

Yogeshwarananda

He said, "Transcendence focus is not possible with thoughts, ideas and the like. The psychology is designed in such a way that one is diverted helplessly by these. Thoughts come from activity which comes from desire. It could be anyone else's desire. It does not have to be your own.

"Focus on the thought energy as soon as there is a formation. Keep the focus on the spot where the thought display occurred. This is elementary focus. It works when the mind is properly rested and the thoughts come in slowly after doing breath-infusion."

February 16, 2003

Satyeshwarananda

He said, "Do not plan to engage in business when you relocate to South America. Keep the austerities as your main aim in going there. Use the critical energy to remove the subtle hard-to-recognize attachments. Do not relate to females sexually when you begin advanced practice. Instead take a female only as a sister, just as Baba does."

February 16, 2003

On this date, I made a notation:

Absorption occurs when the mind or a portion of the mind or the intellect or even the charge subtle energy, becomes focused in a particular way. Sometimes it seems to be a flow of energy in a certain direction at a certain place in the psyche. To practice absorption, one joins one's attentive power to that flow.

February 17, 2003

Kundalini Ma

On this day I saw a kundalini deity. She was in a feminine subtle form. She was in this posture.

Kundalini Ma had no clothing. Her sexual organ was exposed. She said, "Put the organ in here." She indicated her vaginal passage.

I replied, "No Ma. The whole psyche will go in there as a son.

I then emerged with head down as a child does at parturition before birth. Then I felt that the sexual urge in my form, joining the urge in Kundalini Ma's form.

Remark:

Such experiences are rare, but they do occur. One responds not deliberately nor in a planned way but on the basis of how far one advanced.

February 16, 2003

Yogeshwarananda

He said, "This is natural absorption. Learn from it."

Remark:

This was in meditation when the intellect focused itself without thoughts or ideas.

February 17, 2003

Muktananda

He showed me a fire slit in the throat. When doing this, energy comes up from the front belly area.

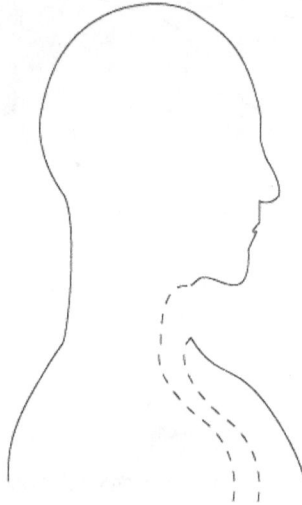

He said, "You will have to sit like this for hours and watch both kundalin1 and intellect. Do bhastrika and other breath-infusion frequently. After some time the lifeforce will give up old habits and cooperate. I did it. Each yogin must curb his psyche."

Muktananda gave some training for dealing with the dakini supernatural lady, Kundalini Ma. He told me to do her bend-over pose. I did it on the left with the left hand on the ground (see page 57). When this is done, one realizes the sex touch-spots. The sexual sensation may flare up suddenly. That will cause sexual arousal but it goes away.

When dealing with the dakini Kundalini Ma, one may assume a tight lotus. She then mounts one's body from the front. She may be in lotus or be in any other posture. This is mostly sexual in the beginning and after some time, one finds that the sexual flavor of it goes away.

Muktananda told me this, "When I went through that phase I got no help until sometime after. At first I could not understand who she was. I did not know she was Kundalini Ma. I thought she was an astral female, with intentions to destroy celibate practice.

Part 3

On this day, Kundalini Devi came again. She did several postures. I followed along doing each in turn as she performed. In each of those postures, she connected her sexuality to mine. Sometimes, that was an actual sexual contact. Sometimes this was done with contact of her sexual organ to other parts of my subtle body. That subtle body was a special subtle form, meant for the purpose. A yogin develops various types of subtle bodies in various dimensions.

When I assumed the rooster pose, Kundalini Ma positioned her vagina in contact with my brow chakra, while her brow chakra was in contact with my sexual organ. This happened because the subtle body she used was interspaced within mine. Her subtle form was able to pass through mine.

When I assumed lotus. She did the same, except that she was upside down, so that the tongue of the subtle body I used, was drawing fluids out of her vagina. And then her tongue was drawing fluids out of my penis. There are questionable tantric actions for completing celibate practice

From the astral world, a yogi called. He said, "Delay no longer. Start today. Use bread, milk, honey and water. Have no fear."

Remark:

This was an instruction to begin absorption practice, and for me to relocate outside the United States. Later that day Muktananda said that the yogi was no ordinary yogi. He said that it was Yogapita, the father of yoga practice.

Muktananda informed me that I should use honey and water or milk and water and sanctify that to Yogapita as a whole meal.

This is done when one is ready to do transcendence practice.

February 23, 2003

Yogeshwarananda

He gave the *Om Bhur Bhuvah* gayatri mantra to use while I drove a car. Some sense impressions and thoughts entered my mind and diverted me from crown chakra focus. The next morning Yogesh said I should use only *Om*.

February 23, 2003

Pushti Ma

She gave a breast procedure for women.

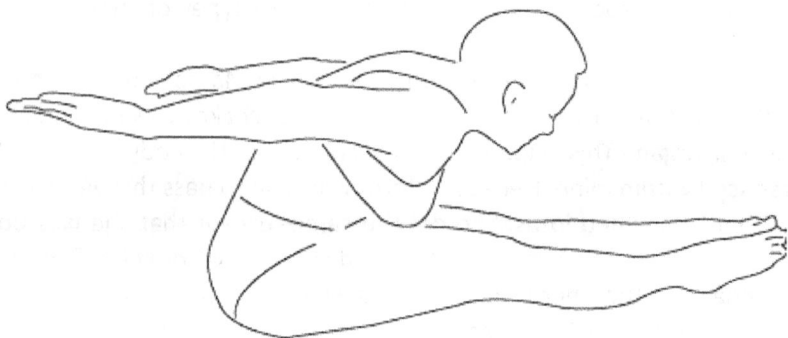

Here is another.

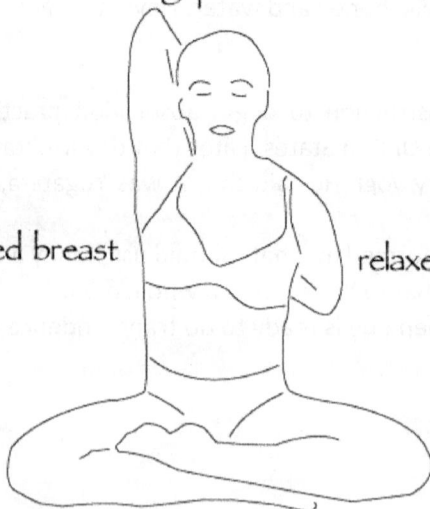

hands intergrip in back

stretched breast

relaxed breast

Here is another.

Here is a woman's arm-pit air-out kriya.

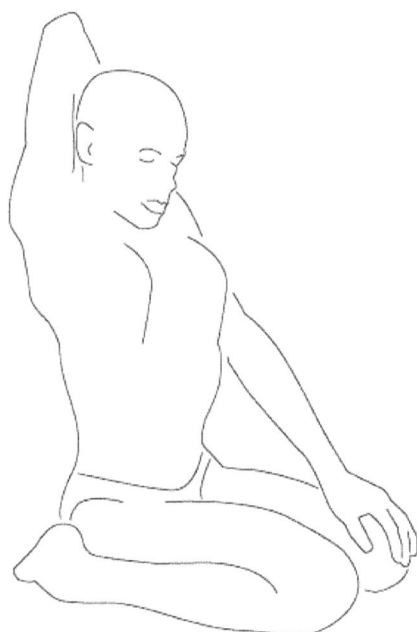

middle finger grabs under armpit
breasts are stretched

Yogeshwarananda

He said, "Engage this part in *ajapa* and breath *ajapa*, otherwise it will wander around for mischief. When it stays still, ignore it, otherwise engage it."

Remark:

Ajapa means silent mental repetition of a mantra. Breath *japa* is when one uses his breathing itself as a mantra, a sound-producing way of concentration and application of attention. The breath is automatically repeated. It is a mantra.

On this day I realized that the kundalini passed through the sexual chakra with no attraction to sexual pleasure. This is because there was no energy in the chakra. That completes celibacy yoga.

Sarasvati Ma

She gave this back-of-the-thigh/under-buttocks procedure.

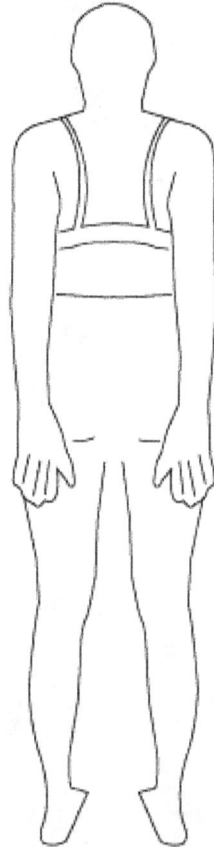

hands on thighs

palms face outward

February 26, 2003

Yogeshwarananda

He said, "Long sitting will be required. Do not think of food. That will be reduced. The whole system will simmer down. As I said earlier this morning, the external-seeking vision must be internalized fully. Then one sees into the supernatural sky of consciousness.

February 27, 2003

Yogeshwarananda

He said, "Build a cave room. Get closed in there for many days. Have lots of air available but no lights."

February 28, 2003

This is a woman's abdomen flex. In this posture, one pushes up the body pivoting on the toes.

March 1, 2003

Yogeshwarananda

He said, "Observe that the slightest thought, idea or picture image, causes the intellect to shift on its own to expand the impression. The self usually sees this after it is done. It deters absorption practice."

March 3, 2003

Muktananda

He remarked, "Nityananda said that if you work hard you can achieve shaktipat capability. To accelerate progress, he blesses you with the association of the Krttikas. They help with the female part of the psyche. You will have to stay in darkness for some time. This will cause the sensuality to settle down more.

Remark:

This is what was seen.

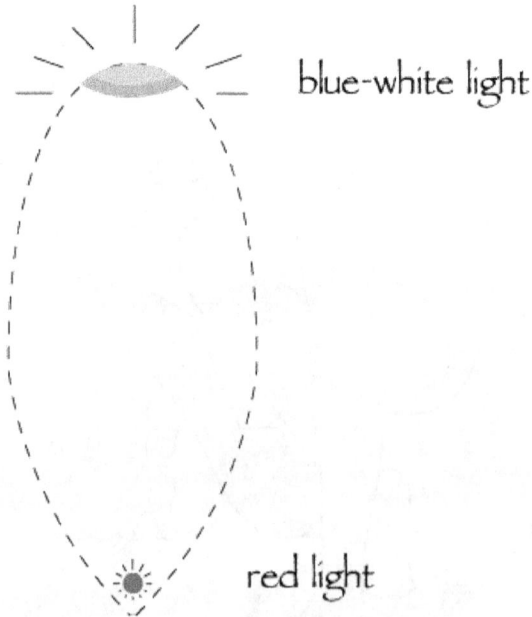

blue-white light

red light

March 4, 2003

Nityananda

He showed how to regain celibate status for shaktipat capacity by removing the genitals and thighs. These involve some special procedures for one-energy kundalini.

Muktananda then said to Nityananda, "You never taught me those methods."

Nityananda replied, "You had no wife. Your organ was not used in a woman's body."

crown hole

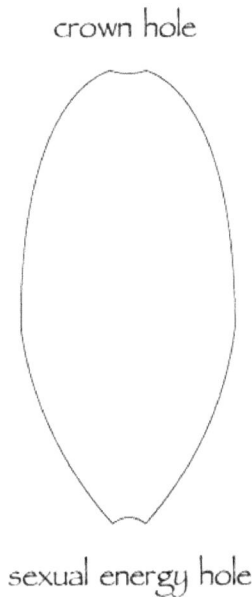

sexual energy hole

March 5, 2003

Nityananda

He showed a technique for breathing through the top of the bubble subtle body. In that form there is no bottom hole for sexual expression. It becomes manifest to yogis, who are honest in celibate efforts. One meditates on the energy distribution through the spray of energy out of that form.

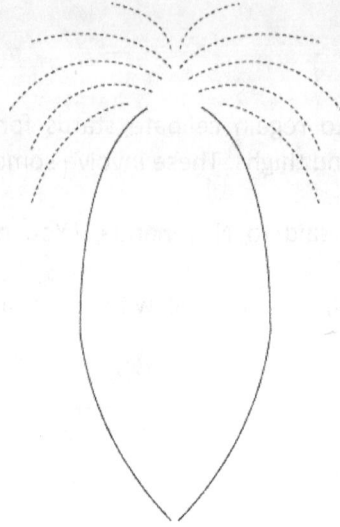

Nityananda (while Yogeshwarananda watched)

This was a practice for breathing through the top hole of the crown chakra in the bubble subtle body. This leads to sensing the subtle channels which originate at that top hole and which may devolve into lower forms.

March 6, 2003

Nityananda

He said, "If one comes in and does not have sexual involvement nor had them before, one uses such a balloon form. Such ascetics do not experience kundalini chakra in a fully expressive display. You resumed such a form again. Maintain it properly."

Nityananda

He gave a yoni-exposure push-out kriya.

This is done with the body in between the heels with raised knees. One uses the hand to push back, while leaning back to turn the vaginal passage out.

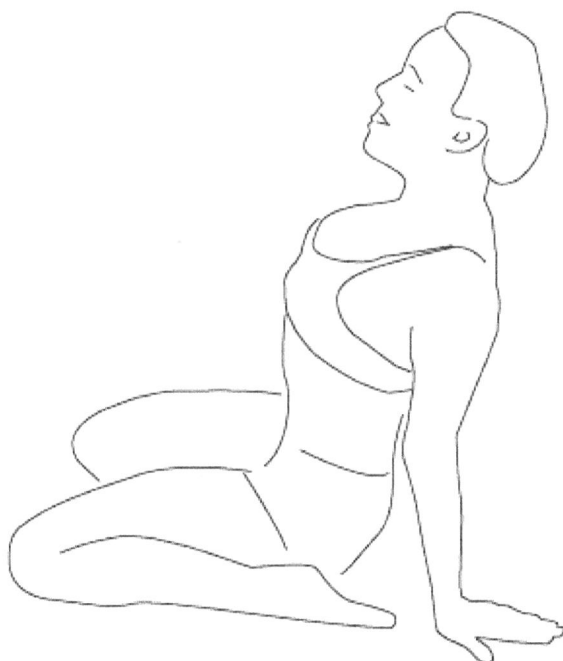

He gave this woman fall-in of the vagina kriya. In this posture, the vagina falls back into the body.

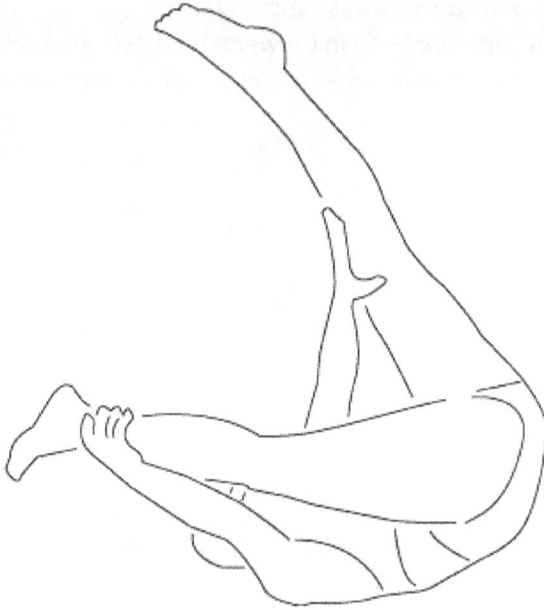

Muktananda said that I should do the lotus posture in brahmin underwear with no pants. He wanted me to use a blanket around the body. He claimed that pants obstruct some of the body currents.

March 10, 2003

Nityananda

He described brahma yoga as follow:

"It has its special aspect which is the perception of the balloon body with its crown chakra hole and the nadis radiating from that. In the case of kundalini yoga, celibacy yoga and purity-of-the-subtle-energies yoga, it is hard to tell where one practice begins and the other ends. These are interrelated. One overlaps the other, beginning with kundalini, then celibacy, then purity-of-the-psyche. In kundalini yoga, the aspirant focuses on the kundalini to first raise its energy by firing it with infused breath energy to create the bhasvara fire light. That fire, like a furnace, is stoked with infused breath while doing rapid breathing.

"Celibacy yoga uses the expertise gained in kundalini yoga. It brings into play front kundalini. Back kundalini is infused breath kundalini which involves fresh air pushing polluted energy and sexual power. Front kundalini involves sexual energy and nutritional power, especially nutritional power. In celibacy yoga, these play a part as you experienced.

"In purity-of-the-psyche yoga, the focus on kundalini and celibacy is relaxed. One focuses on the whole subtle psyche. At first, in brahma yoga, in the balloon body, there may be three or four holes but no more. One at the top, one at the navel and one at the sexual area. Sometimes, there is one in the heart chakra tunnel area. Gradually the lower holes convert into scars. Then the scars disappear. The highest hole, the crown chakra, cannot be adjusted."

March 14, 2003

A woman's breasts air-draw-through procedure. This draws air through the nipples and breasts tubes of the subtle body.

fingers grab
shoulder blade

this breast
is stretched

fingers pressed on floor

A woman's back-thigh and vaginal-hormone release procedure.

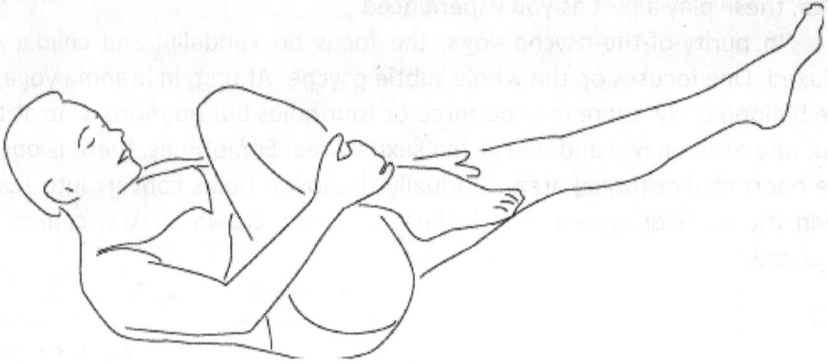

March 16, 2003

A woman's vagina-thigh stretch. This stimulates the pregnancy apparatus and the delivery of child system. When I practiced this kriya some women came from the astral world. These were disembodied females. They did this exercise with me. They are were taking possession of the energy which exuded from my subtle body.

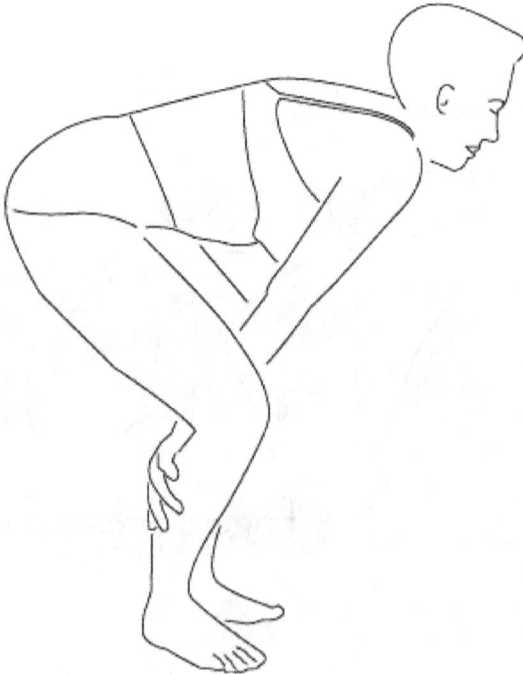

This is a chaste woman's rooster pose. This is done with the hands outside the thighs as shown in the diagram.

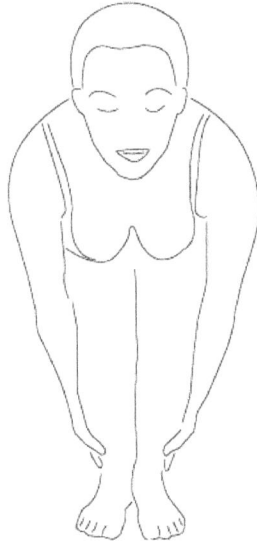

There is also another pose to be used by women who are addicted to sexual intercourse. In this one, the hands are placed on the inside so that the vaginal jaws are spread apart.

March 21, 2003

Nityananda

He inquired, "How did you avoid fame?"

I replied, "I hid under the goddess the way chicks hide under a hen, when predators come near. Small animals who avoid being eaten usually hide away."

He remarked, "For transcendence practice, you should sit for hours. It was so sad to see many come, practice and then go away when only four hours more of sitting would give results. Do not be impatient. Pay dues and succeed.

"Sit in lotus for longer periods. That is the first stage of full transcendence absorption after the balloon form becomes manifested. This sitting will settle the mind and quiet the lifeforce. Then full absorption comes."

He gave a chastity-pull woman's technique.

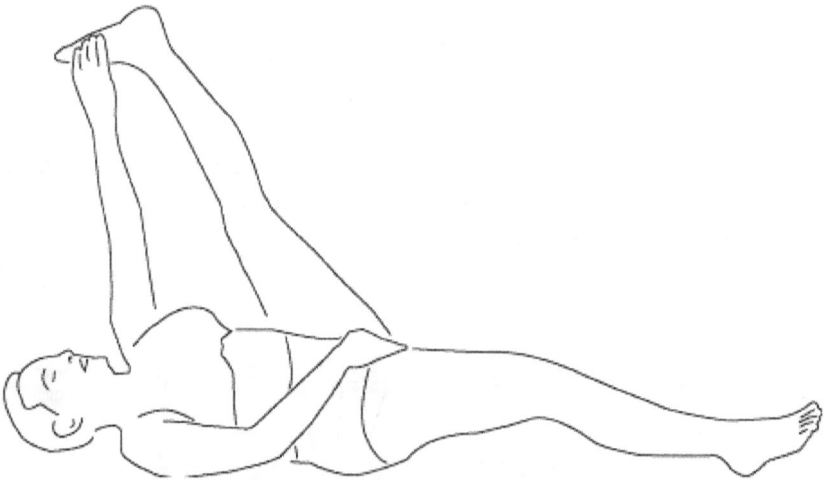

March 28, 2003

Shivananda

He came out of a light of core-selves. He was cautiously viewing my subtle body since he did not want to perceive the kundalini lifeforce or the kanda in my subtle body. He said, "When kundalini yoga is completed, then automatically brahma yoga begins."

By his proximity, I realized that the sky of consciousness cannot be accessed without stopping the disturbing sensuality.

March 31, 2003

Shivananda

He showed that the kundalini parts were sourced in the balloon body originally. When the kundalini chakra develops the balloon body disappears, just as when a seed is used in producing a tree, the seed disintegrates. After years of staying on the astral plane, in a parallel world, Shivananda retreated to the causal level to complete yoga practice.

November 3, 2002

On this day there was an urge to make notation for future yogins. For those who are sincere the pains of yoga postures are positive.

The pains of asana postures if tracked from within can help the yogi to find the tubes in the subtle body. The thoughts which arise during meditation lead the yogi to the imagination orb and eventually he learns how to control and convert it into the intuition eye. A yogi must learn from repeated efforts at meditation, that the mind must have an anchor. This anchor is the naad sound which pours through the right or left ear into the subtle head.

November 8, 2002

Babaji

He said, "Despite the unfavorable environment, do the procedure."

Remark

I was in Guyana to find an isolated place but at the said date in November of 2002, I had not located it. There were many radios and stereo equipment noises and other forms of disturbance. I was doing an absorption practice, where there is a slit opening in the intellect. Through that slit, naad sound entered into the intellect to influence it to give up the attachment to this side of existence.

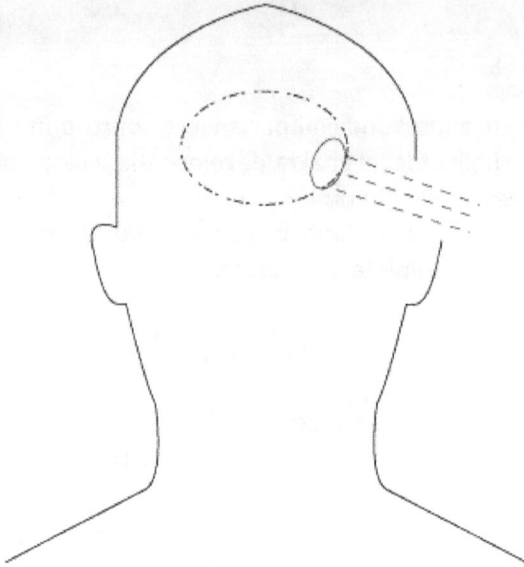

December 23, 2002

Yogesh commented that the early morning before sunrise is very conducive to truth-yielding (rtambhara) intellect focus."

Remark:

One has to mold his life in such a way as to facilitate yoga practice. A yogi should get away from all people, places and things which put down or retard yoga. He should live in such a way, that the practice can be done efficiently. For instance, sexual indulgence kills off yoga practice. A yogi has to make up his mind to either continue with it or leave it aside for others to perform. Actually the yogi is not needed for sexual life. He should leave it and let others who are enthusiastic complete it. In that way he can use his time and interest for spiritual life. Anything, sex or anything else, which is an impediment should be left aside.

If one is engaged in sexual intercourse during the night, he will be reluctant to rise early in the morning. In addition sexual indulgence is such a strong force, that the mind will continue thinking of it. The yogi will have to forego the practice. In addition his energy level will be reduced since so much energy is consumed in sex involvement. A yogi should make up his mind as to whether he wants to make an all-out effort for yoga. We have to understand that there will always be people who want to pull us back into sexual indulgence and into other things which are counterproductive towards progress in yoga. At some stage, for success, one should ignore these persons, increase the resistance and attain full celibacy.

Basically I am against sexual indulgence, except for the purpose of begetting children. A person who says that he is my disciple or that he is my friend even, and who does not subscribe to this idea is actually my sworn enemy. I am not saying that a man has to be absolutely celibate but my proposal is that he must be striving for that absolute compliance in his life with the idea of no sex if there is to be no child.

As fated, a yogi, under pressure from ancestors, supernatural people and even human beings, may be compelled to be sexually-linked. That is the lever of fate which claims the yogi. Aside from this, the yogi even when compelled should maintain the interest in full celibacy, even though his body is owned conjointly by others who have contrary interests.

In terms of meditation, Yogesh said that at noon, it may be conducive to the brow chakra opening. In the afternoon it may be conducive to the listening of the naad sound, and pulling the intellect into that sound backwards in a straight line.

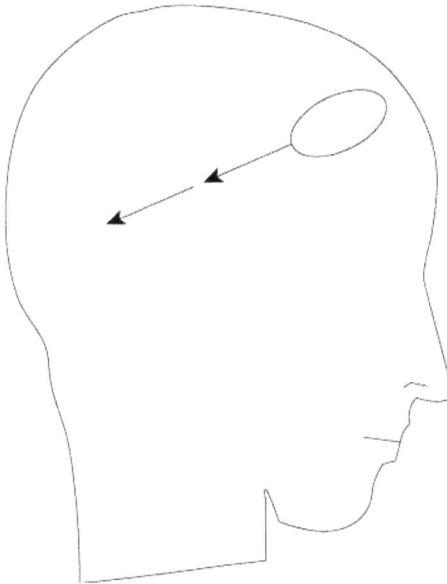

Remark:

The point is that one has to make this yoga practice the focus of one's life. It has to be a persistent practice.

December, 25, 2002

Bawra

He said, "It should have a support. That is why. Give it that as an alternative support. Even though it has two legs, it hops on one only. It alternates. Just give it that as a support."

Remark:

This is an explanation of the nature of the mind which has to rely on chitta or the mento-emotional energy. When the mind touches or makes contact with the chitta energy, impressions which are embedded there come out. The mind then becomes preoccupied with the impressions and their sequential formations. A yogi should train the mind to substitute the naad sound for the mento-emotional energy. This means the mind must be trained to develop an instinct for turning to naad sound.

Despite the importance of gurus, each yogin must train his mind. The student himself must train himself and spend many hours in meditation doing this to indoctrinate and orient the mind to take shelter in the right back side of the head where the naad sound manifests. The mind must be trained to develop an instinct for turning away from the presentations of the mento-emotional energy.

January 18, 2003

On this day, one of the Shivas gave a posture to be named Madhvasana. When one perfects certain stages of yoga, one may sometimes reach a mahayogin who will give one a special asana posture with instructions that one should practice this and name this after oneself. In some cases the said posture may already have the name of another great yogin, just as a city street may carry the name of a famous politician and then be renamed for another.

This pose was awarded to me because of the successful effort to make my present body celibate. It was a momentous achievement, considering the genetic background of the body which was derived from parents who were unfamiliar with yoga.

When this posture is done, one must keep the testes and genital organ in the back. From this one gets the idea of how to live without sexual expression.

This pose is effective to lift liquid from the subtle bulb-shaped organ which holds the subtle semen which may be emitted into the body of the angelic women who meet a yogin for sexual interplay.

Gorakshnath used to show this asana to his favorite disciples, the ones who were totally convinced that absolute celibacy was the way to exist from then onwards. It is a fact that if a yogi is not properly prepared, he will become stalled in the angelic world for sexual enjoyments. All yogins must be forewarned. One has to achieve a high degree of celibacy before giving up the gross body or one should hide in the subtle world while completing the yoga austerities after leaving this body, otherwise one will become linked with angelic women in a sexual way. It cannot be avoided merely by wishful thinking, nor by protection from yogi gurus.

In this world, there may be many students who study under a sannyasi renounced monk. Such a teacher may keep a tightly regulated ashram or hermitage, where no females are permitted to go. Still we find that even under such circumstances, the students wander away to find women. Most of all the teacher though expert at physical protection cannot guarantee astral isolation. Hence the students may sometimes remember wet dreams in which they find themselves having subtle sexual intercourse. Many students boast that they have no such dreams, but these same fellows cannot swear that they remember all astral experiences. Can the teacher protect one if one's subtle body slips into a parallel world?

A yogin must be very advanced in celibacy at least to the point where he dries up or eliminates the subtle sexual liquids on a permanent basis before leaving his physical form. Or he has to hide in the subtle world after leaving the physical body. Then one may continue the celibate procedures there.

I regularly meet some great yogins who stay either in the astral or causal world in some dimension, hidden there. They do not meet angelic females who may disrupt the practice. A yogin can stay with such yogins and continue the practice after leaving the body.

If unfortunately one slips into a dimension where one meets the angelic women, more than likely, one will have sensuous affairs. One will lose track of the practice and be lured into taking another physical body after some time.

January 18, 2003

Yogeshwarananda

He said, "Use the pains which occur in the lotus posture, to put the mind in the center of feelings. That leads to full transcendence absorption. Gradually each day, tolerate the cramps and other pains when you sit to meditate."

I said to him, "That was not written in your books." He replied, "Some things are learned from a guru directly. It is not all routine knowledge."

May 17, 2003

Gorakshnath

He said, "Disregard the mystic abilities which contravene introspection. Siddhis which give expression in that world and its subtle supports, should be left aside by the student. Resistance to their expression is itself a mysticism of worth."

Remark:

One should be alert that mystic abilities may become an impediment if one becomes preoccupied expressing them. One should by all means, not use a psychic power except to advance the practice of yoga. Yogesh showed a trick of using a power to invest in yoga and to refrain from letting others know that such an ability is present in one's psyche. He said that just as a selfish capitalist will invest all profits to expand the business further and will not even let his employees know how much money he accumulated, so a great yogi should invest his mystic power in further practice without letting anyone besides his teachers know how far he progressed.

January 15, 2003

At a building site of a house in Guyana, Gorakshnath appeared, riding a bull. At first I mistook him for Shiva who uses a bull on certain occasions. Gorakshnath is known to ride a tiger.

He said, "This place is suitable. Use it. These fellows are not yogis but they are helpful. I will come here later. In the meantime maintain the practice."

Remark:

Gorakshnath maintains a yoga siddha form which is made of subtle light. He is available for assistance in hatha yoga austerities. Some great yogins may be mistaken for being Shiva. Some use insignia which is usually ascribed to Shiva.

January 30, 2003

Hariharananda

He showed what he considered to be the 2nd kriya. This is a gentle focus of or gathering of milky light in the fontanel, the front forehead. He gave a list of preliminary practices as follows:

- listening to the naad sound in the right side of the subtle head
- memory suppression by locating where memory organ is located, and by achieving an objective separation from it
- no stress energy in the mind or in the emotional zones
- proper rest of the gross and subtle forms
- living a lifestyle which facilitates yoga practice
- nadi cleansing
- sealed celibacy

He showed this 2nd kriya as being what is depicted in the diagram below.

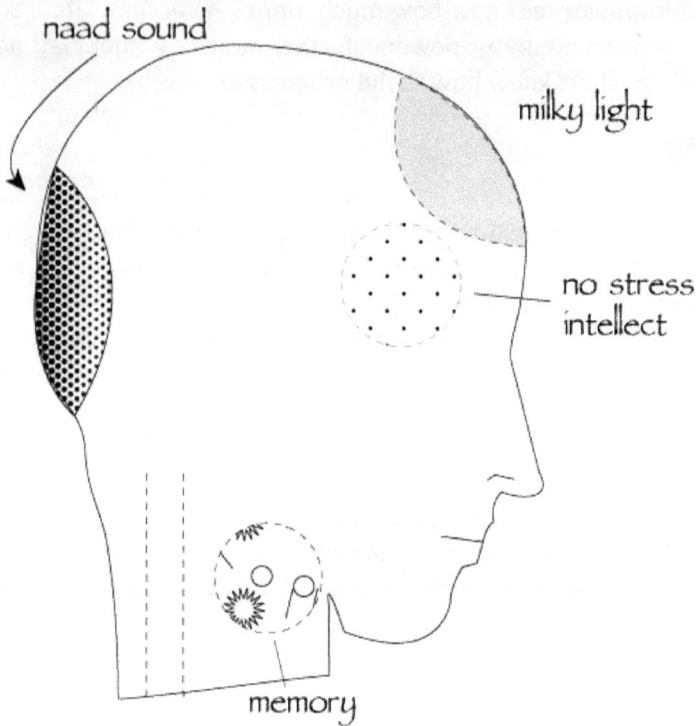

Remark:

The number of procedures and the order in which they are given, varies from one yogic tradition to another, all depending on the system established by great teachers. In books, like the *Yoga Sutras*, and the *Hatha Yoga Pradipika*, various methods (kriyas) are given either directly or indirectly. It depends on which teacher one is drawn to or which one is assigned by providence. There is really no contention, because if one is given the wrong technique, it will not work or it will work sometime in the future after one completed certain preliminary practices.

I will discuss the preliminary procedures given by Hariharananda. This is a colleague of Yogananda, which means that their spiritual master was Yukteshwar, who is in the Babaji lineage. These yogis follow the system given by Babaji. I also took instruction from him and associate with him in the astral world. He is very kind yogi even though his association is hard to achieve.

Hariharananda's procedures are explained below.

- listening to the naad sound.

This is the sound heard on the right side of the subtle head near the right subtle ear. It is also heard in the physical head but only when the subtle body is interlocked into the physical one. This sound is also heard on the left side of the head or on both sides, or throughout the entire head. Some yogis say that this sound originates in the subtle spine which is the sushumna nadi channel.

Sometimes if one is in a quiet place, one can hear this sound by closing the eyes and biting down on the right jaw as if to squeeze both jaws together on the right side. One will hear a screeching sound, an Eeeeee sound. As soon as one relaxes the muscles, that sound will change in frequency to a blended high pitched sound. That is the naad. One may hear this if one is in a dark place which is remote. One may hear it if one's physical body will die shortly.

Yogis practice a deliberate focus on this sound, but the mind usually rejects it and seeks out pictures, images, sounds and echoes from the external physical world and from memory of the world. A yogi tries to stop the mind from wandering away from this sound. He trains the mind to drink or absorb this sound. After long practice, the mind develops a liking for this. Then, it tries to avoid mental imaging and other mental and emotional impressions which distract it from this. Some yogis feel that this sound comes from outside the subtle body and enters into it. But others feel it is from inside the subtle form.

Both views are reconciled, since in some experiences, one feels this sound pouring in from the outside of the subtle right ear. It enters the head and influences the mind space. On the other hand, if one masters kundalini chakra, the sound may come from the cleansed kundalini energy, from the cleared sushumna nadi, which would then be on a higher level, closer to the primordial subtle energy which borders the spiritual world.

Krishna gave Uddhava a procedure for contacting this sound. That instruction is in the Uddhava Gita (Canto Eleven of Srimad Bhagavatam).

- memory suppression.

Patanjali made it clear that memory is one of the vritti operations of the mento-emotional energy. For success in yoga, it has to be suppressed. There is no way around that. The problem is that the spiritual master cannot help the disciple much with this, because the memory is so close to the core-self, that only the core itself can suppress it. Except for its fault of allowing the psychic equipment to operate automatically, the core can get his memory under control, but it will require a sustained effort for a long time. The automatic operation of memory must be deactivated.

One should locate where the memory is in the subtle body. That is the first objective. This is done in meditation by observing from which subtle place, the memory of previous occurrences emerges. After careful observation with detachment one gets to identify that place. It may be argued by different yogis, that this place is here or there but that is beside the point, for wherever one finds it, one should learn how to suppress it there. If one mistakes its location, then eventually one will realize the fault and find its true position.

In my own case, I located it in the high chest area with its opening by the esophagus. I am able to suppress it there. Once located, one must learn how to suppress it. Usually an advanced yogi will come into one's subtle head and show one how to squelch it. Thereafter one should practice to change the habits of the psyche in relation to the automatic operation (vritti) of the memory. Success in such practice is denoted by achieving a separation from the memory whereby one is no longer obliged to look at its presentations forcibly but can reject them as soon as they arise.

It is a fact, that a yogi who has not achieved this memory suppression has not mastered dharana transcendence focus which is the 6th stage of yoga.

- no stress energy in the mind or in the emotional zones.

Even among yogis, it is commonly said that one should be in the material world in the midst of hustle and bustle, but one should remain unaffected by stress. This is so much of a false statement because it underestimates the mind's susceptibility to external gross reality. The mind is affected. Therefore one should go to an isolated place to do yoga. Most of the ancient yogis did that, and they were not in a highly industrialized society.

If there is stress on the mind, it will affect the yogi as soon as he tries to internalize. He should live in such a way and maintain such association which permits him to be stress-free.

- proper rest of gross and the subtle bodies.

This is achieved by doing a daily kundalini yoga practice, through which the gross and subtle forms become surcharged with fresh pranic energy.

Physical, psychological and emotional over-exertion which is necessary or unavoidable on occasion, should not become the habit of a yogi. If he is to be successful in yoga, he should leave that aside as well as all association which produces that. One should be away from gross sounds, videos, and people in general, so that the psychology can be free from internal interactions with so many impressions. One should not over-work physically like a beast of burden, unless of course one is compelled by providence.

- living a lifestyle which facilitates yoga practice.

This is understood when one realizes that one's diet may either facilitate or deter yoga. This understanding forms when one masters the abdomen lift exercises. In the advanced stage one realizes that unless one curtails all non-yogic association, one will not reach a more advanced stage. Then one seeks isolation and becomes humble to the human beings who can disrupt one's practice. This humility takes the form of respecting them from a safe distance.

- nadi cleansing

Nadi cleansing is achieved through various practices in breath-infusion. The primary means is by doing bhastrika rapid breathing in various postures and observing minutely how the feelings moves in a breath-energy saturated subtle body.

- sealed celibacy

Sealed celibacy is achieved from being without sexual contact for three years while doing bhastrika breath-infusion with the intention to lift the sexual fluids which naturally course downwards in the gross and subtle bodies.

Just as a child may have no idea of the sexual energy of his body nor of its sexual potential, a person with a sealed celibate form, forgets carnal knowledge. His sexual organ becomes to him or her, only a urinary instrument. To a male in this condition, all women or females are like mothers or sisters. To a female, all men are like fathers or brothers. One then regains the childhood innocence about sexuality, but with the insight about the potential of kundalini.

~~~

The second procedure which was given by Hariharananda as the gentle focus or gathering of milky light in the front forehead, is done as the chief method given by Babaji. This is simply sitting with eyes closed or half-closed in a quiet preferably shaded or dark place and holding one's attention gently at the space between or slightly above the center of the eyebrows.

If there is milky white light there in specks or in masses, then gradually this may converse or be transformed into a tiny dot or star in the distance. A question may be asked as to what action should be taken if one sees no light there or if the light is speckled colored dots or gyrations and is not a milky white. The answer is to keep the focus there nevertheless.

After focusing for a time in meditation, if the focus is consistent and steady, one will get results and further instruction from a more advanced personality, either physically on this side of existence or in the subtle world.

January 31, 2003

After careful inspection of the subtle body, during the stretching of a posture, because of the granthis or knots and blockages in the subtle tubes which course through the lower parts of the subtle form, I saw that the effects of such stretching does not reach the crown chakra in the subtle body,. This means that those yogis who feel that stretches and postures are sufficient for yoga, have drawn a wrong conclusion.

Yoga cannot mean just stretches and postures for toning the gross body. Patanjali listed eight stages of which asana postures is the third only. To clear the nadi tubes one must do breath-infusion, specifically bhastrika rapid breathing.

The crown chakra is a hole at the top of the subtle head. This is only activated in a yogi who moves kundalini energy complex into the subtle head.

There is a special asana posture shown below. This is used to achieve a sealed celibate condition, and to regain sexual innocence, which is so necessary in higher yoga. In that posture, when a male does it, the sexual organs remain at the back, squeezed there by the heels.

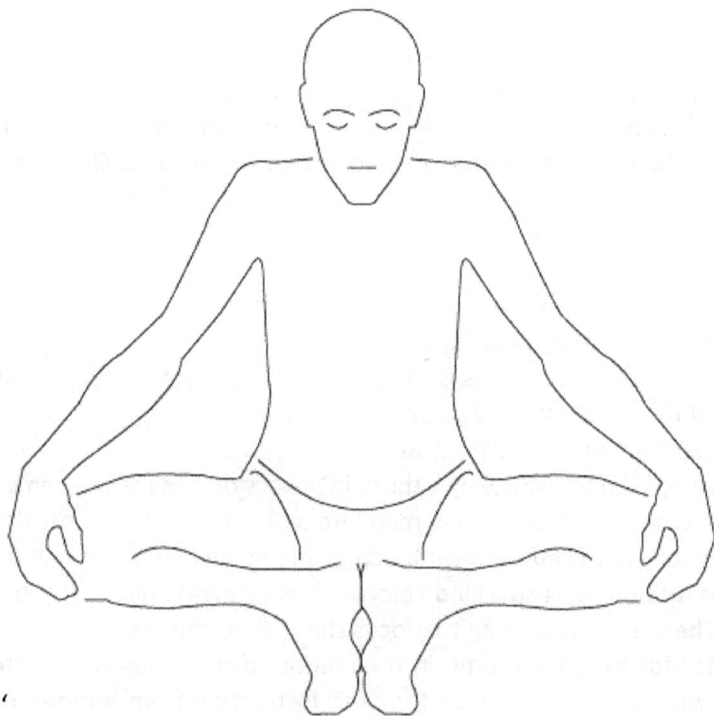

February 1, 2003

There is a technique that may be used with effectiveness for compressing impressions in the memory or for causing such impressions to be neutralized, so that they do not illustrate pictures and sounds to remind one of mundane encounters of the present and past material existences.

One may use *Om Namah Shivaya*, while stamping it into the memory chamber. If in one's case, the chamber is located elsewhere in the psyche, one can still use it on the memory there.

We should realize that so long as the memory operates automatically, there is no chance for attaining higher yoga and for becoming liberated, since such a memory will keep reminding us to act in the social material world.

February 2, 2003

The discriminative faculty is part of the same psychic unit which converts into the naïve or duped faculty. Patanjali alerted that besides memory, there are four operations of the mento-emotional energy, which must cease before we can attain full absorption practice.

Another one of these unwanted operations is the discrimination faculty which brings on correct knowledge and invalid interpretation. However both of these may be considered to be like two gears in a gear body. To use one, you have to go to neutral before shifting to the other, except that the shift to the duped or alluring one occurs quickly and automatically like the automatic transmission of a car.

When in neutral the self blanks out. It realizes the shift to the duped status only after it finds itself involved with erroneous judgements, which hurt and embarrass it. This process of shifting can be controlled after long practice to observe how the subtle mechanism operates.

February 18, 2003

Gorakshnath

He said, "Do not use the organ."

Remark:

This referred to the analyzing concluding orb of the intellect. This is a pratyahar withdrawal of a bothersome faculty. It is a practice completed by yogically-sealed celibates only. Others may practice but results are forthcoming for those in higher yoga only.

Patanjali

He said, "From the naad footing, identify the attention light which is mingled with or locked into the intellect's focus. Once it is identified, unlock it. Unmingle it. Separate it."

Remark:

There is a complexity with the various organs of perception in the subtle head. These psychic adjuncts of perception cause confusion for those who are new to yoga and for those who practiced much, and who for some reason did not progress into higher stages.

If however one becomes situated in the naad sound which is usually heard in the right side of the subtle head, one may have a chance of sorting through the various parts of the intellect.

The naad footing which Patanjali discussed is important because it is the replacement for mantras, which in themselves are a distraction mostly. One or two mantras, and very short ones, are very useful in higher yoga, otherwise mantras do not help, and must be abandoned at some stage. In the case of the naad sound, there is required no endeavor to vibrate an audible or inaudible mental or otherwise sound. Thus the energy used for the mantra is conserved. It is put directly into the required focus at whatever stage the yogi reached. The naad sound is there. It does not have to be vibrated. It is there for the convenience of the yogi to be used as Patanjali indicated, as a footing.

February 27, 2003

On this date, I saw Hariharananda who is deceased. He was with a friend named Surya. Surya smiled and then disappeared. Hariharananda made a complaint that Surya did not practice sufficiently. After Surya left, Hariharananda entered my brow chakra and showed how to use Patanjali's unlocking of the attention instruction. Apparently he did not get far beyond daily repeated attempts at doing this. At present he did not have a yoga-siddha body. He used an astral form which looked like his old body which he recently abandoned.

March 14, 2003

Shiva

He gave a crown chakra mantra: *Shivoham*

This mantra was given by Rama Bharati as my grhasta sannyasa mantra. Shivoham is an abbreviation for *shivah aham*, which means I am *(aham) shivah* (Shiva). But Shiva told me that in that usage, the word shiva assumes its ordinary meaning which is auspicious. He said that it means that someone is free from the material energy's dominance. Some swamis claim that shivoham means that the person is the supernatural controller named Shiva. That is absurd

Shivoham is the mantra to be used when one is transferred into the very top of the subtle head during meditation. This mantra may help a yogi to be stabilized, otherwise he will not be able to stay there for very long unless kundalini chakras remains there for some time.

The mantra for remaining centered in the head of the subtle body, on the intellect organ, is *Om Namah Shivaya*. In this case, *Shivaya* does mean Lord Shiva. *Namah* means that you offer your respect to Him because he is the supreme pioneer of yoga. This mantra is used if one finds that one cannot station oneself there and one feels a need for a support to hold oneself there.

March 15, 2003

Here is a diagram with detailed notes for study by yogis.

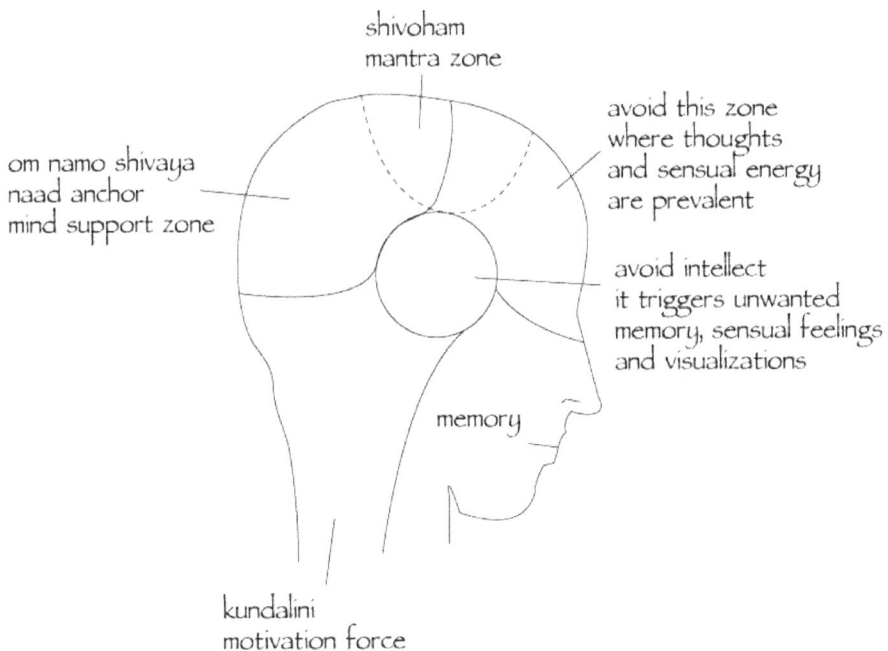

shivoham
mantra zone

avoid this zone
where thoughts
and sensual energy
are prevalent

om namo shivaya
naad anchor
mind support zone

avoid intellect
it triggers unwanted
memory, sensual feelings
and visualizations

memory

kundalini
motivation force

This is a kriya to be used by those who attained a footing in listening to the naad sound. As mentioned this takes much practice, for the mind must be accustomed to the sound, as to be attached to it. If one finds that the mind is indifferent or is repulsed or disliking of the sound, it means that one has not practiced enough.

Once one has that footing on the naad sound one should stay behind in the head or on the right side mostly and look. This would mean of course that one developed the ability to retreat from the frontal part of the subtle head.

Initially the mind needs a brace or prop. It gets that from the external world. By nature, the external world is designed to suck the energy of the self. In the conditioned state one likes this.

When a yogi graduates to higher yoga, he abandons the external world, at least, most of it. But then there arises other problems because the internal world Is itself filled with impressions from the same external creation. Thus initially, one finds that meditation causes one to return to the external world. The memory, imagination and sensual energy, are programmed to enforce the entry into the external world.

Hence we must find another brace internally. That other support is the naad sound. It is the only part of the psyche which will give definite and free assistance initially. The chitta or mento-emotional·energy is dangerous. At least this is what Patanjali indicated. He advised its complete restraint.

March 18, 2003

I made a notation on naad sound to inform students that the mind becomes attached to the naad, when one tunes into it easily, even when there are other sounds heard by the physical or subtle hearing mechanism.

The pratyahar sensual energy restraint practice, becomes successful when the mind-attention complex becomes detached from the strong attraction to the external sounds in this physical dimension.

Introspection practice does not end there but a portion is completed at that stage. This is the portion regarding the withdrawal of the subtle mechanism from the need to constantly feed on the external world. At that stage one has to go within the psyche and continue the retraction in reference to the sensual energy, memory, imagination, calculative intelligence and lifeforce.

March 20, 2003

Yogeshwarananda/Patanjali/Gorakshnath

Under their combined influence, I realized certain hindrances to transcendence practice. These are:

- memory
- imagination faculty
- extrasensory hearing and other perceptions like clairvoyance
- analytical faculty

In higher yoga, there is a laya point consideration. This laya means dissolution of objectivity. The mind regularly moves through a dissolution point in which one loses objectivity. However when the mind does this, it involuntarily relocates to a lower plane of consciousness. This is a handicap for yogins. They must study the psyche and understand how to dodge this.

July 18, 2003

Rama Bharati

He said, "You must monitor it yourself, just like the guru did. No one can help you. Later you may guide others. I am on the other side watching."

Remark:

This was in reference to the transcendence absorption process, which was pioneered by Yogesh. These notations are the fulfillment of that instruction to monitor the progression in detail.

July 26, 2003

Lahiri

He instructed, "Forget the Uddhava sutra about the sound from the heart. Do what is for you. Bring cramps from the thighs up to the front of the body. Keep the connection with the naad sound which comes from outside. It will connect of its own accord."

Remark:

On this day I used an instruction given to Uddhava by Krishna. However as in all cases, one may not use every instruction found in scripture. Lahiri advised that I use the cramp feeling from my thighs as I sat in a tight lotus, connecting that with the naad Eeeeee sound which came into the subtle body through the right subtle ear. While doing this, the stream of cramp energy connects into the naad sound. This makes for an effortless linkage of the mind to a higher concentration force, which is dharana practice, the 6th stage of yoga.

July 29, 2003

Durga

She showed a sexual-slime extracting method (kriya). This is for women, who have a vaginal passage which holds thick secretions. Such women can hardly become yoginis, but if they endeavor, it may be possible. The posture below is used with rapid breath-infusion Then the yogini stands while applying all yogic locks. She then does the down-draw breath.

In that posture, one uses the little fingers on the tail bone of the spine, while resting the fingers on the anus and vaginal area.

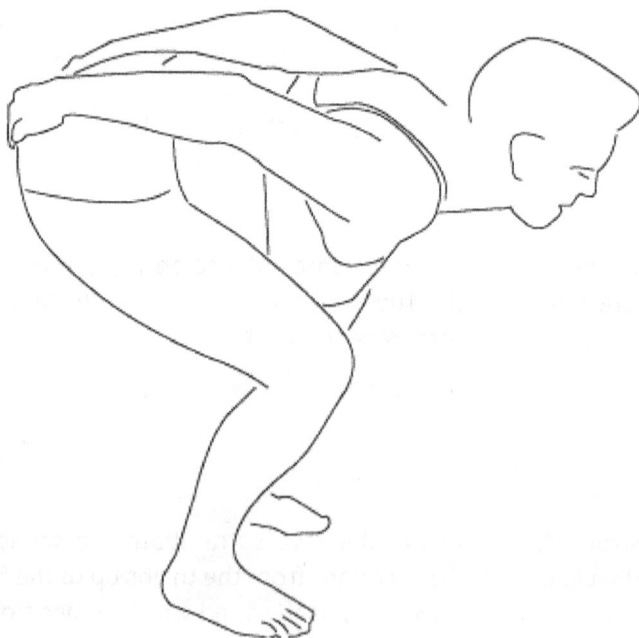

May 8, 2003

Hariharananda

He said, "I noticed you but I could not advise. If I show favoritism others may gripe. Here, use this. Teach him this."

Remark:

This was an instruction to tell a student named Balyogi to use the tongue curl-back and neck lock exercises. That practice aids in the channeling of the kundalini chakra through the neck and into the brain. In brahma yoga practice, the tongue curl-back causes energy to surge and circulate more in the subtle brain. By it, one discovers other passages for kundalini power and jyoti-light passages.

Persons who do kundalini yoga must learn to apply the neck lock consistently while doing bhastrika and other breath-infusions. That is required.

Hariharananda made a remark about others who would gripe if he spoke to me in private during a visit. I went to his ashram in South Florida. During that visit, he spoke superficially to me. However it is a fact that disciples may restrict their teacher by regulating his time with others who do not live at the ashram.

Disciples become jealous if a spiritual master mentions anything new to anyone besides themselves. Sometimes the teacher says something that they are familiar with but since by nature, they are envious, they conclude that he said something new which he never discussed with them before. Since they serve him or his mission from day to day, they suspect that he may give to others, something that is rightfully theirs.

In yoga it is the practice that counts. Even if one lives at an ashram where an accomplished master is resident, another person who lives elsewhere may make more advancement and be worthy of higher instruction because of practice. This means that the guru is not the crucial factor. It is the practice.

However if one is distracted from practice, then one will form false ideas about yoga. One will digress repeatedly. This is all part of the course of yoga, because when the yogi realizes that he or she is the cause of his or her own lack of progress, that person may take steps for self-reform. In the Bhagavad Gita there is advice.

उद्धरेदात्मनात्मानं
नात्मानमवसादयेत् ।
आत्मैव ह्यात्मनो बन्धुर्
आत्मैव रिपुरात्मनः ॥६.५॥

uddharedātmanātmānaṁ
nātmānamavasādayet
ātmaiva hyātmano bandhur
ātmaiva ripurātmanaḥ (6.5)

uddhared = uddharet — should elevate; ātmanā — by the self; 'tmanaṁ = ātmānam — the self; nātmānam = na — not + ātmānam — the self; avasādayet — should degrade; ātmaiva = ātmā — self + eva — only; hyātmano = hyātmanaḥ = hy (hi) — indeed + ātmanaḥ — of the self; bandhur

= *bandhuh — friend; ātmaiva = ātmā — self + eva — as well; ripur = ripuḥ —
enemy; ātmanaḥ — of the self*

One should elevate his being by himself. One should not degrade the
self. Indeed, the person should be the friend of himself. Or he could be the
enemy as well. **(Bhagavad Gita 6.5)**

बन्धुरात्मात्मनस्तस्य   bandhurātmātmanastasya
येनात्मैवात्मना जितः ।   yenātmaivātmanā jitaḥ
अनात्मनस्तु शत्रुत्वे   anātmanastu śatrutve
वर्तेतात्मैव शत्रुवत् ॥६.६॥   vartetātmaiva śatruvat (6.6)

*bandhur = bandhuḥ — friend; ātmā — personal energies; 'tmanas =
ātmanas — of the self; tasya — of him; yenātmaivātmanā = yena — by whom
+ ātmā — self + eva — indeed + ātmanā — by the self; jitaḥ — subdued;
anātmanas — of one who is not self-possessed; tu — but; śatrutve — in
hostility; vartetātmaiva = varteta — it operates + ātmā - self + eva — indeed;
śatruvat — like an enemy*

The personal energies are the friend of the person by whom those
energies are subdued. But for one whose personality is not self-
possessed, the personal energies operate in hostility like an enemy.
(Bhagavad Gita 6.6)

Part 4

Babaji

He said, "Reach it in, out or at the entrance. When it is strong it pours in, otherwise as it is proportionately weak, it seems farther away. Note the entrance like a gap in a wall."

Remark:

This refers to the naad Eeeeee sound which pours in the right side of the subtle head. A yogi is supposed to master the first mystic action of brahma yoga by focusing on and into this continuous sound. This is not a mantra. The yoga does not say this sound. He merely hears and takes support in it.

Vishvarupa Universal Form of Krishna

This day I was at Osan Air Force Base in South Korea. The son of my body was stationed there. I visited with his mother. The Universal Form showed how to release responsibility energies which then return to the cosmic pool of such subtle force, or go into the psyche of others, causing them to complete the said duties. When a yogi, after repeated efforts at yoga austerities, becomes very detached, without being attached to laziness or irresponsibility, he gets a waiver from the Universal Form of Krishna. He is released from many social duties.

He progresses in transcendence-contact practice. Some ascetics, after some transcendence, act as mission teachers or world saviors, as they are directed by the same Universal Form, all depending on the compassion and affection energies in their psyches at the time.

Patanjali indicated that one has to transcend the dharma-megha type of absorption, otherwise one will again take social duties. Those great yogis who perceive the rules of savior-ship in the dharma-megha or the cosmic cloud-like pool of rules for responsible social interaction (dharma), which concern spiritual development, may return into the world to uplift a sector of humanity.

Buddha

The Buddhist religion is prominent in South Korea as is Christianity. As arranged by the son of my body, I visited a Jogye-sa Buddhist temple in the place of Dongdeamoon, South Korea. Buddha showed me a method of calming the frontal chamber of the subtle head.

This forehead area is susceptible to sounds and pictures which affect meditation attempts negatively. In that method given by Buddha there are two procedures as shown in the diagrams below. One moves one's attention back and forth as indicated by the arrow. The root of the nose is the place where the nose intersects the face under the center of the eyebrows.

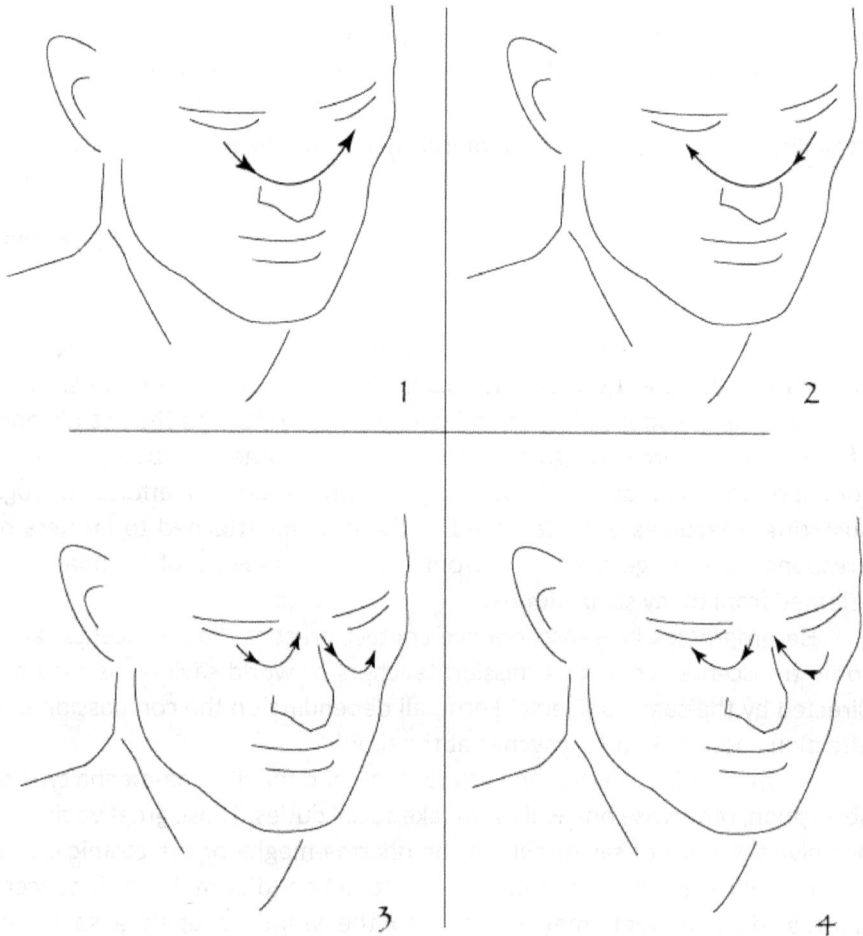

July 7, 2003

Babaji

He said, "Meet naad sound at the entrance, or inside or outside. Listen to it there. Keep the sense-of-identity there for the duration of the meditation. In cases where it is outside, enter out and then go through the window to penetrate the chit akash sky of consciousness. If it is at the entrance, you may stay there. It will usually not move in or out for that meditation. When it is on the inside, it will stay in. You should meet it wherever it is."

Remark:

It is not easy to locate the sense of identity. It evolves when a spirit makes contact with the subtle material energy. Ramana Maharshi of Arunachala used to put a question to visitors with the remark, "Who am I?"

It is a good inquiry, because most persons know themselves only as their developed cultural identity. However, besides the cultural self, there is the identity which is known in Sanskrit as ahankara. This identity is just a speck on the mystic plane, but it is a very powerful energy. Everything we do is centralized on it.

In a large city like London or New York, there is a central building in which political decisions are made. Such a place may not be the largest premises or it may not be located in the busiest part of the city, but still it is very important since the laws governing the behavior of the citizens are made there. Similarly the speck-like sense of identity is central to all participation.

In brahma yoga, we learn to isolate that speck identity. When one focuses on and eventually learns how to transfer one's core self into the naad sound, one gets the technique for isolating the sense of identity. By ripping it away from the intellect organ, the memory, the sensual energies, one trains it to remain in the naad sound. This training causes it to cooperate with the core-self in the quest for kaivalyam which is the separation of the core from its psychological equipment.

Usually, the sense of identity remains attached to the mental and emotional fluctuations. These are the personal energies which comprise what yogis call the antah karana abstract senses. This attachment is so strong that it may be compared with the attraction felt by a sixteen year old boy with a fifteen year old girl who are in love with each other. Eventually by practice, this attractive force may be reduced for a particular yogin.

July 5, 2003

Babaji

He said, "Observe its approach to fill the mind space on the right side. It may fill the entire space during some meditations."

Remark:

This pertains to the same naad Eeeeee sound, which in some meditations increases in intensity and extent.

July 15, 2003

Rama Bharati

"The lifeforce must become calm. It must enter a small localized stillness (pralaya). This is done by the reduction of desires, a sincere introspection practice, quieting of the various inner voice-activating mystic beings within who sponsor the involvements, the assumption of long periods of padmasana lotus posture sitting for suspending the mobile energy in the thighs, legs and feet. Regular practice of this causes the assumption of transcendence states.

"Do not plan to make a living. Food and such things will come by the grace of Shiva. Use the sannyasa mantra daily. Say it on your sacred thread. Use this loop."

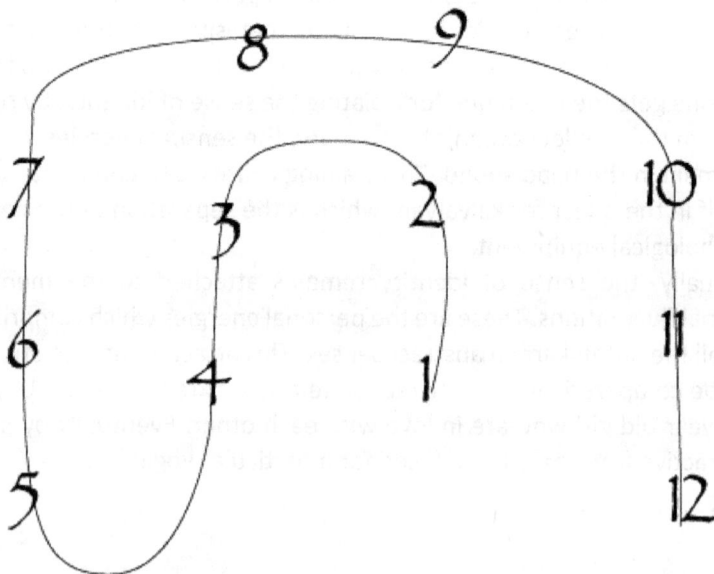

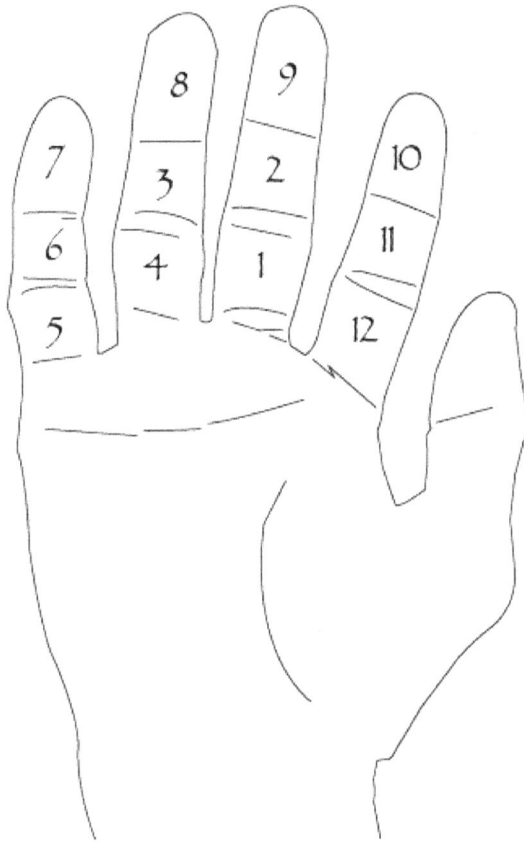

Remark:

In transcendence practice, the lifeforce enters what is called a pralaya or an immobilization of its operations.

The reduction of desires have to do with avoiding social life and reducing psychological connections with anyone who is involved with such life, and transferring one's allegiance to the siddhas who practice yoga in the astral world. In yoga, as in ordinary life, everything hinges on association. If one stays with the siddhas, then one may become a siddha. The desires for mundane social life gradually reduces.

A sincere sensual energy internalization practice is required. Through that, one retracts whatever procuring senses one protruded into the environment. Just as an infant has no desire to eat very sour food or to drink liquor but as the same infant would develop such desires in the course of time, so we developed a variety of procuring senses which cause us to chase after a variety of things. This must be reversed, so that the senses which are outgrown are pulled inwards until they digress into the psychology into nothingness, into non-activation. Then a yogi becomes freed from those things which attract him to the social environment of these lower worlds.

The quieting of the various voice -activating supernatural beings within, is done in higher yoga in a direct way, and in low elementary yoga indirectly by ignoring or refusing to respond to certain inspirations within the mind and feelings. Students must identify those inspirations which are harmful to yoga. They should ignore these.

In advanced practice, one sees the mystic persons (devas/devatas), who are speakers behind such inner voices. By an industrious yoga practice, one gains a power to dismiss them from the psyche.

The assumption of long periods of padmasana means long periods of sitting in lotus posture or even in easy pose, sukhasana. For those persons who use bodies which cannot assume those postures, it means sitting on a cushion or in a chair or even laying down.

The suspension of the mobile energy in the thighs, legs and feet, pertain to retraction of the mobile power which is regulated by the desire energy in the mind and feelings. This energy causes human beings to develop fast modes of transportation. All technological developments like automobiles and airplanes, have to do with the uncontrolled expression of mobility. A yogi curtails this by extracting the mobile energy from the thighs, legs and feet. Deep absorption is not possible unless this energy is suspended, since the kundalini chakra would not enter into a short or extended stillness nor cease its survival interest on this plane of existence.

The sannyasa mantra is *Shivoham*, which means *Shivah aham* which is to say *I am auspicious* or *I became auspicious*. Behind that is the true celibacy. When a yogi reached the boy stage in relation to sex desire, then he becomes auspicious.

The sannyasa mantra is said twelve times on the fingers in a loop as follows. The thumb is used to count as the sacred thread is looped around the thumb once. The real significance of that loop is that one goes through his day of twenty-four hours without sexual involvements, subtle or gross. Thus the celibate loop of energy in the subtle body is not broken. Sometimes however as forced by providence or through a loop hole in practice, one breaks the loop. Then it is immediately reformed because of the strength of the celibate habit. Any slight or intense flirtation which is incidental or intentional causes a breakage in the loop. And thus for a time, one loses the auspiciousness of celibacy. Eventually a yogin has to get out of this zone if he wants to close the celibate energies. In this region there will always be one or two persons, who from time to time, carry an energy which breaks the loop.

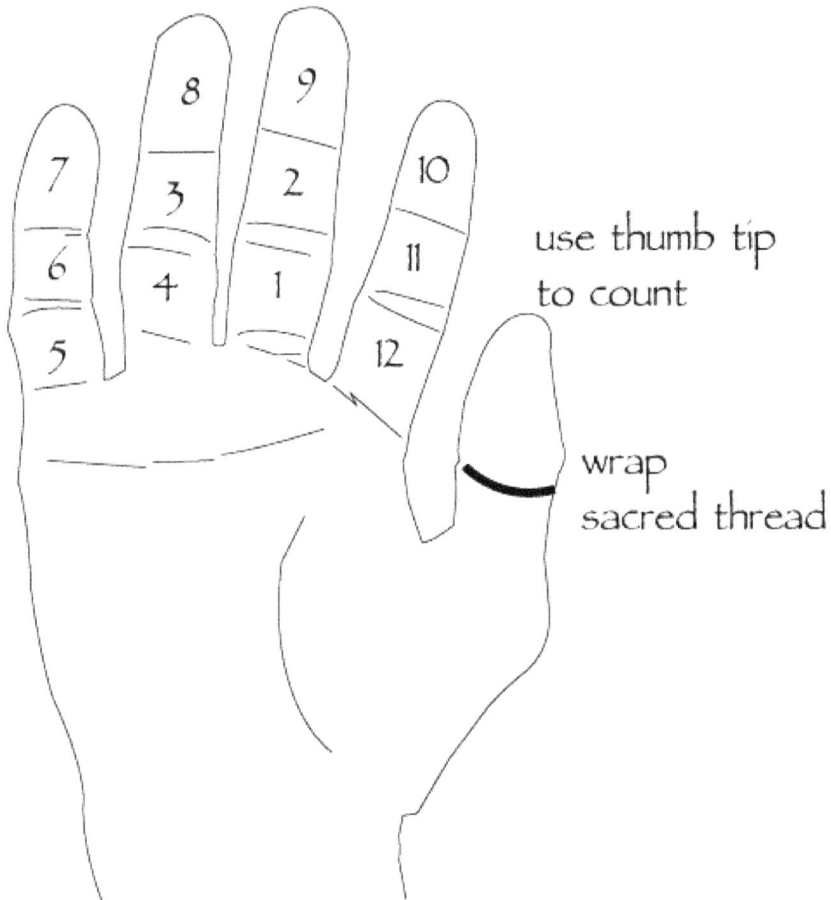

use thumb tip
to count

wrap
sacred thread

July 16, 2003

Rama Bharati

On the full transcendence absorption process, he stated, "Internal response to thoughts should cease. Ignore those who send such thoughts. Let them do as they please. Stop the internal response mechanism and the detection devices. Kick out the supernatural persons who operate the mental radio response controls. People on the outside, the enemies of yoga, cannot attack if those supernatural operators do not respond to entreaties.

"Once the thoughts stop, absorption practice begins in earnest. This will be the preparatory stage of surcharging the kundalini-less subtle body, and sitting for hours in padmasana posture."

Remark:

For the sannyasa process, I adopted many gurus. Rama Bharati is one of them. These gurus mastered absorption practice. They shared their knowledge, giving relevant techniques at various stages. The kundalini lifeforce has a value up to the full transcendence absorption stage and then it loses so much of its significance, just as a fuel depot has value to a pilot before the aircraft leaves the ground. Once the aircraft is refueled, the petrol station does not have the same significance. One must master kundalini yoga. Then it will be possible to focus on full transcendence absorption, which is the means of practicing brahma yoga. That is the highest yoga one may practice with this physical body. If one wants to go further, he can do so by using a yoga siddha form, either before or after leaving the physical form.

The enemies of transcendence absorption are both within and without the psyche of a yogi. The external enemies are insignificant. Their power is magnified by the internal ones. The internal enemies are twofold as the lower internal nature and the supernatural persons who regulate that from within on a mystic plane. If these are dealt with, success is assured.

To go to the spiritual place, one has to pass through or peer into the spiritual sky which is known as the paravyoma, the superior environment (vyoma). It is also called the chit akash or the atmosphere which comprises bliss-yielding spiritual energy.

All thoughts on this side of existence must stop before one can develop the insight vision into the spiritual sky.

July 16, 2003

Shiva

He marked my subtle body with three-lined tilak and a trident tilak on the right side of the trunk of the body.

Remark:

This is a body mark for sannyasis, who leave aside the external religious process and take wholeheartedly to the internal austerities through which one can progress into the spiritual sky.

July 16, 2003

On this day I made a notation, since a grandfather of my body had a terminal heart attack and lung deterioration. He was a very materialistic man but he was pious nevertheless feeling that righteous lifestyle, as he understood it, was the ultimate aim. Due to his transfer to the astral side some obligatory energy which he transplanted into my psyche was reinstalled in his subtle body. This relieved me of certain social responsibilities to which I was obligated because I took a body in the family which descended from his form. That relieved me of some ancestral obligation.

July 16, 2003

Rama Bharati

He stated, "Once something is sensed, if by training you are at a stage where you do not respond, the supernatural being who detects it within, will again bring it to your attention by using a memory signal. He will attempt to discuss it in a pleasing or interesting way. If your resistance is developed, you will again reject him, otherwise you will listen, be influenced by his comments about it, and subscribe to the idea or encourage its development."

Remark:

This happens in higher yoga, that even though one may reject something which forestalls the practice, still, later one may subscribe to it. A yogi should realize that there are miniature supernatural people living in the psyche. Many of them are against a firm yoga practice.

Shiva

He said, "Very subtle dishonesty, very subtle violation of morality; these stop the manifestation of deep transcendence. Be on guard."

Remark:

Patanjali stated in the Yoga Sutras that after long practice, finding and eliminating impediments, the yogi succeeds. An impatient person or one who wants to be blessed with full transcendence absorption without having to earn it, cannot be a successful yogin.

In regards to what Shiva said, he directed me to a book called *Jain Yoga*, by R. Williams. This book has a survey of the mediaeval sravakacaras. It describes the austerities practiced and recommended by Mahavira, one of the Tirthankara teachers of the Jain faith.

Babaji

He instructed: "Holding it, attune the respective orb to it. The other orbs will not hold it. Some, because they require changing excitements. Others, because they do not pick up sound. Hold it there. From there, the other features of chit akash will be manifested, usually beginning with sight within the intellect."

Remark:

This refers to holding the attention within the naad Eeeeee sound which usually pours in through the right subtle ear or which may come into the subtle body from another orifice. The attention orb is to be held to it, for some time, as the first kriya in dharana, dhyana and full transcendence absorption. In terms of how these develop, dharana, dhyana and full transcendence absorption are sequential. The sequence is called *samyama* by Patanjali.

The orbs which require changing excitements are the lower subtle senses. The ones which do not respond to the sound are the higher subtle senses. The lower ones work in conjunction with memory. These usually distract a yogin from the naad focus, which serves him as both a footing and a mantra, a position from which he may stabilize the attention and wait patiently for the imagination orb to be converted into a seeing-eye for peering into the chit akash, the spiritual atmosphere.

July 19, 2003

Yogeshwarananda

From a distance, he said, "All that includes paravairagya. Details were given but you will discover the whole of it. Some of us did not have the same hang-ups as you do, or as others do or did. Each must work on the discrepancies which hamper full detachment."

Remark:

This relates to fine-tuning the aspect of keeping the intellect organ from reacting with what happens in the world. It is a total self conquest, self-checking, self-criticism and true self-help. Little by little one can achieve this. One should be patient with the self.

Notation

I made a notation of the supernatural being who resides near the evacuation pouch. After eating he came up and said, "Now do breath-infusion. Fill this with infused energy."

He pointed to an empty chamber which was shaped like a capsule. Because they are under the dulling and passionate influences, people ignore this instruction time after time. They perceive the instruction of that person as an urge which may be ignored without consequence.

August 1, 2003

Yogeshwarananda

He showed the mobility orb which operate the feet, and the minor mobility orb which operates the sexual apparatus. He said, "That is the result of not eating for sexual purposes for the last three years. That caused the orb to move up and out of the legs, due to it not being fed subtle hormones."

Remark:

This orb has to be de-activated for full absorption practice. So long as certain subtle energies are in motion to act in the material world, one cannot experience full transcendence.

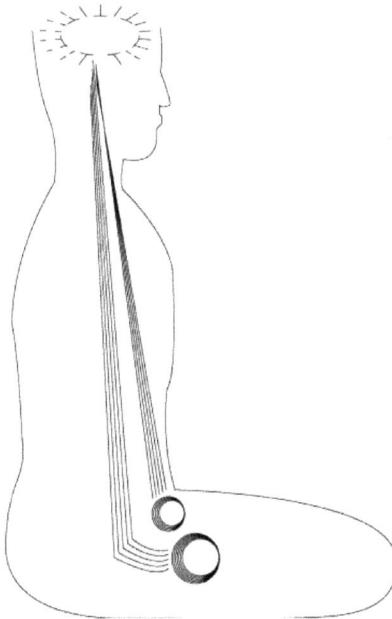

Yogeshwarananda

By his grace, I observed the movement of the mobility and sex functions orbs, both being retracted into the throat orb, which appears to swallow them. The mobility orb was swallowed first.

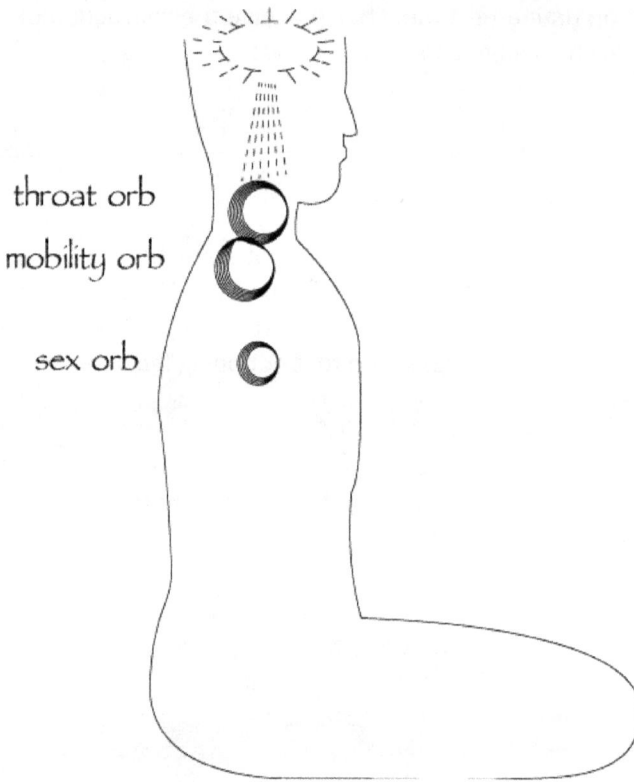

throat orb

mobility orb

sex orb

Remark:

It should be noted that as they advance, some yogins pass through these stages without a visual understanding, just as persons sitting in a jet may not see the clouds or landscape as they pass through the sky. One should be observant, and must have mystic vision.

I noted that visualization of things which pertain to the earth zone, occur in the mind space which is in the frontal area of the subtle head. Modern people are too preoccupied with the physical format. They take steps to affirm the physical brain and to deny the subtle head.

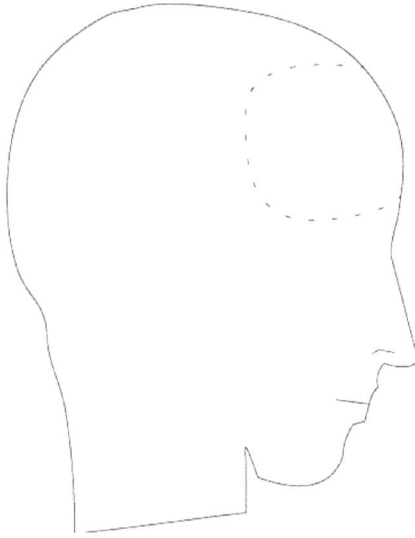

August 9, 2003

I made a notation about realizing advanced pratyahar sensual withdrawal. One should have experiences or visions of certain thought transferences, without these being muddled or being flashed too fast for coherence. If one retracted his or her sensual energies sufficiently, the tendency of the mind to present muddled or haphazardly mixed sounds and images, ceases for the most part.

I was in an aircraft when I made this notation. A lady sitting in one seat of the plane, thought of herself in a very attractive form. She used a crude body which looked like a human adaptation of a hippopotamus. Still, she conceived of herself in a slim sexually-appealing form in a short skirt, being panty-less and standing with the bottom of her buttocks exposed. She conceived of that in reference to me and other males on the aircraft, as a way of attracting us.

Due to mastership at sensual withdrawal, I clearly saw what she did mentally, even though that mental conception took place effortlessly in her mind space, just as if she was an expert at introspective focusing practice.

Another passenger, a male, imagined himself standing to remove his luggage which was stored in an overhead rack. He did not stand, but only mentally conceived of doing this. He wanted to retrieve something from his luggage. He daydreamt at the time. This is an example of a transcendence focusing practice, which is the effortless linkage of the attention to something. Of course in yoga, we practice to do this in reference to higher persons and powers.

These incidences usually occur in a sponge-like area of the mind environment, in the right or left frontal part of the subtle brain. For the yogi these may occur in a clear persistent flash or in a slow-motioned series of formations.

Lahiri

Nabhi kriya expressions

He showed a four-fold nabhi system, which is the natural system of distribution of nourishment which is automatically carried out by material nature.

Nabhi means navel. For all purposes our feelings are controlled, regulated and destroyed by the navel chakra, which is the primal place for nourishment of material bodies. Except for a yoga siddha body, all subtle and gross forms are controlled by the navel whirl chakra. Even the kundalini chakra is to a greater degree regulated by the navel. This is realized when a yogi perfects kundalini yoga and gains control of diet and air intake.

Mother-to-fetus nabhi kriya

This is compulsory for persons taking birth in a material body or in any other realm where it is necessary to enter into a female psyche for entry into those places.

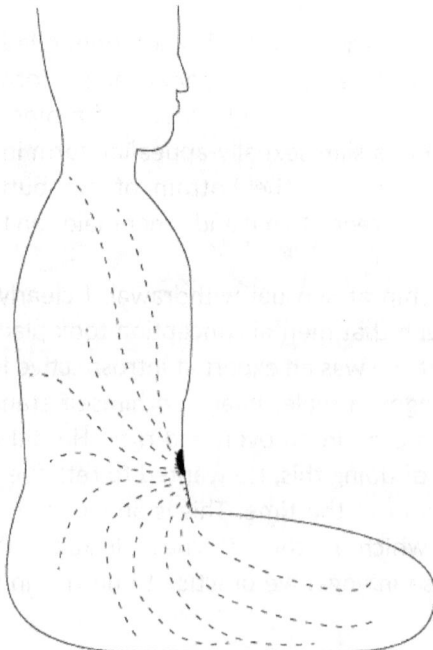

Even though such intercourse was required by a father and mother, in this nabhi kriya, the energies are not primarily concerned with sexual intercourse. It is concerned mainly with creating a form for movement and feeling ability in the particular world of manifestation which the form is to manifest in. What is experienced as sexual attraction by the parents, is experienced in a converted-way as being a need of a form by the child to be. The child develops an attitude of dependence on the would-be parents. This attitude is experienced as lust or sexual need in the parents' emotions and minds.

Nabhi kriya after birth.

This is the natural system of energy distribution just after birth. It is the conscious pull for food nutrients.

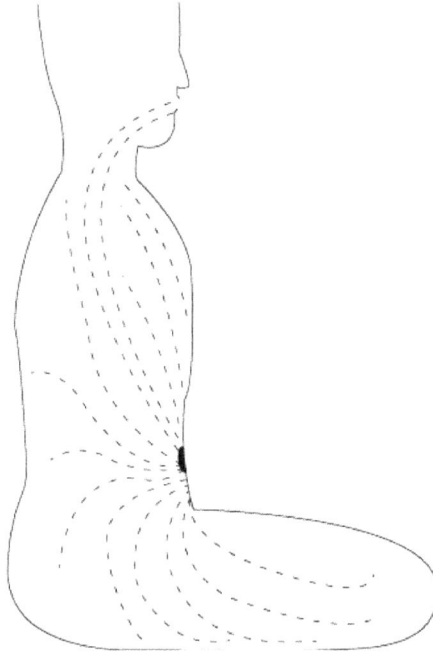

Distribution system kriya

This has two configurations which are the lung-heart pump distribution and the abdomen-intestines-colon apparatus. The vein-arteries system mediates between the lung-heart pump and the abdomen-intestines-colon system.

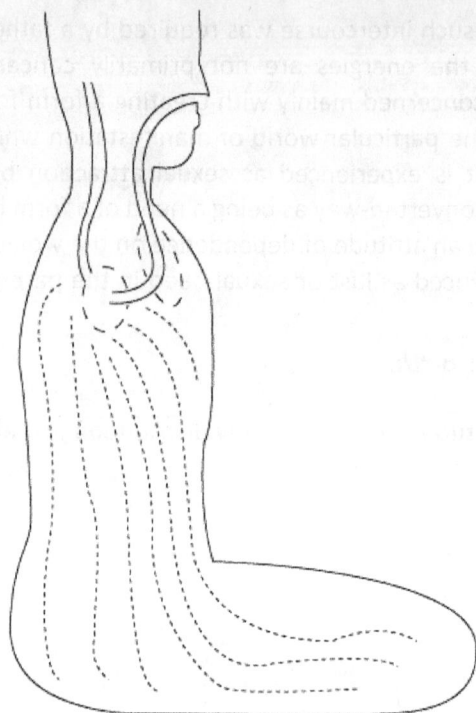

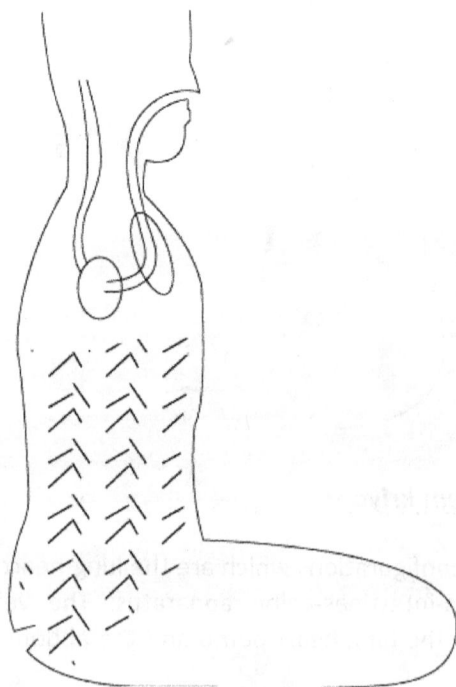

Yogically-improved nabhi kriya

This system is developed only in yogis who practice postures and breath-infusion. It is very effective in freeing the psyche from lower energy intake.

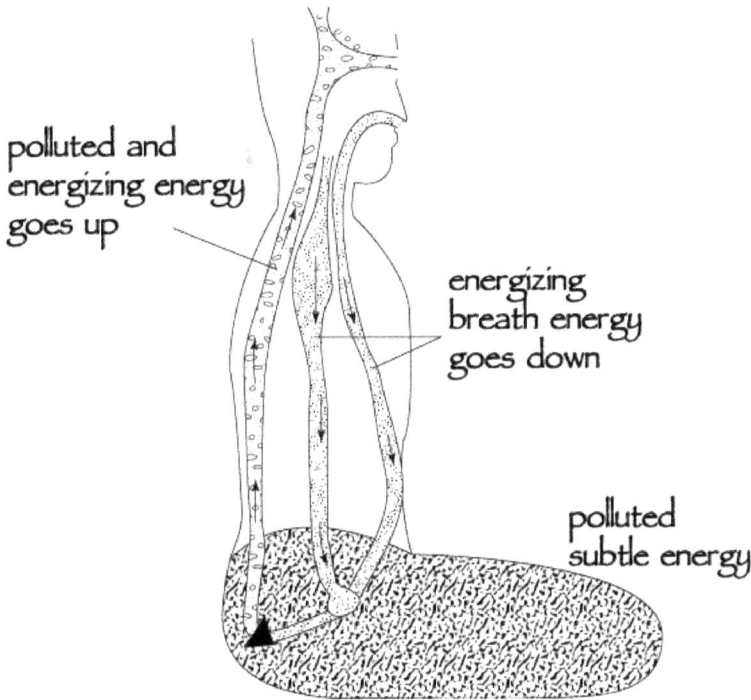

polluted and energizing energy goes up

energizing breath energy goes down

polluted subtle energy

August 11, 2003

Yogeshwarananda

Pulling up lower sensual orbs

He showed how to elevate some lower sensual orbs. Initially one becomes concerned with pulling in the sensual energy which exudes from the head of the subtle body. Later one perceives that there are some other orbs, which escaped from the intellect organ long ago, and which function from far away as its satellites. These orbs are elsewhere in the subtle body.

In the case of a donkey, the orb which is for grasping is lodged in the mouth, while for a human being it is in the fingers mostly. Sometimes in a human being the orb for sexual intercourse comes into the mouth and then there is intense kissing and a resistance for sexual contact. But the orb moves into the sexual organ where it finds its full expression. In the case of a mouse in the dark, the orb for vision is in its whiskers, while in a human being that orb will try to get information from the feeling orb in the hands and feet.

These are orbs of energy which must be retracted for a complete introspection. Once a yogin realizes how long and intricate, the path of yoga is, there is a likelihood that he may turn from the practice. When they discover that yoga is detailed and scientific, a few persistent ascetics are encouraged to continue.

There is a sensual orb which operates the intestines, as well as one which operates the feet and sexual organs. These must be retracted otherwise transcendence states will not be experienced.

Yogacharya Vacaspati (Dr. Ashoke Kumar Chatterjee) has made it clear in his book *Purana Purusha,* that so long as the dynamic prana moves, there is no full transcendence absorption. He said that one should shift into the still energy.

This means that so long as the sensual orbs are operating on this side of existence, one cannot enter into their dissolution or de-activated state. Thus one cannot enter into or even peer into the sky of consciousness. One has to shut down the sensual orbs. Patanjali stated this in another way, explaining that the operations of the vrittis of the mental-emotional energy (chitta) must come to a standstill for there to be real yoga.

There are some kundalini yoga practices which help in the retraction of the orbs which are in the intestines, sexual organs and feet. These are done with bhastrika rapid breathing while the fingers are pushed against the anus/perineum area

August 11, 2003

Yogeshwarananda

In this respect, having to do with the sensual orbs which originally came out of the intellect organ, Yogesh is the master of the process. Other yogis mastered this but not with as much precision and detail.

Here is a diagram for doing a posture which helps to pull back the mobility orb. While doing this, do bhastrika rapid breathing, but pull all pain-energy back into the brain. This action trains the mobility orb to move into the intellect.

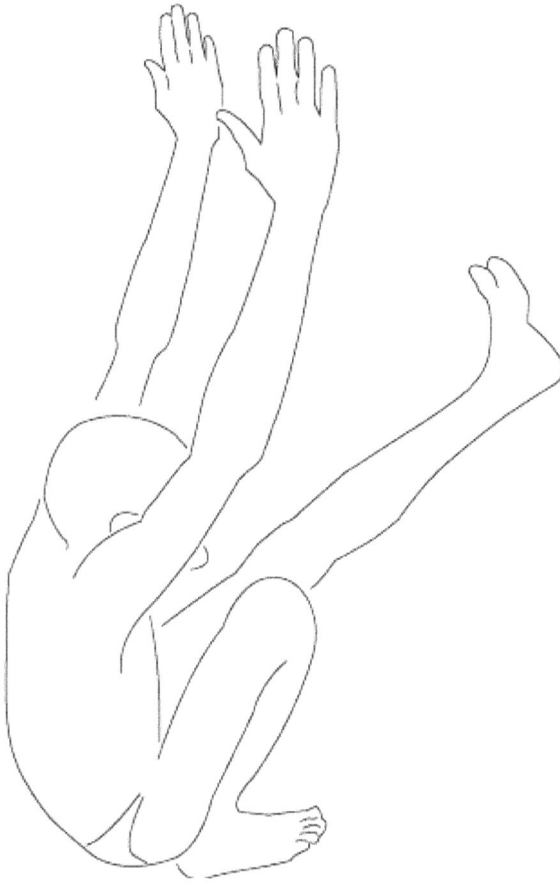

This second posture is an easy one but it requires for the eyes to be closed for increased concentration on the movement of the subtle energy. One should breathe the air down into the lower belly.

One will notice that after controlling the diet for a time, it permanently adjusts, and one can eat one main meal early in the day, with a light snack later. Initially if one tries to do this, one may have wind pain or some other problem, in addition to emotional disturbances. When these ailments cease, even if one does not eat frequently and even if one greatly reduces, one can understand that the nourishment orb is being retracted. When the orbs are curtailed, there is a great reduction of random energy movements all over the body, resulting in deep absorption.

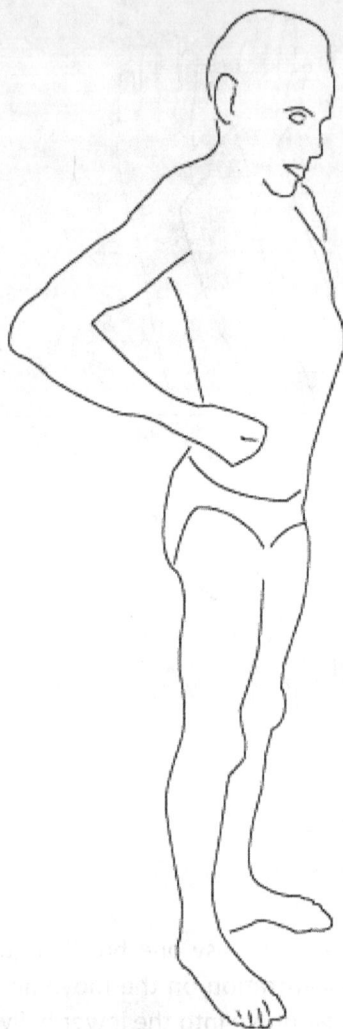

August 12, 2003

Here are some foot orb into sex orb, into intellect organ mystic actions. These concern the portion of foot energy which is empowered for sexual interest. This energy causes a person to travel for miles if possible to have sexual intercourse. In some cases a disembodied person will travel through the astral distances a very long way and even pass through several dimensions for sexual indulgence. There is the case of Pururavah who pursued the angelic queen named Urvashi exactly for that purpose.

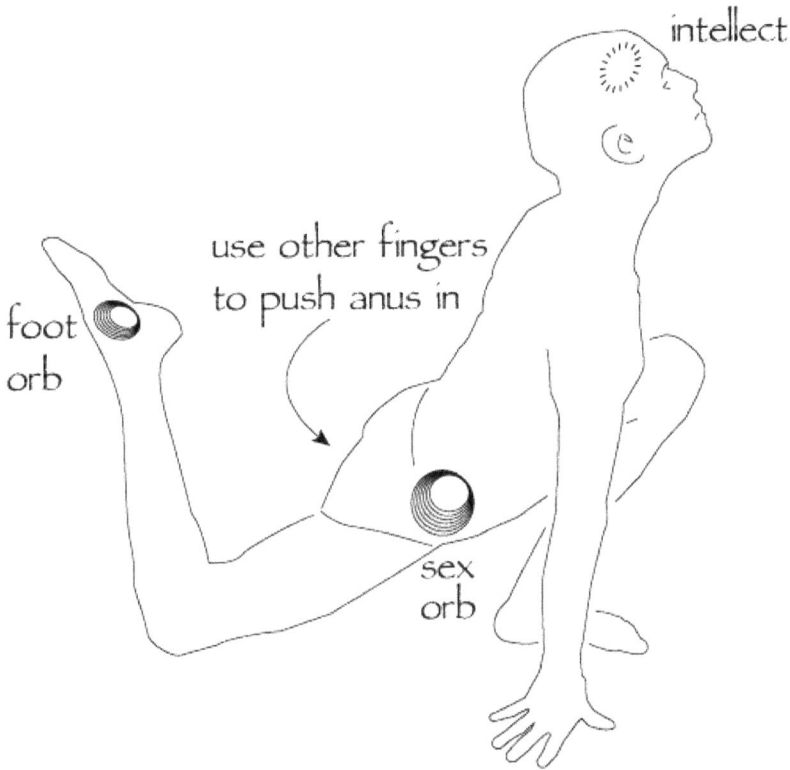

August 17, 2003

I did a food-orb withdrawal, having to do with food needs of the feet. This orb is withdrawn to the intestines first. Once in the intestines, it is pulled out of the navel chakra. Look at the two postures below. These allow one to find this orb mystically.

In yoga practice, a particular posture may help a yogi achieve one experience today and another a year after. It depends on the stage of his advancement. Yoga is not boring if it is done progressively. The same posture may be used from day to day, while achieving new skills as proficiency increases.

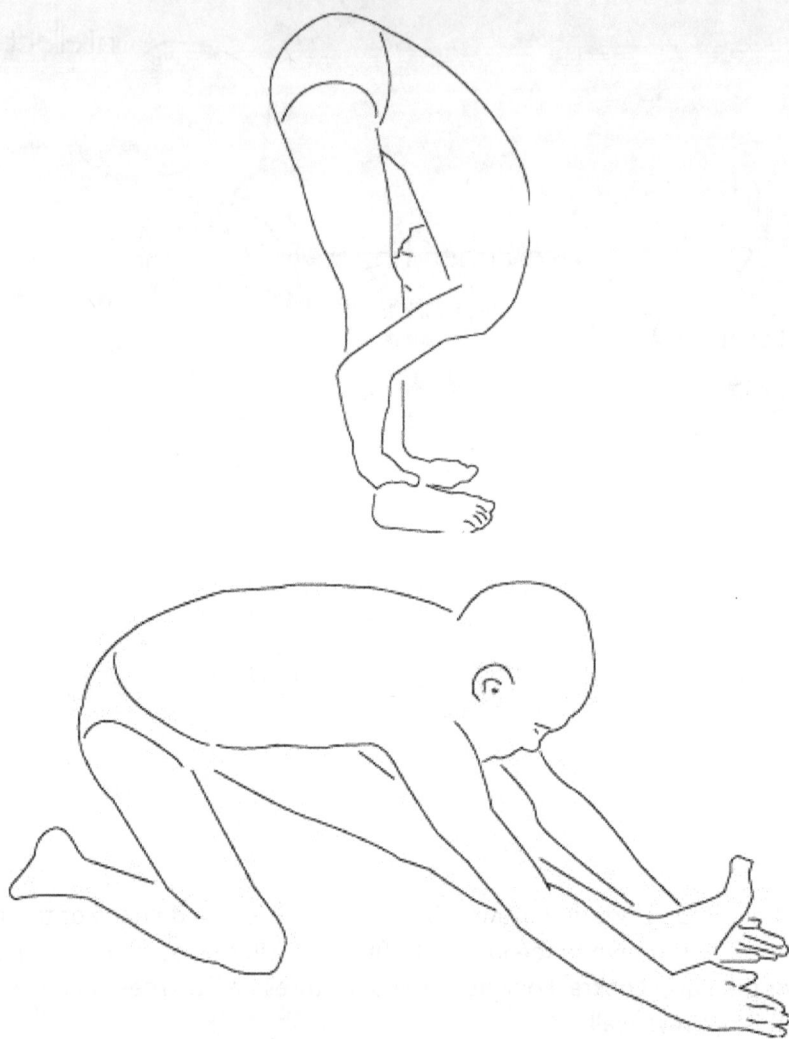

Pulling the food orb in the foot or in other parts of the subtle psyche, is part of advanced interest-retraction practice. One who does this, attains nirvana or the blowing out of material existence, which is simply a way of saying that one closes out his existence on this side of the living range.

Initially sensual energy retraction practice is done by pulling back the sensual energy which courses out of the psyche through the eyes and ears. Later, one must zero-in on other aspects, one by one. Each yogi must work for deliverance step by step.

On this day, Lahiri and his disciple Panchanam Bhattacharya, were talking. As permitted, I happen to hear the conversation. Lahiri said, "One cannot cheat."

Panchanam replied, "Gradually a yogi is purified. Each practice must be done sincerely."

Retracting an air ball from the foot-leg-thigh apparatus into the lung. This is for controlling the mobility mechanism which causes the body to go here and there in various materialistic pursuits. This is required as a preliminary practice before doing full transcendence focus.

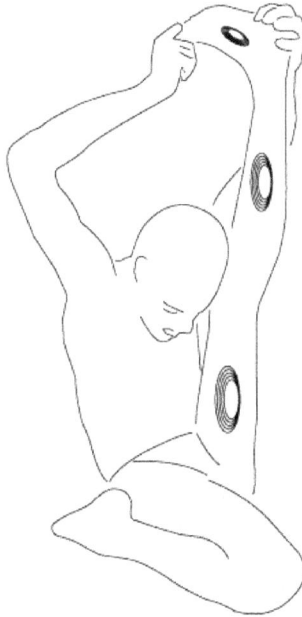

foot, leg and thigh
orbs

Lahiri showed an *omkar* kriya. This curbs subtle energy. There are diagrams below. When this was given to me I stayed with a disciple of Rama Bharati, my sannyasa guru. Incidentally the formality of sannyasa does not mean anything by itself. One has to be capable of celibacy by virtue of having mastered kundalini yoga. Superficially sannyasa by a ceremony has nothing to do with the mastery of kundalini yoga.

A guru is much. A yogi-guru is much more than a mere guru. But even with such a teacher, one cannot succeed if one does not have the grace of providence. One must be a favorite of the Central Person in the Universal Form. Then one can sidestep the social obligations, which contravene yoga.

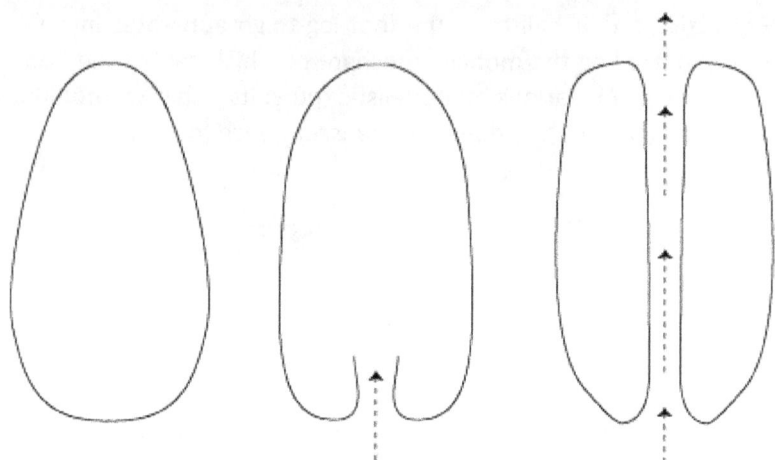

heart chakra penetrated by kundalini force

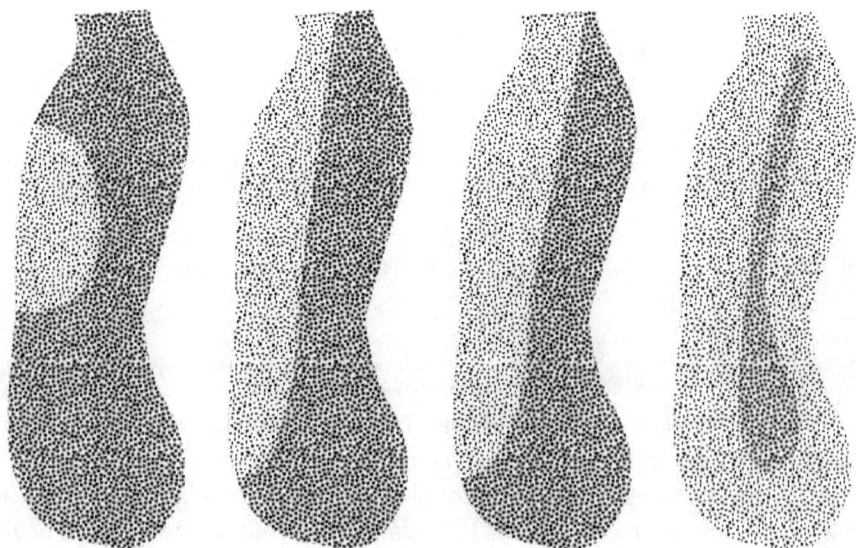

increasing proportion of energizing energy due to pranayama breath-infusion

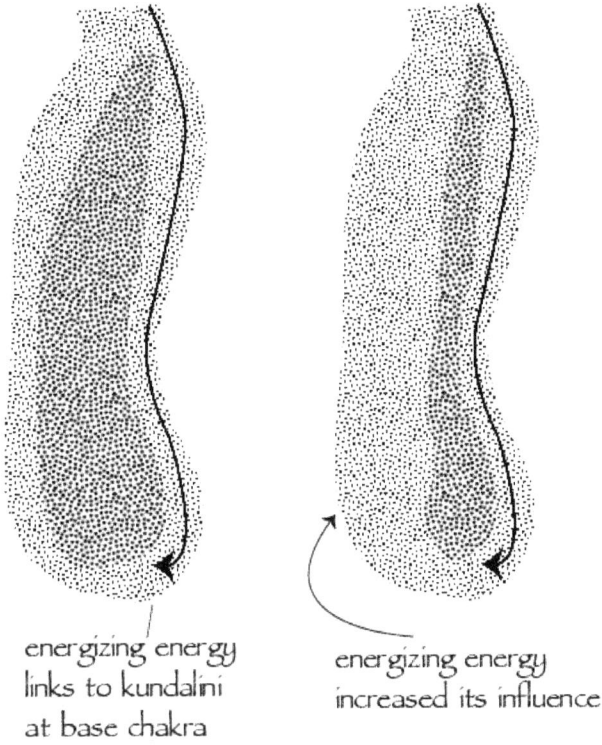

energizing energy
links to kundalini
at base chakra

energizing energy
increased its influence

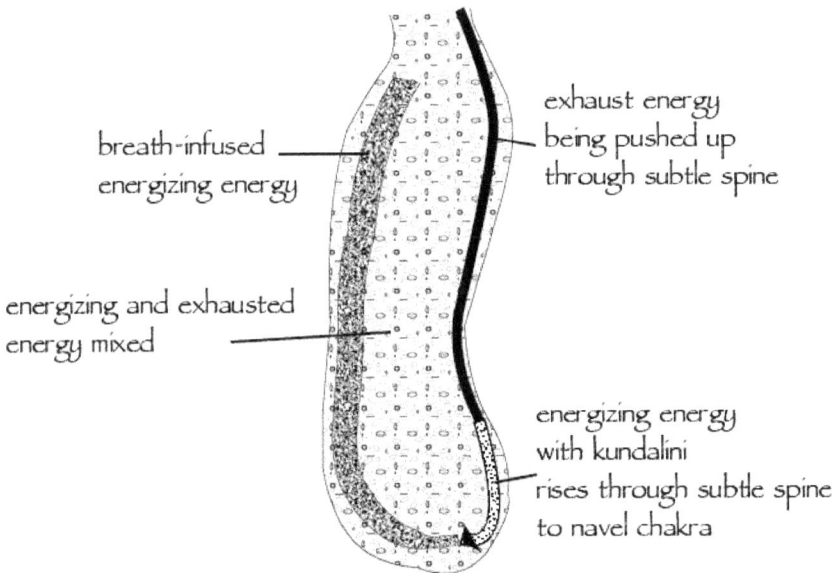

breath-infused
energizing energy

exhaust energy
being pushed up
through subtle spine

energizing and exhausted
energy mixed

energizing energy
with kundalini
rises through subtle spine
to navel chakra

exhausted
energy

energizing energy
links to kundalini
at base chakra

energizing energy
increased its influence

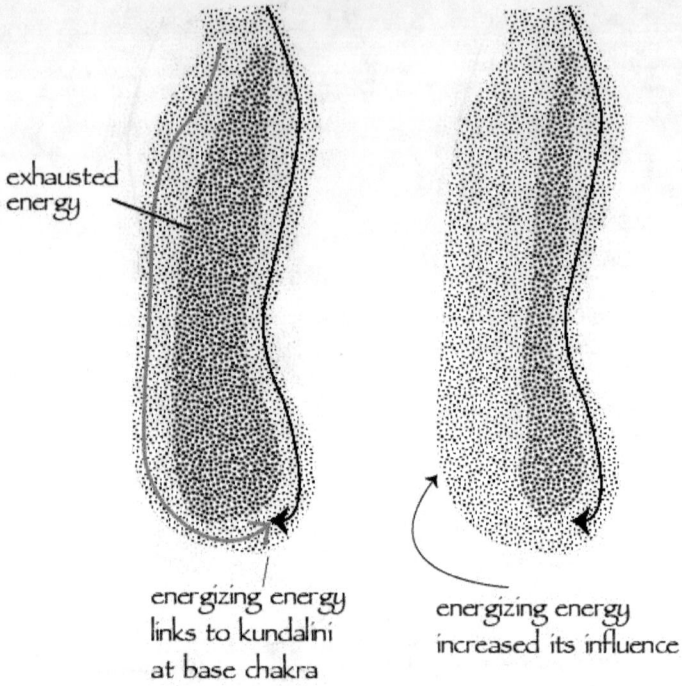

These diagrams below are a sequence

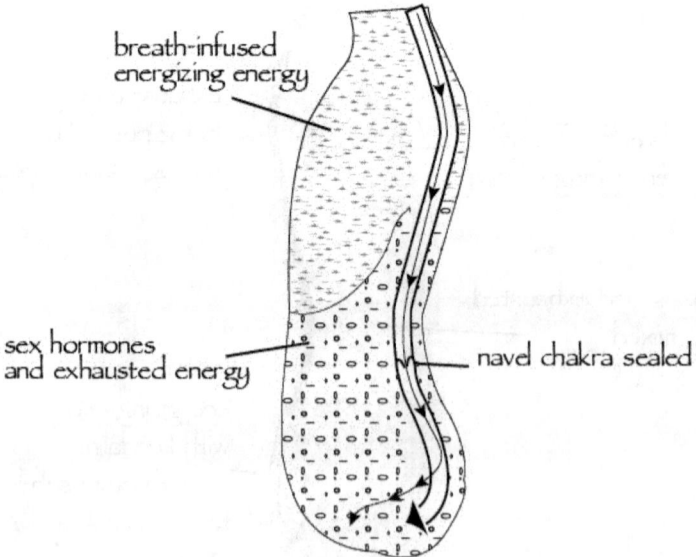

breath-infused
energizing energy

sex hormones
and exhausted energy

navel chakra sealed

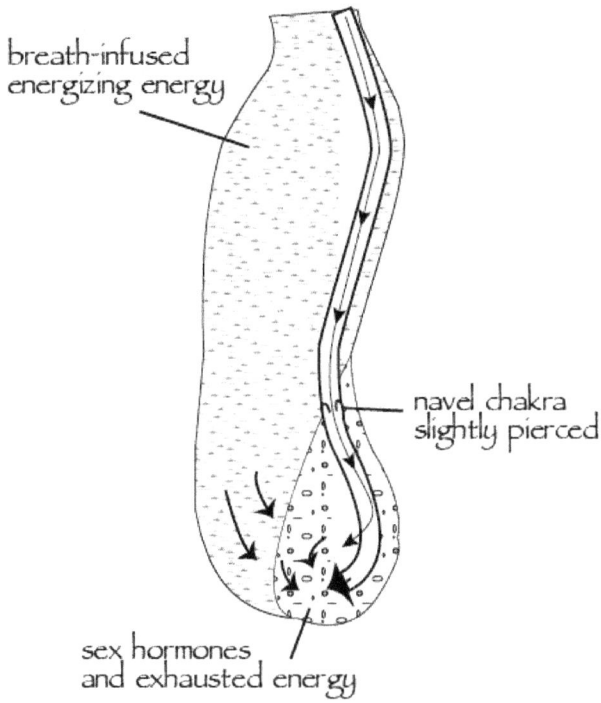

breath-infused
energizing energy

navel chakra
slightly pierced

sex hormones
and exhausted energy

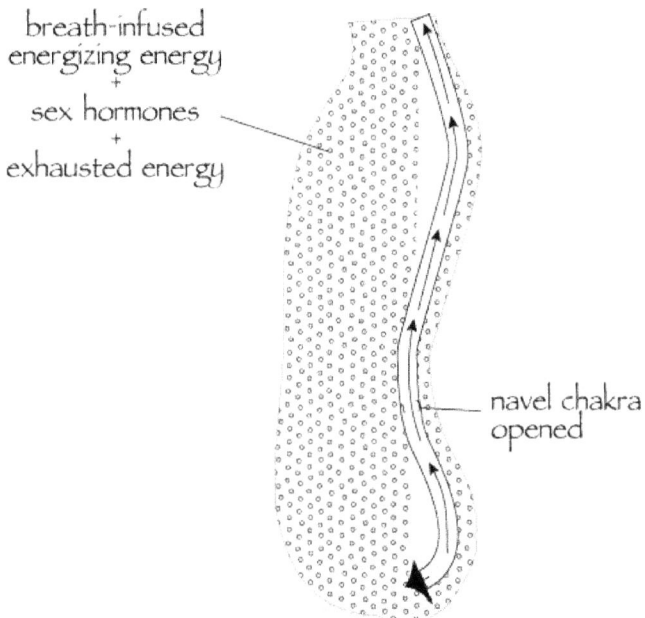

breath-infused
energizing energy
+
sex hormones
+
exhausted energy

navel chakra
opened

August 19, 2003

Lahiri

He said, "Only after full celibacy with no formation of semen, does the heart lotus go up. Otherwise sex energy pulls the petals downward.

He gave this instruction:

Take down the intellect light-gas energy and mix that in this region.

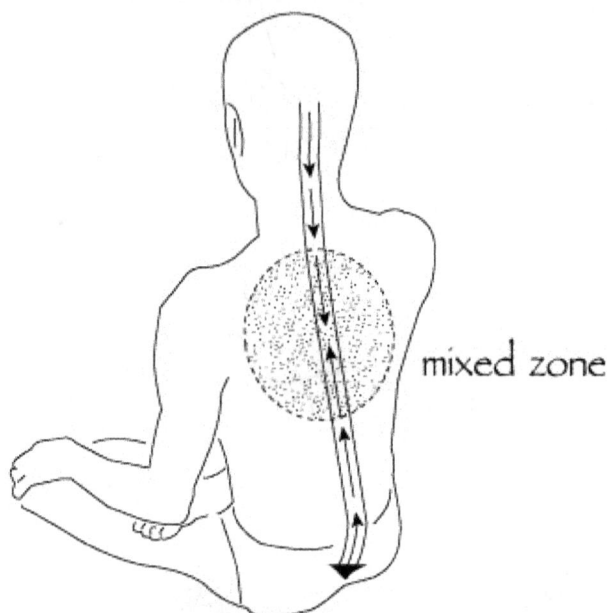

mixed zone

He stated further that *omkara* contact is not always a hearing technique. It may be a position or feeling, or even sight technique on occasion.

August 20, 2003

Lahiri

He gave an anus orb withdrawal. This is used to reduce food intake and to force the anus controller to cooperate with the plan of yoga. This goes along with curtailing meals and reducing food intake to one meal per day, with liquid or light snack at other times.

A yogi should remove himself from the busy schedule of human civilization. This is necessary for full success. See the posture below. One stands, arches over, and does the one-jerk breath, while pushing on the anus region. One-jerk breath is a sudden pull of air inwards, followed by a sudden push of air outwards. One does this for about 15 to 20 such in and out breaths at a time. The fingers are pushed in the anal area. This causes a reduction in the energy used by the anus orb, thus freeing the kundalini chakra from the base chakra.

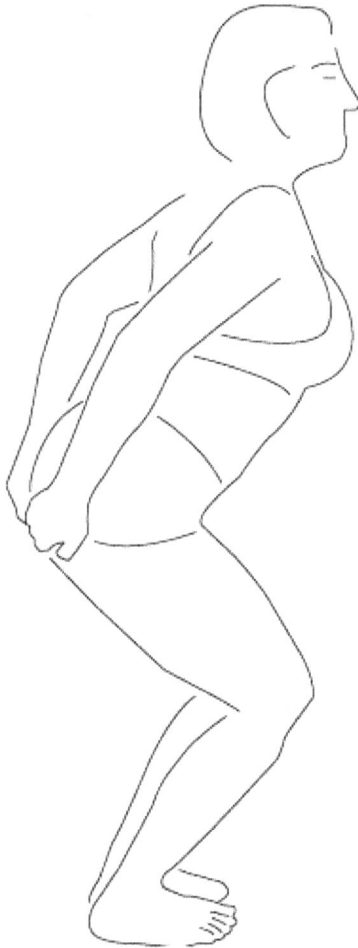

Lahiri commented that the foot, leg, thigh stretches in hatha yoga, awakens the kundalini energy in the correct manner.

Sushumna perception meditation

This is done to check to see if the sushumna subtle spinal passage is cleared. In the average human being, it is dark because the energies are dull due to involvement in animalistic activities. A yogi should rate his progress.

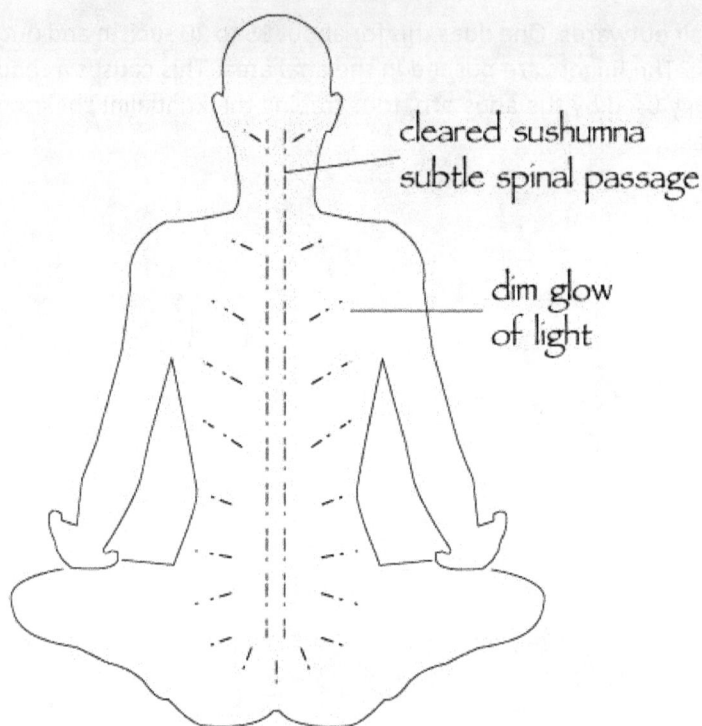

cleared sushumna
subtle spinal passage

dim glow
of light

August 23, 2003

Yogeshwarananda

He said, "You are not ready. You are in the wrong environment."

Remark:

I was at an unfavorable place. The environment was noisy. It was geared to material activities. Yogesh was in a queue of yogis, being the 5th yogi in the line-up. Seeing me practicing he made the remark. At the time, I planned to relocate outside the United States. The actual incidence may have occurred one year sooner than the date above.

Lahiri gave an omkar practice on that day of August 23, 2002. Here is a diagram.

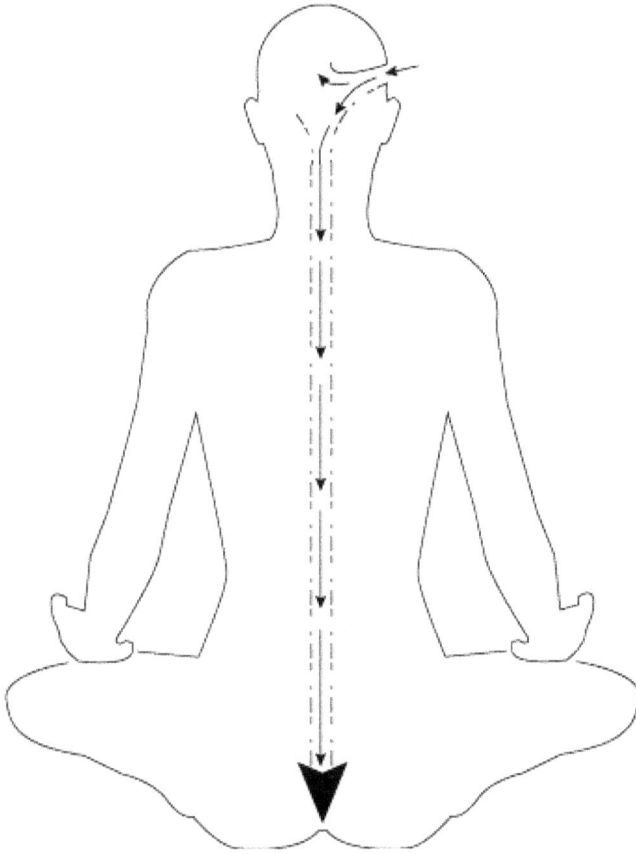

On the following day, Lahiri said that as the naad subtle sound leaks into the right ear, it may be directed into the sushumna passage in the spine. From there it may spread and expand into the bubble body.

Remark:

The bubble body is a pranamaya kosha, or a body which comprise energizing subtle energy.

Lahiri made a remark. He said, "Hatha yoga is wonderful for awakening kundalini. The stretches stimulate the chakras, open the sushumna nadi, allowing union and cooperation between the lifeforce and the intellect. These organs cease fighting each other and cooperate for the yogi's development."

August 25, 2003

On this day, I saw the excitement lobe. It is a small light in the subtle body, in the intellect which consist of glowing and flickering lights. The excitement orb is in the attention energy. It is very fleeting, very illusive. It is subtler than the attention energy and more forceful in making the yogi deviate from practice. Due to this orb, great ancient yogis like Vishvamitra were diverted from yoga objectives, and spent many years with diversions, before they became perfected. Usually that excitement orb is about this size:

O

It may shrink or expand on occasion.

It is usually believed that women cannot become successful yoginis, but this is not true, even though generally women are not fitted to the rigors of yoga. It is because they are prone to excitement. They fall under the influence of that orb. Many great yogis warned that a man who is attached to women cannot become a great yogi. The reason is that generally women are prone to the excitement orb.

It follows then, that those men who are attached to women, would of necessity, be engaged in pleasing such females, which means working under their impulsion which come from the stimulus of the excitement orb.

Conversely a few lucky females may get away from the influence of excitement if they fall under the influence of a yogi who is resistant to the orb and who stands his ground and does not budge to its impulsions. To this, a yogi should have the association of higher ascetics who are stronger and more resistant.

Lahiri gave a technique for suppressing the excitement orb. This is an interiorization technique. As readers can observe, I do regress to pratyahar sensual energy withdrawal from time to time. This is necessary as one advances. Whatever a yogi failed to achieve previously, is brought to his attention as he progresses. He must complete each part of the practice which was neglected before.

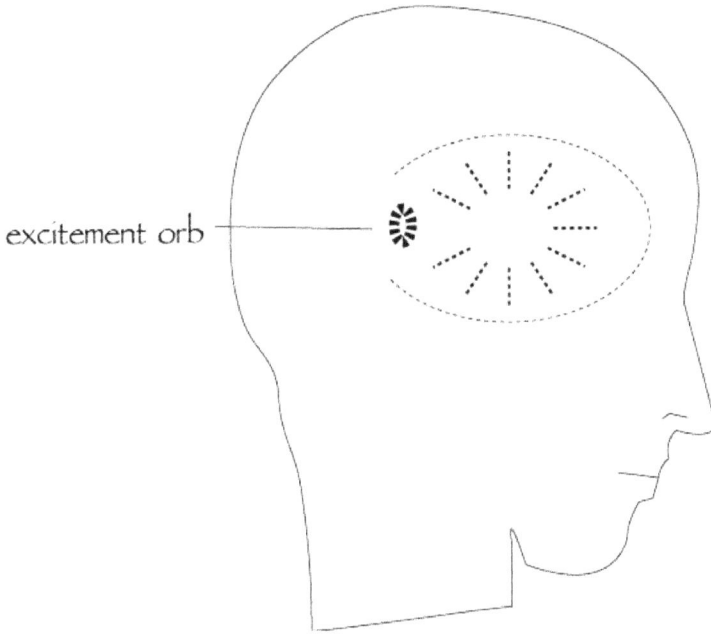

excitement orb

When the suppression of the excitement orb is mastered, one notices that it stops the tendency to pass through the focal consciousness point. It removes one's inability to perceive automatic memory and image transfers. What does this mean?

The focal consciousness is a vanishing point for the objective consciousness. If one checks carefully with the eyes closed in a dark place, one will notice that every so often, or even irregularly, one loses objective consciousness, even while awake. It may happen for a split second or for longer. As soon as one gains objectivity again, one notices that the mind has already developed certain ideas. One stares within to see such visualizations or sounds. This happens frequently. Great yogins like Ramakrishna indicated that for success in yoga, one has to conquer this tendency of being forced through the vanishing point of objective consciousness. It is not an easy attainment for a yogin. When one masters this, it is said that one reached the 4th plane of consciousness or the turiya.

The imagination orb usually operates in conjunction with the memory orb and with the sensuality mechanism. Their conjoint function is to keep the core-self entertained within the mind. Unfortunately, these apparatuses are so expert at their functions, that the core remains perpetually enthralled by their schemes. This is to be regretted.

That is all I can say. The same God who awarded that seemingly uncontrollable sensuality, will give one the strength to control it, but one has to practice ardently.

Part 5

Yogeshwarananda

On this day he informed that the excitement orb really belongs to the lifeforce. He said, "It is not part of the intellect mechanism. Send it down. It merely goads the intellect. It thrives in disturbed states. It chases sensations. It rides the intellect piggy-backed."

He also stated, "Pain is needed to internalize hatha yoga. Without pain, the mind will externalize more and more, to avoid the internal world of the psyche, except in the case of dirty emotions."

Remark:

This is an important information. Every yogin should consider this.

Yogeshwarananda

He said, "Krishna discussed it in Chapter two of the Bhagavad Gita discourse. Everyone does it but does not realize what transpires. It is a transcendence absorption"

Remark:

This is a talk about the 7th stage of yoga, which is dhyana. This is what Krishna said:

ध्यायतो विषयान्पुंसः
सङ्गस्तेषूपजायते ।
सङ्गात्संजायते कामः
कामात्क्रोधोऽभिजायते ॥२.६२॥

dhyāyato viṣayānpuṁsaḥ
saṅgasteṣūpajāyate
saṅgātsaṁjāyate kāmaḥ
kāmātkrodho'bhijāyate (2.62)

dhyāyato = dhyāyataḥ — considering; viṣayān — sensual objects; puṁsaḥ — a person; saṅgas — attachment; teṣūpajāyate = teṣu — in them + upajāyate — is born, is created; saṅgāt — from attachment; saṁjāyate — is born; kāmaḥ — craving; kāmāt — from craving; krodho = krodhaḥ — anger; 'bhijāyate = abhijāyate — is derived

The act of considering sensual objects, creates in a person, an attachment to them. From attachment comes craving. From this craving anger is derived. (Bhagavad Gita 2.62)

A yogi must study the operations in the psyche to understand what to do to achieve pratyahar, dharana and dhyana. These, being the 5th, 6th, and 7th stages of yoga, are operated automatically in the psyche. Thus one can understand them from nature itself.

For instance, if we study how we got this body and how it developed in the father's body as a speck of semen and then developed further as an embryo in the mother's form, we can understand what the reversal of introspection is. Now if one goes back further and understands how we lost the last body and how before entering the subtle body of the would-be father, we were reduced to just about nothing, we could understand nature's process of introspection.

Nature has the ability to either express or suppress the sensuality. The suppression is introspection, being done for us forcibly or desirably by nature.

Dharana means a deliberate focus, such that the attention is attached to something else and is kept there on the basis of a desire. Nature also operates much focus in that way, but we have to study its methods. Take for instance, a toddler's repeated attempts to walk. Even though frustrated repeatedly, the child focuses on walking over and over, for days or months or even for years. This operates by a focus on mobility.

In this way one can learn from nature how to do higher yoga, since nature is itself executes subtle actions.

August 30, 2003

Lahiri

He gave an *omkara* kriya. A yogi should hear subtle sound which usually resonates on the right side of the subtle head, near the right ear.

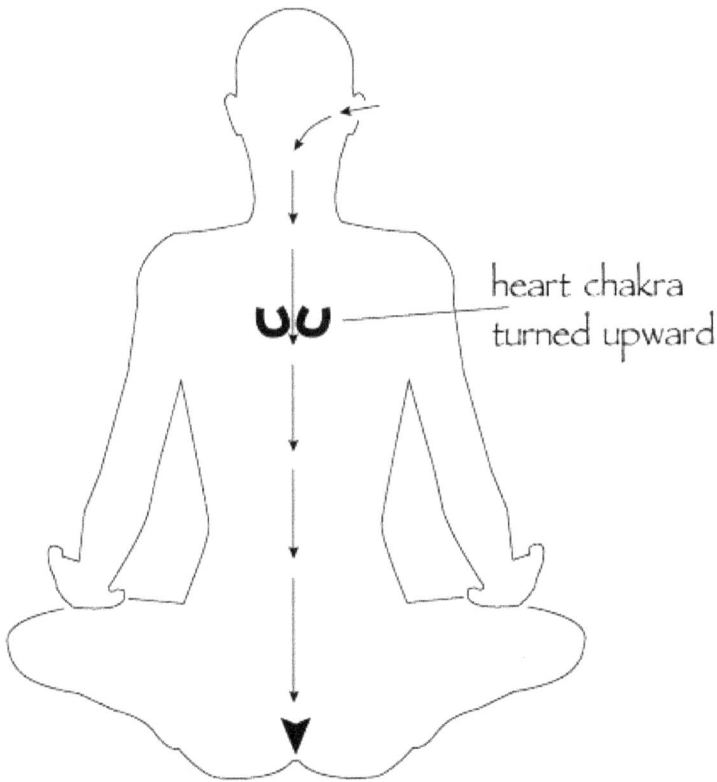

heart chakra
turned upward

September 2, 2003

Lahiri

He showed an *omkara* kriya which extends the naad sound into the abdomen. This conditions the low energy in the abdomen area to naad sound.

Yogesh mastered these techniques, for he described them to me, but he did this by using supernatural energy from the causal plane instead of the naad sound. On occasion though, he used the naad sound.

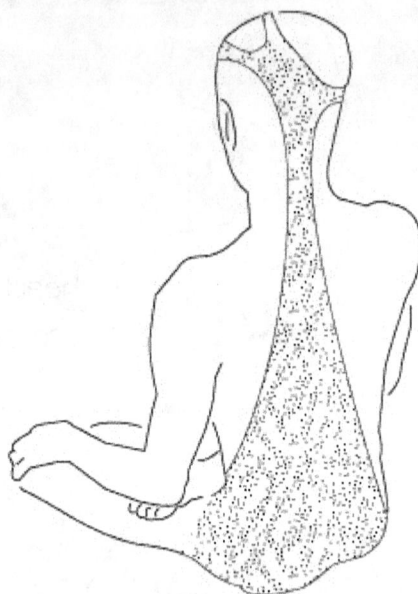

naad sound in head,
neck and trunk

September 2, 2003

Yogeshwarananda

A sex hormone pull-up

Remark:

This is just one of the methods for this purpose, all depending on what part of the body one retrieves the hormones from to do this. One does rapid breath-infusion while sitting on the soles of the feet, which are together. A male places the head of his sexual organ between his big toes and squeezes it there. A female places her fingers where the thigh meets the groin area. One pulls up the hormones through the nadi tubes shown in the diagram.

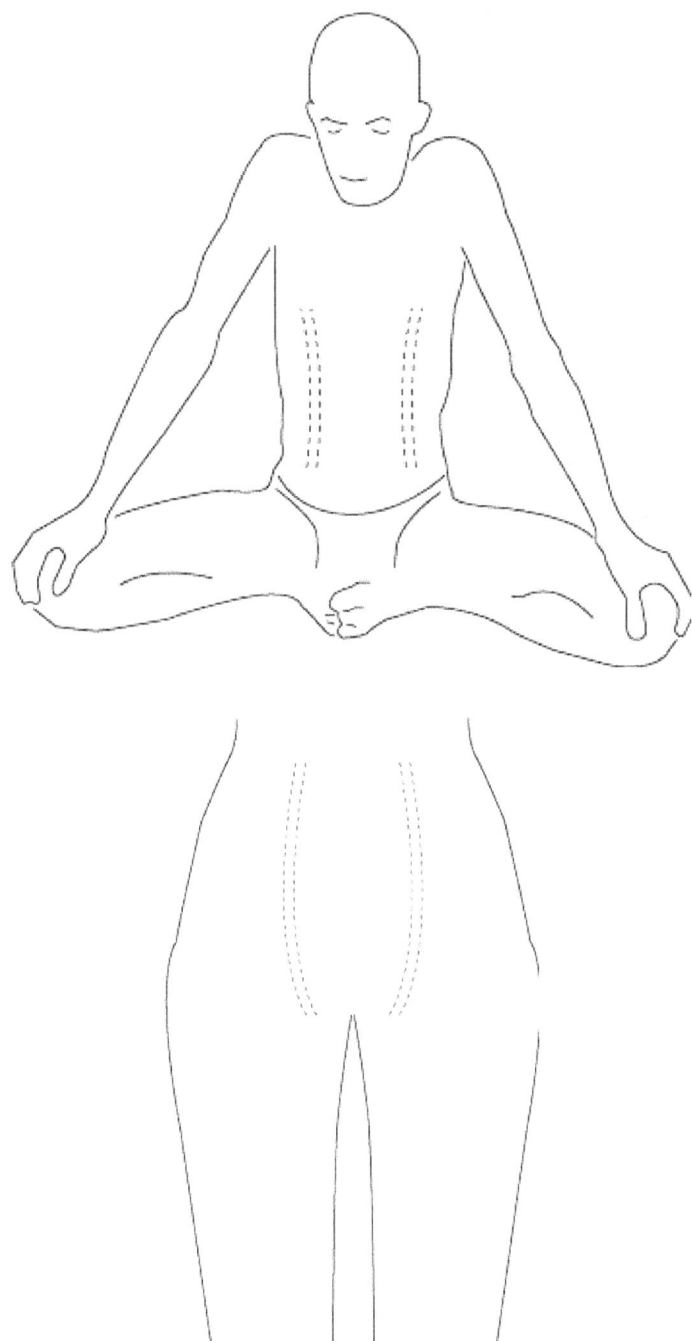

September 4, 2003

Lahiri

Remark:

In this practice, once the yogins gets hold of the naad sound, the Eeeeee screeching sound, he allows it to leak over into the head of the subtle body and down through the spine to spread into any areas which were penetrated by charged energy during the bhastrika breath-infusion breathing session.

Some attempts at this may fail since the sound which enters the right air may refuse to follow the attention of a yogin as he moves his focus through the charged energy. However he should try to do it. During some practice sessions, he will experience that the sound follows his attention, while during others it does not, but remains outside the right ear of the subtle body.

When the sound does not follow, the yogi can leave a trail of attention energy and that will carry impressions from the naad sound to those energized parts of the subtle body

September 5, 2003

Lahiri

He gave a procedure for *omkara* kriya during rapid breathing. This should only be done by yogins who are very much used to hearing the naad sound. While rapid breathing, one will not be able to hear the sound. Thus one applies this on the basis of having experienced it in meditation and knowing its position outside the right ear of the subtle body.

Lahiri gave entry points for the naad sound, as being the right ear, the brow chakra and the crown chakra aperture (crown chakra).

Yogesh advised that a yogin should chase the imagination orb after each thought or picture expressed by it. He should find it, hold it still where it is, in the ideation sponge-like mental energy. The yogin must also restrain the excitement orb by insisting that it ceases sensual interest and memories.

September 5, 2003

Yogeshwarananda

Excitement orb, attention energy suppression

This shows that the excitement orb or excitement energy which pushes the psyche to investigate sensual contacts, may be pushed down into the sushumna channel and kept slightly above the navel region to be quiet and inoperative there:

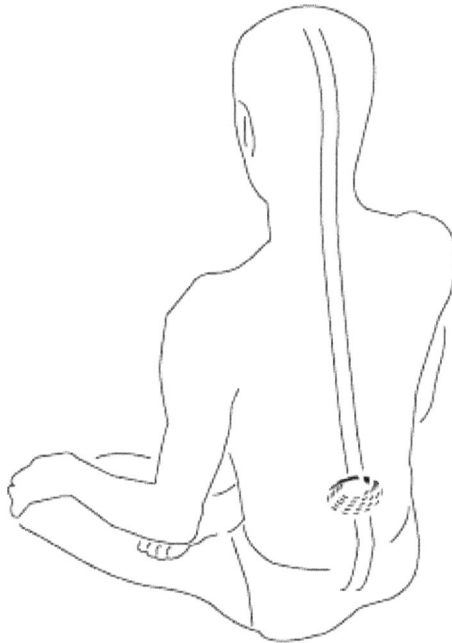

orb suppressed
in sushumna

The attention energy, when freed from the dictatorship of the excitement orb does not project itself, nor remain in a state of anticipation or anxiety.

September 8, 2003

Yogeshwarananda

As indicated by him, I discovered the analytical orb on the bottom of the subtle tongue. It has a light-yellow greenish color. I withdrew it into the front part of the intellect.

The analytical orb is possessed by a need for news. It controls speech. It creates and promotes gossip. It forms and divulges conclusions.

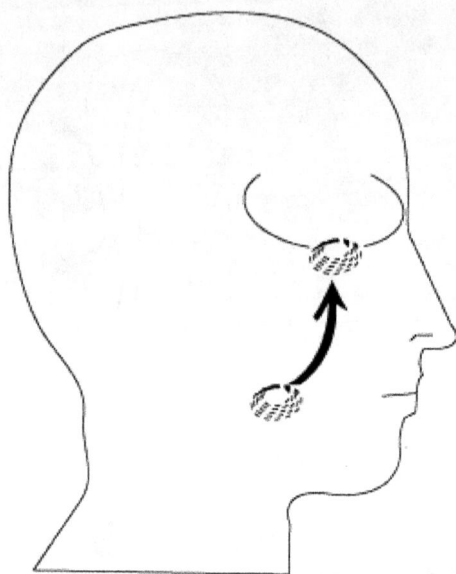

retraction path

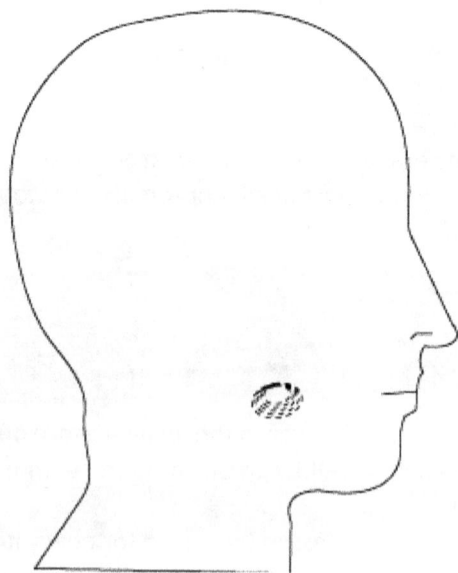

September 8, 2003

Shiva / Vishvarupa

On this date some persons were mentally searching for me, thinking that I would escape their vigilance if I entered a forest in South America. I hid behind the Vishvarupa Form of Krishna in a darkness on his back side. Their mental outreach energy could not detect me. After sometime, their mental focus dissipated.

Soon after Nandi, the bull of Shiva, appeared in a sculptured form that I acquired months before this happened. I got that from some ritual priests at the Venkateshwara Temple in Chicago, USA. On this sculptured form, the horns were chipped. The base was also chipped. In established temples, there is a rule that a cracked or chipped or otherwise damaged murti is no longer serviceable.

That Nandi was in the book shop which was closed on that day. After waiting at its door, a lady came. She agreed to open the shop. I asked about the sculptured form but she said she did not know the price, or even if it was for sale. I asked her to check with the authorities. A priest came and told me I could take that *murti* for US $15. It is one of marble stone.

After hiding behind Vishvarupa and seeing the Nandi, I picked up that form and started walking in the undergrowth of a dense canopied forest. Suddenly an eight-inch Shiva appeared on the bull I carried. I kept walking down the path. Ma Durga appeared there with Shiva on the back of the bull and then Ganesh, joined them. Skanda appeared in front of the bull holding a rein.

When Skanda came, I began walking at the side behind him. The bull was to my right.

Buddhi and Siddhi, two wives of Ganesh appeared ahead but seeing Skanda, they disappeared. Ganesh dismounted and went to get his wives.

Then Mother Durga dismounted and said that it was a good place for me to stay.

Remark:

It appears that Buddhi and Siddhi, the two wives of Ganesh, are not permitted to disrupt the celibate condition of Skanda Kumara. They keep their forms out of his vision at all times.

Female forms may have the power to disrupt the celibacy of an ascetic. This is possible. However, some yogins especially those who were involved sexually, and who overcame and walked away from it, do develop resistance. Shiva had once gave a condition that if Skanda Kumara were to stay with Goddess Durga, or with Ganesh, no other woman except Goddess Durga should be seen by Skanda.

September 9, 2003

Yogeshwarananda

Under his supervision, I held the analytical and excitement orbs at bay. During this practice, there was a pulsation of a dark light at the brow chakra.

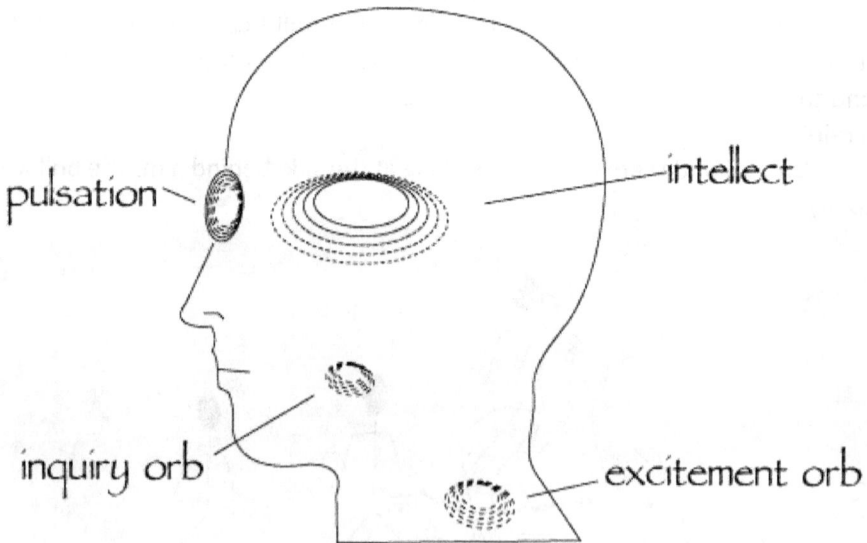

pulsation — intellect

inquiry orb — excitement orb

Heat build-up withdrawal

Due to food hormones and climatic conditions, the subtle body, as well as the gross one will accumulate heat. A yogi should do breath-infusion in order to expel this, otherwise it will be converted into sexual energy which will distract one's attention and promote sexual expression.

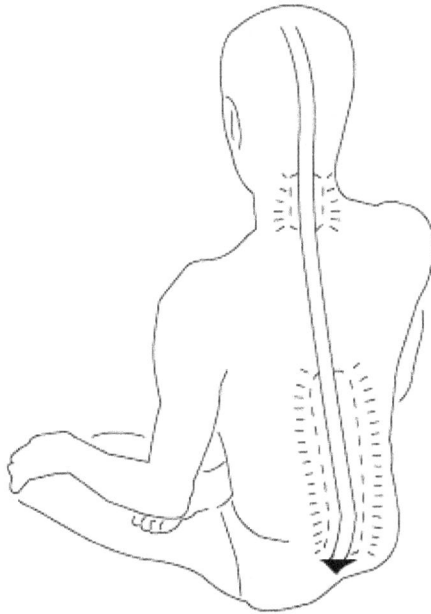

heat radiation

September 9, 2003

Yogeshwarananda

He showed how to catch the imagination orb which was near the throat. At the time, the attention energy was centralized in the intellect as a blue-white little star, having the capacity to entertain the self by visual and audio images. In the throat there is mento-emotional energy, in which the imagination orb may be imbedded for the purpose of converting memory signals or sensual data into motion pictures within the mind.

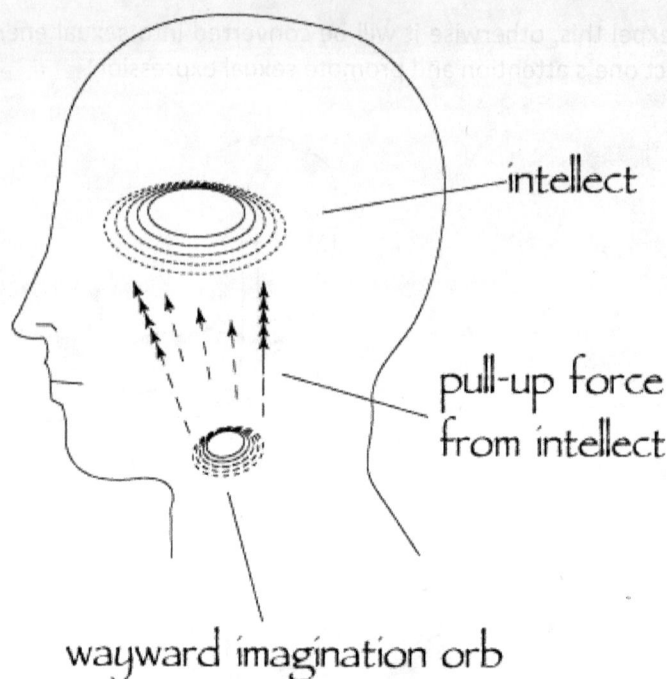

intellect

pull-up force
from intellect

wayward imagination orb

September 14, 2003

Mahavira

Mahavira was a Jain teacher, a great yogin, who lived in the time of Buddha. Mahavira is known as a tirthankara. He gave a web-like pick-up technique which is used in some instances by yogis who want to attain full transcendence.

Yogeshwarananda gave a similar pull-up and push-down·technique having to do with the causal body in terms of pulling energies into it from the subtle one.

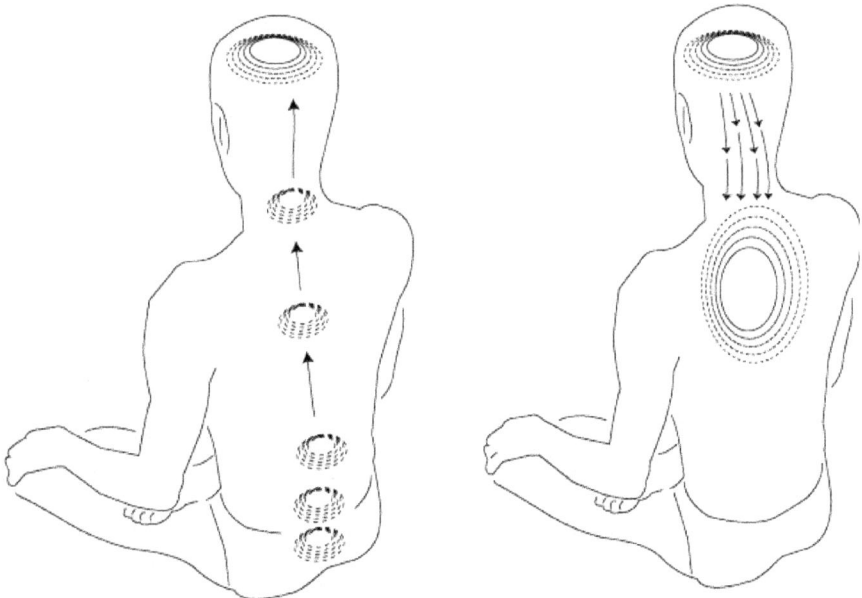

Mahavira

He said, "See how far they travelled. We saw the progress, long before their Christ was born. We turned around, because as you travel you acquire baggage as you proportionately put down the self. They should turn back and relinquish the baggage as they pick up themselves."

Remark:

Mahavira appeared some 600 years before Jesus Christ. He explained that the elevated Indians realized that if one invest in material advancement, one will do so at the expense of spiritual focus and not otherwise. One can develop one or the other. If perchance one cannot foresee this and one neglects spiritual cultivation, then sooner or later, one should realize the miscalculation and reverse oneself by decreasing the interest in materialism.

Kirpal Singh

This yogin was in Western countries in the late 1960's and in the 1970's. I have not seen him for many years. He stressed the listening of the naad sound.

He told me, "Without breath-infusion, the attention energy has little interest in the naad sound. The attention defocuses from naad and focuses on thoughts. However persons who do not or cannot do breath-infusion should still make the effort to force-feed naad to the attention energy. Sometimes, when the sound seems deep, the attention develops an interest in it, a curiosity to go into it deeply to see what it is and where it originates. By pranavision the attention may see tiny sounds making multi-colored dots and hear a rich blend of little sounds which comprise the naad."

Yogeshwarananda

He advised that the memory should be controlled by not allowing it to use former images. If perchance images arise during meditation attempts, one should stop the intellect from creating associative ideas. If one fails to do this, the intellect will indulge in a series of images and one will be forced to observe these, thus thwarting the meditation.

A yogin should stop the intellect from accepting or appropriating the images, otherwise he will never achieve higher yoga in terms of deep absorption.

September 19, 2003

On this day I observed the unity between the memory mechanism and the analyzing part of the intellect organ. These psychological instruments work together to keep the spirit entertained. As though hypnotized, the core-self usually becomes absorbed in their presentations and awards them psychological energy to enact further plans, by using the material body to manifest schemes. A yogin however, should put a stop to their consultation so that he can free himself from the imaginations which they inspire. A yogi must learn how to intercept the energy which seeps from the memory and goes into the analyzing part to goad it, to form conclusions for survival through dominance

Breath-infusion is necessary, since if the psyche is not properly surcharged, the core-self finds that it is unable to separate the memory from the analyzing part. It is forced to become preoccupied with the intellect alone. To expect full cooperation from the intellect is the way of a foolish yogi who does not understand that the mind is designed for insubmission. One should take assistance from the naad sound which pours in through the right subtle ear. If one finds that the mind is not interested, one should move in the mind with the attention energy alone, and keep oneself as close to the naad sound as possible, then one will develop a detachment from the mind and its compelling mechanism and be able to curb the memory and the analyzing part.

September 16, 2003

Using techniques shown by Yogesh, that most loving and blessed guru, I saw the operation of two sex orbs in the eyes. In males (not effeminate males) the right eye has one orb and the left eye has another but the right is larger and more dominant. In females (not domineering females) the left orb is larger and more dominant.

The larger sex orb is ever vigilant to catch colors in the external environment. These help it to locate sexual opportunities. To a greater degree nature sponsors a color show for sexual purposes, even in the case of plants with colorful flowers for pollination.

The larger orb takes energy from the heart-chest area, from the waist, from the pubic and from the thigh areas. It accepts that energy the way a government accepts money from citizens as mandatory taxes.

These sex orbs which are in the eyes, do not retract into the intellect. When they are retracted, their energy is diffused into the various parts of the psyche from which they derive power, and in the lifeforce directly.

eye orbs from back of body
right orb bigger in males
as illustrated below
left orb bigger in females
not illustrated

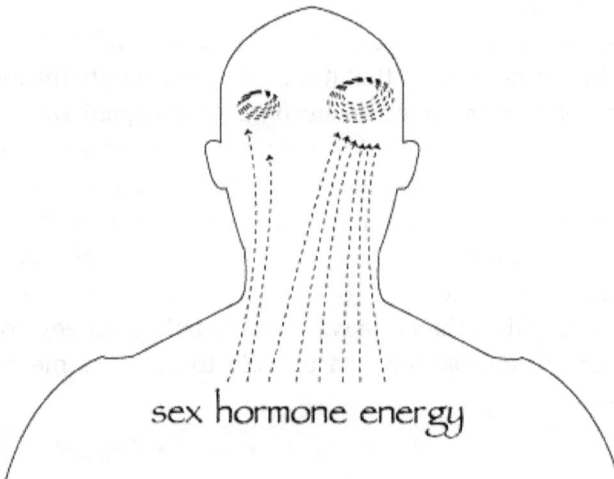

sex hormone energy

September 27, 2003

On this day I discovered a mist energy which is always dripping down through the psyche. This energy moves down into the heart-lung area and mixes with the kundalini energy at the base, then it comes up into the head through the sushumna central channel. Sometimes this mist energy, mixes with the Eeeeee sound, the naad sound. Both when mixed form into a higher concentration force which is used by yogis for transcendence absorption practice. From in that mixed energy, one may perceive some orbs in the head but these seem to be like dark orbs when seen from that prospective.

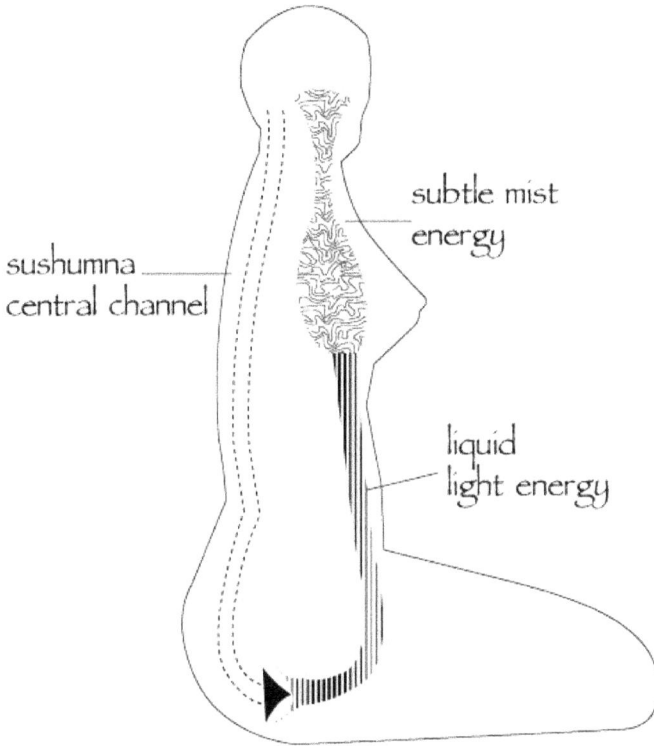

sushumna
central channel

subtle mist
energy

liquid
light energy

September 30, 2003

I was in Denver, Colorado on this date. I did a pratyahar withdrawal of the architectural-needing part of the psyche. This part wants to see and appreciate, to create and produce, architectural wonders in material nature. Each living being has this part to his psyche, even lower creatures like birds, bees and trees. Birds build wonderful architectural nests.

Such tendencies must be withdrawn before one can become liberated, otherwise one will have to stay in the material world to fulfill urges.

On this day, Rama Bharati reminded me of the need for isolation or some cave-like darkness for absorption practice and for chit akasha vision.

October 1, 2003

Muktananda

He said, "To make the senses immune to the electromagnetic influence of the subtle elements a yogi will require darkness for meditation. They are five in all, plus their innumerable combinations. These five are:

1. smelling odors
2. tasting flavors
3. seeing colors
4. touching surfaces
5. hearing sounds

"To put these in the dark in this dimension, a yogi should do the following, but note that when you get into isolation, start with 3 days, then I week, then increase after a time to ten days, then two weeks, then three weeks, then one month. At that stage absorption energy will show the way.

1. to darken smell, remove odors even incenses
2. to darken flavors, use a simple bland diet in conjunction with a rigorous posture and breath-infusion practice
3. to darken colors and shapes, stay away from electric power and lights , natural or man-made
4. to darken surfaces , do not contact the opposite sex, get rid of the need for luxuries and comforts
5. to darken sounds , be away from the noises of human civilization

"In addition, a yogin should check and limit the inner voices."

Remark:

The inner voices are the voices within the psyche. Some are the talk or influence of the miniature supernatural persons who live in the mind or feelings.

October 5, 2003

Yogeshwarananda / Muktananda

On this day under their conjoint influence, I saw energy seeping from the mento-emotional energy reserve into a psychic pouch of impressions which was to be manifested in this life. This occurs and then the seepage of psychic information prompts for fulfillment. When it is about to enter the pouch, one can see it or read it, just as a horticulturist knows the potential of particular seeds or sprouts.

However the seepage of energy has an inducing potency which charms the viewer. A yogi transcends that if he curbed the inquiry, excitement and need orbs, otherwise as is normal, he is compelled to act in a way as to fulfill the urges. That causes the person to work in the socio-cultural environment, thinking that what he does, is important.

Muktananda commented as follows, "Karma yoga may be done by a yogi who cannot stop the seepage. That yogin works under the patronage of the Universal Form which Arjuna saw. Working like this, he will eventually get the required detachment, and then he may get an exemption from such work and become liberated by strenuous austerities. All such work falls under the jurisdiction of the Universal Form and particularly under the supervision of the Dharma demigod, who is represented in the Mahabharata as Yudhishthira. But one cannot become liberated directly by working like this. Ultimately one must side-step this. Still it is better to work for Dharma, than to work in a so-called free-way and become implicated without any coverage from the supernatural authorities."

October 11, 2003

Muktananda

He instructed, "Go where the thoughts arise. Perform the absorption there, where the pleasure energy would be experienced. Tie the attention there, as a man wooing a woman-friend. Let the two energies intermingle with joy."

Remark:

This pertains to a meditation practice. After tracking to the location where thoughts or images arose, but while ignoring the thoughts or images, one will notice that one has an instinct to do the tracking. This is important, since initially a neophyte feels that it is unnatural to practice. He should develop confidence in the process of doing this, otherwise one will become disheartened and will give up the practice, condemning yoga as imaginary or impossible.

Once the emotional energy is linked to the attention which tracked it, there will be an ease. This may be experienced as being in an airless atmosphere. Suddenly there may be light to the right, left, before or behind. There may be a soothing light or a flash, then total darkness or nothingness. A yogi should not be disheartened. His main aim is to practice. That is what he should be self-convinced about.

Muktananda

He instructed, "As ideas arise, anchor the attention to them. Feel as if an ocean with tidal waves calmed with not even a ripple."

Remarks:

This instruction means that when one sees, hears, or otherwise becomes aware of ideas during meditation, one should focus the attention so that it moves into the place where the images or sounds occur. It does not mean staying at a psychic distance from the idea and looking at it, or giving it attention. If one remains at a distance, one will be entertained by the idea. When one puts the attention into the place where the idea occurs, it stops immediately. Ideas cease developing. The place turns blank.

In other words, the same mental place which was lit by the idea or sound, will turn dark, blank or may be filled with speckled lights. One must hold the attention at that same place and note where it is in the psyche.

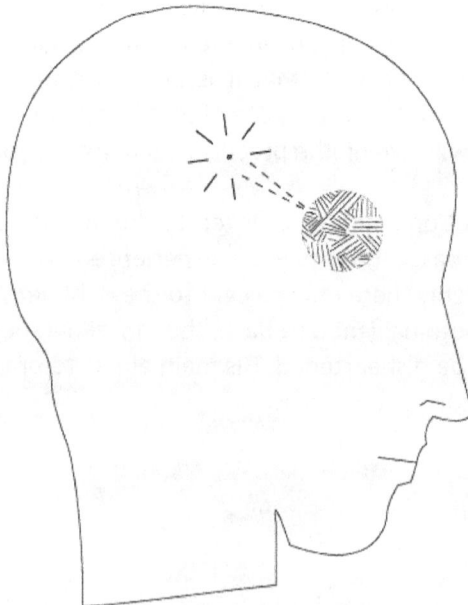

October 11, 2003

Yogeshwarananda

He remarked: "Linking the willpower with a natural or ordinary concentration force is where the practice of spontaneous absorption begins. It has to be effortless linkage as contrasted to deliberate focus which requires exertion.

"A yogi begins where the psyche is, with normal impressions and memories. Link or connect the willpower to the place where the visualization/imagination occurs. On occasion there will be a little sweetness to it. Gradually the attention will curve inwards of its own accord."

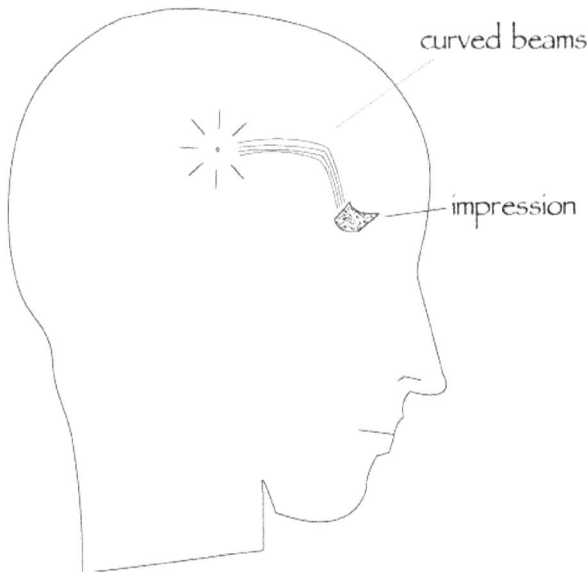

curved beams

impression

October 17, 2003

Experience of naad sound

In this experience a yogin realizes that so long as one is attentive to this side of existence, he does not positively hear the naad sound. Under this cultural identity, one has no interest in anything but this world. This means an interest in this physical world and its subtle counterpart. Those who are materialistic have no interest in the subtle counterpart of this world. Beyond that subtle basis is the chit akasha or the real world of consciousness.

October 21, 2003

Yogeshwarananda

He stated that when a yogi works with the subtle sponge-like energy, having ideas and thoughts, he develops an instinct for locating the imagination and for avoiding its blown-up images. After repeatedly doing this, he gets a natural detachment and control over the orb. Later, after sufficient practice, one develops an eye of intuition. This is a psychic light, which disappears often.

April 18, 2002

Kirpal Singh

Deliberate transcendence focus / 4th kriya

He said, "Open top. Keep it open. Do not close it. Use this and that opening. Then wait."

Remark:

This refers to using the naad sound as the basic foundation for deliberate transcendence focus practice. One keeps the crown chakra at the top of the subtle head open. One notes the opening through which the naad sound pours into the subtle head from the right side. One remains absorbed in the sound and those two openings. One waits in meditation for the chit akasha sky of consciousness to become manifest.

In some practice, that sky does not open, but the yogin does not become despondent. He practices patiently.

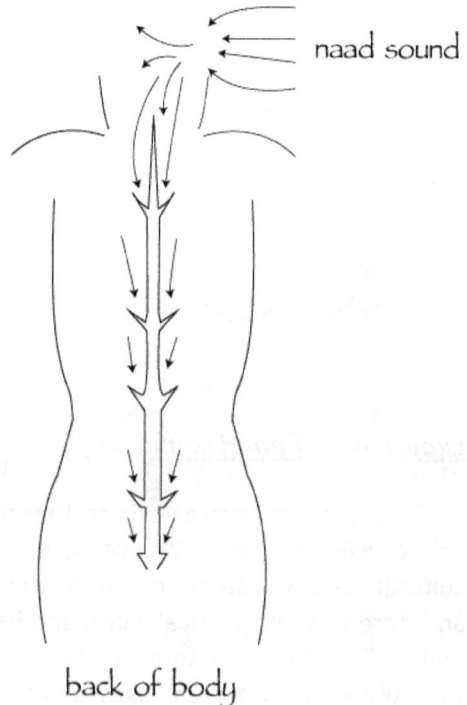

naad sound

back of body

April 21, 2002

Muktananda

He gave a whole deliberate transcendence focus procedure for the bubble body. In this practice, one traces pockets of energy as numbered 1 through 7 in the diagrams. Some yogis may not experience this sequence but the point remains that one should make particular note of whatever experiences one gains during practice.

Muktananda explained that this vision is the intellect piercing the darkness with no removal of it, like seeing through a misty atmosphere.

Remark:

This refers to the intellect vision, piercing to see something with no third eye vision and no clearing of the darkness in the subtle head. Intellect has the power to pierce through the darkness. It may perceive even without the aid of the brow chakra. This is difficult to operate and to control. Normally it happens haphazardly on its own. A yogi should study this to understand the conditions under which the intellect assumes this supernatural visionary power.

One can for instance, study my notes in this *Yoga inVision* series. But one should apply oneself to master this. Through concern, I assumed this body, lost spiritual and supernatural insight, made efforts to regain that, took these detailed notations, just to show the way. Still, a yogin who takes my assistance will be required to endeavor by himself or herself.

Here is that bubble body kriya.

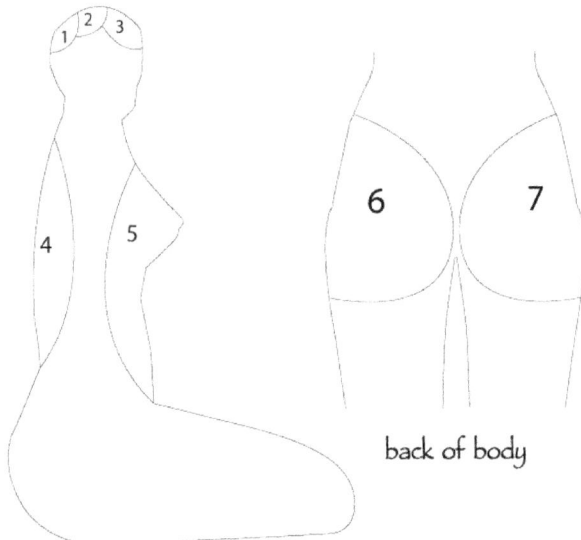

back of body

April 28, 2003

Yogeshwarananda

He advised that using the naad sound as a tie point I should do a special interiorization practice. In this one first establishes a link to the naad sound. When the link is strong and sure, one takes each of the senses and links it to naad. The question may be asked as to how one can grasp a particular sense. One may begin for instance with the hearing sense. One tries to find the center of it. When one locates that one takes it to naad. After a time when it remains settled in the naad sound energy one waits there in the naad and becomes sensitive to identify any other sense. It may be the taste sense, the sight sense, the smell sense or the touch sense. Any one which arises, would then be brought to the naad sound. One after the other one may bring the senses into the naad energy and link them there. On some days, one may bring two or three or four but not all five senses. One or two of them may remain invisible and seemingly inactive, especially if there is no stimulation or related sense object.

A sense like the smelling sense may be hard to locate if one does not have a fragrant object in the vicinity. That sense may remain unmanifest until its particular object of pursuit is within a range. Still, a yogin should endeavor to capture it. It exists even when it seems to be invisible or dormant. A yogin should be sensitive enough to capture it even when it is not manifested. This takes practice. At first one should learn how to capture the imagination orb by studying its position when it displays an image or sound. Wherever that display occurs in the mind, one should go there and hold that blank space, knowing fully well that the orb is there. With this confidence if one practices one will in time develop supernatural vision.

Periodically during these practices, the imagination orb will convert into a vision tool, a supernatural vision tool. Sometimes it will seem as if one moved into a video show, whereby one enters another place and is present there invisibly like the thin film on a soap bubble. On a soap bubble one sometimes sees images of other things, or one may see unusual colors. In the same way one may exist supernaturally in another place, like a thin film, and one will perceive that other place clearly. This may happen during these practices. This may happen for just a split second. These spontaneous occurrences are vital to yoga practice. These are the beginning of spiritual vision.

May 18, 2003

Muktananda

He said, "The imagination orb works by itself in the tamaguna chit shakti portion of consciousness. Teach it to retreat from that into itself and into I-ness, as well as into naad sound. From that the rajaguna chit shakti and sattva guna chit shakti vision and atmosphere will develop.

Remark:

This instruction may be followed by those yogins who saw the chit akasha on occasion. A question arises as to what is the chit akasha, and as to where it is. This is complicated in a way. This is also simple. Let us think for instance of a pilot in an aircraft. But somehow, long ago, after he travelled for many years, he began to realize that he must be in a cloud, for he could see nothing clearly ahead of him. He could see within the aircraft because there were lights which were powered by the engine. Somehow he got a hunch that he must be in a cloud. He was not sure but he felt by some intuition, that his condition must be based on being in a vast but limited cloud.

Suddenly he passed through a clear space in the sky and saw transparent light, but as soon as this happened, clouds surrounded the aircraft again. He did everything he could by going upward and downwards, to the east, west, north and south. He veered the aircraft around and still remained in clouds. He could not find clear space. This is similar to what happens when we make progress in meditation.

In this example the aircraft is the material world which we perceive. The cloud is the darkness in the subtle head, a darkness which is perceived when eyelids are closed in a dark room. The clear space which was haphazardly experienced by the pilot is the chit akasha. Normally the pilot can see things in the aircraft just as we can see things in the material world. So long as the engines operate the pilot can see because there are lights in the aircraft just as we have the sun, moon and electric lights for physical vision. But the lights in the aircraft cannot penetrate the clouds. The only way that the pilot can see beyond the clouds is to enter into clear space. However he is unable to do so. He does not have the power to do so. He has to develop that ability.

A yogi must develop the power to see outside the stupor energy (tamaguna shakti) and passionate force (rajaguna shakti). It will not occur by wishful thinking. It may happen haphazardly as one practices but to make it happen on demand is an entirely different matter.

May 24, 2003

Nityananda

He said. "Look! See this further."

Remark:

I was in the Port Charlotte, Florida. A man looked at a woman who passed on the street with a stroller in which a child was pushed. The woman wore short pants, so short that the lower part of her buttocks protruded. Nityananda showed that in another dimension, the bottom part of her buttocks was full of wriggling worms, feasting on flesh and sexual secretions. There were many hereafter people at her sexual organ. They were in miniature forms, living there, waiting for opportunities for rebirth. As she moved down the street many men were attracted to her due to the invisible potent force of the hereafters. I noticed that in my own body there was a sexual arousal on seeing her. I ignored it.

August 20, 2003

Janmashtmi Day

On this day I did an attention-beam retraction, but it led to Babaji. I also did a mystic pull on the 3rd eye chakra, the brow chakra. This was done without using the willpower energy. The attention beam which is covered in intellect energy originates from the sense of initiative, ahamkara.

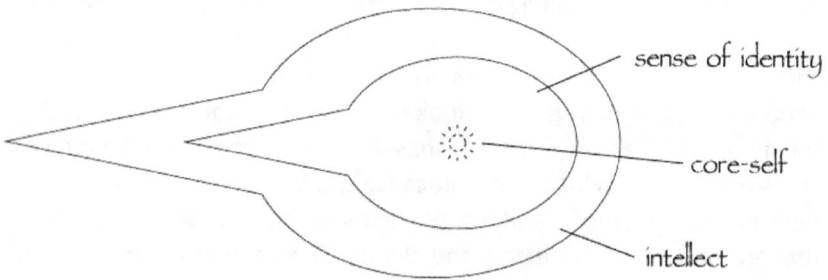

sense of identity

core-self

intellect

August 23, 2003

I did a Babaji procedure combined with a Gorakshnath method. This is a funnel shape attention energy return, while holding naad sound. This gets one to the sense of initiative energy. In the conditioned state, one is force to lump these energies together without being able to distinguish one from another. In higher yoga, one can sort them.

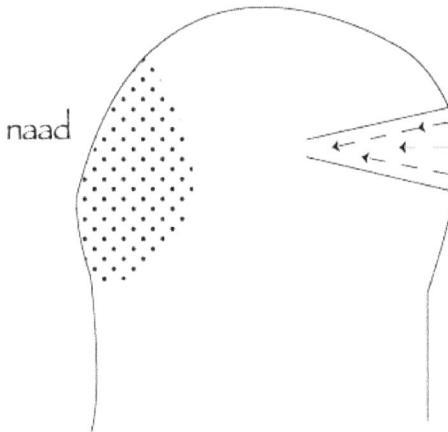

naad

August 24, 2003

On this date, I realized that there is a hunger for subtle light. This is why people get frustrated with meditation and give up yoga practice. It is primarily based on this hunger for light impulse. This impulse is dominant. If one does not see light in meditation, one gives up yoga after a few tries. When one attempts to practice dharana, one finds that there is only darkness in the subtle head, This darkness is usually interrupted with images and sounds which are based on mundane existence, on what is stored in the memory or on what registers through the senses. Otherwise one gets no experience. Subsequently one ceases meditation and returns to ordinary religion which is reliant on mundane experiences which are definite and certain, as sure as the material world.

However the recommendation for those yogis who will persist is to rely on the naad sound. If one sticks to this sound, there will be flashes of light and break-through into the chit akasha. Initially this will be sporadic. If one is impatient, one will not stick it out for success. Nityananda lamented that neophyte yogins go away before doing sufficient practice. Sometimes he said, "O how unfortunate! He left yesterday to resume social life. He had only 5 more hours of practice left before he would experience the spiritual reality. His impatience got the better of him."

September 20, 2003

Subtle posture

Postures can be done with the subtle body. These may be done while the subtle body is in the gross form, as one does exercises. Or they may be done in the astral world with the subtle body. Those yogis who find themselves doing yoga practice in dreams may consider themselves to be lucky since that indicates that when they leave the physical body permanently, they may continue the practice. The subtle body is habituated to pleasures, vices and social interactions of all sorts. If one finds that his subtle body changed from these tendencies, he should encourage himself and regard himself to be lucky, as there is every likelihood that he developed or is developing a yoga siddha form.

On this day I did an exercise in the subtle body. I sat on the soles of the feet, which were together. Then I placed one hand on one knee and the other hand on the middle of the thigh near the same knee. In that posture I did rapid breath-infusion.

Part 6

I did a deliberate transcendence focus practice for gathering sound and light alternately. One takes the assorted tiny sounds heard in the psyche and tries to put them together. This is like a blend of various musical notes. One then takes all the assorted lights or specks of light and puts those together.

Before this practice, one must do a session of breath-infusion, so as to fully charge the subtle body. If one fails to energize the subtle body, thoughts and images will interfere with the focus. It is the nature of the subtle body to apprehend impressions from images and sounds. Thus one has to do something to affect this tendency. This is done by breath-infusion practice. Each yogi has to practice for himself and judge what each discipline may accomplish.

September 24, 2003

Muktananda

He said, "It is part of pratyahar interiorization. If nature can do it to us, can we not effect it ourselves?"

Remark:

He made this remark in reference to celibacy. His idea is that since nature produced full celibacy in boyhood, it must be possible for a yogin to deliberately cause his body to be celibate even in adulthood. He feels that once a yogi trains his body to forget about sex, just as an infant has no idea about sex pleasure, the yogi can advance further and apply the same training to more subtle vices like imagination and memory usage.

Patanjali gave the yogis the ultimate instruction to stop the imagination and memory usages, just so they could attain to higher yoga practice in full transcendence absorption.

September 26, 2003

On this date I saw some response orbs which were activated at various chakras. These orbs are fatiguing to a yogi and cause him to be remain hogtied to the social world. There are many beginners who dream of reaching higher yoga. Some of them talk of yoga in glowing terms and make fun of persons who know little or nothing of the practice. Still, such boasting will not help. This is because in the psyche, one has enemies in the form of various tendencies which are counterproductive to success.

Playing God does one no good for yoga success, neither does playing missionary. One must tend to self-development by constantly endeavoring for full purity and by finding all subtle faults in the nature.

There was some bad energy coming from others. It was reached me while I did breath-infusion practice. This energy reaches a yogi during meditation attempts as well. Sometimes when a yogi has a plan to meditate for half hour, he spends twenty minutes suppressing such bad energy which enters the psyche. He finds that when he has a plan to meditate for 30 minutes, he can only do so for 10. He is helplessly challenged by bad energies in the mind space.

There are response orbs on each of the chakras in the subtle spine. These accept vibrations which come from others. Once these vibrations are received by the orbs, they are sent into the brain where they are converted into pictures and sounds, just as radio and television waves are converted for our hearing and viewing. The yogi may be forced to see these within the mind. This forestalls meditation practice.

While doing asana postures and pranayama breath-infusion, a yogi should be attentive within to the movement of subtle energy. However, the response orbs interfere with this, by receiving information from others and then converting that data into signals which strike the imagination orb which in turn converts such signals into pictures and sounds. These pictures and sounds baffle a yogi, who then tries to read them, and respond to them fittingly. This is all failure for yoga. It is a wonder that some yogis, even though they are just beginners find time to play God or to act as missionaries.

September 27, 2003

Bengali Baba

This person is one of Rama Bharati's gurus. He made this remark, "Willpower has little to do with it. Ego makes one feel that it does and one neglects to work patiently with the lifeforce to change habits, thus wasting time, following ideas of hope, following confidence religions or beliefs which lead nowhere. Willpower is just like a little switch which can or cannot turn on a big machine."

Remark:

Willpower does have application in yoga but not in all instances of the practice. There are some important and very vital stages of yoga, in which willpower has no effect whatsoever. Each student must study this and come to the proper method for each phase of the practice. Of course we must all take assistance from greater yogins like Bengali Baba. They give hints but in some applications, we must study the situation carefully to see what is effective and what is a waste of time. Willpower will help but in terms of reaching the chit akash it will do very little.

Peering into the sky of consciousness is more a matter of purification and stoppage of our engagement with the rajaguna passionate force and the tamaguna dulling mental energy. Hence mere willpower will not help. Whatever we may conceive of, no matter how great it is, if we are doing that in the passionate or dulling mental energy, we will not be able to reach the chit akash. No matter how much we exert it, the willpower will do nothing to help us. We have to separate ourselves from the passionate and dulling emotional and mental energy completely.

The problem is that we do not understand that our considerations on this side of existence are done in and with those two lower energies.

September 29, 2003

The kundalini lifeforce

In another dimension I had an encounter with the Kundalini Ma, the lifeforce personified. This was sexual. Sometimes one must engage like this during the progress of yoga. Muktananda had some experiences like this which baffled him, but he was rescued by some advanced yogins who explained the normalcy of such experiences. There is no danger with experiences of this nature, provided these are with Kundalini Ma or another yogini who is on par.

In this experience I was in another dimension where I was in a yoga posture squatting on the soles of the feet, Kundalini Ma was in a posture with her knees near her breast but she was in midair. Both of us were without clothing.

Her sexual organ became linked to mine. Sexual fluids from the subtle spine of my body flowed into her form passing through my sexual organ. All fluids in the spinal chakra from the neck down were discharged, as these were drawn out by the pulling force in Kundalini Ma's body. It was a crystal clear fluid. She said nothing to me but wanted more and more. This went on for about ten minutes in the time reckoning of that place.

When I returned to this dimension, I check my physical body but it showed no signs of sexual stimulation. There were no sexual emissions. My physical body was completely out of touch with the body I used in that rare dimension. A yogi should check on experiences of this nature, to see if the information from a parallel world is feeding back into this gross existence. These experiences should be discussed with higher yogins who can explain these in terms of yoga progression.

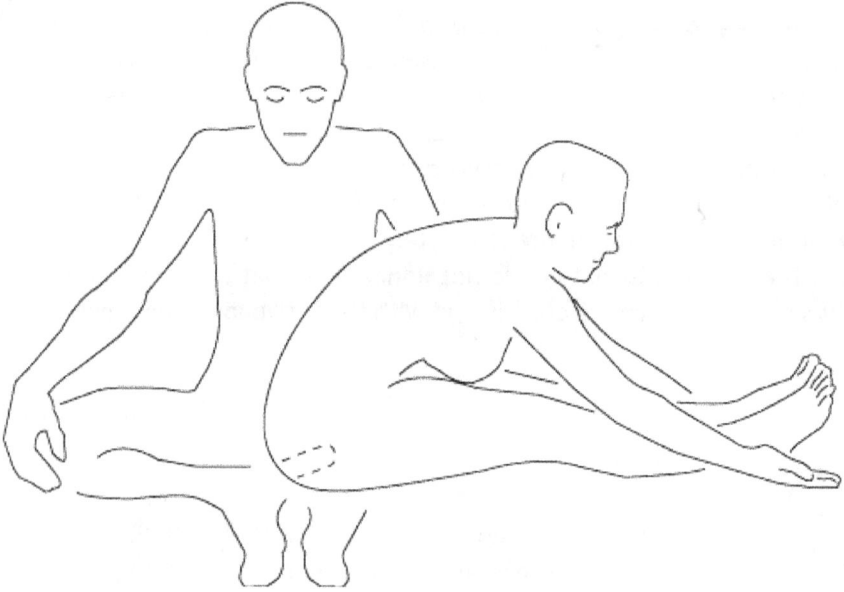

September 30, 2003

In the Anu Gita portion of the Ashvamedha Parva of the Mahabharata, Krishna told Arjuna that after completely giving up mundane life, a yogin succeeds in attaining the spiritual place in six months.

एतावदेव वक्तव्यं नातो भूयोऽस्ति किंचन
षण्मासान्नित्ययुक्तस्य योगः पार्थ प्रवर्तते

etāvadeva vaktavyaṁ nāto bhūyo'sti kiṁcana
ṣaṇmāsānnityayuktasya yogaḥ pārtha pravartate (4.60)

etāvad = etāvat = this; eva – so; vaktavyaṁ - what is said; nāto = na (not) + atah (thus); bhūyo = bhūyah = being; 'sti = asti = is; kiṁcana – anything; ṣaṇ - six;

māsān – months; nitya – consistently, regularly; yuktasya – of proficiency; yogaḥ - yoga; pārtha – son of PÃthā; pravartate – accomplishing

This is all that is to be said. There is nothing beyond this. O son of Pṛthā, one who practices proficiently and consistently for six months accomplishes this yoga. (Anu Gita 4.60)

Six months? Well that is what Krishna said. It hinges therefore on the time it takes to completely give up mundane existence. That is where we consume much time and effort. But once we accomplish that, it should be six months.

On this day I again saw Kundalini Devi in a parallel world. She was buttoning up her vagina. It had six buttons. She was an attractive woman but with a sense of responsibility and some self-respect. She had a cream colored very attractive body. She was semi-serious and semi-flirtatious.

After returning to this plane of consciousness, I considered that encounter with Kundalini Devi. I thought, "To be sure, something like that should be buttoned up forever, never to be opened again."

But that was wishful thinking. There is no telling which world one may appear in and what sort of sexual or nonsexual experiences one may be committed to according to the type of body one acquires.

October 1, 2003

Muktananda

He assisted with the struggle with Kundalini Devi. He took me away when she stood before me on one foot with her organ exposed and when she called for vaginal intercourse from behind.

He said, "Clean these areas instead. Ignore her. Do not entertain nor play with her. Ignore her subtle requests, her idleness and antics. Push on for full success."

While he said this, even though we both turned away from the direction she was in. I still saw her before me. She was on both feet with a slimy vaginal passage, but she was facing backwards.

This facing backwards happened because I was working on the base chakra, the muladhar chakra.

Muktananda said, "Make notations of these experiences. Others may learn of it and know what to expect. I did not leave details because I was a brahmachari celibate student when similar experiences afflicted me. Since you are a father it is not improper for you to speak of this. Tell the others so that they may prepare themselves."

Muktananda

He showed how relationships are usually conducted through and by the kundalini energy. We took miniature forms and entered into my sushumna passage. There we saw many touch points which were emotions on the physical level. These are kundalini energies but when one is on the outside of the sushumna one usually mistakes these for expressions of affections.

Most yogins fail to mention or to take into consideration the emotional body. This is because they are usually making efforts to suppress it, to ignore it, since it is troublesome and impulsive. It is also confused with the intellectual form, the vijnana maya kosha. The emotional body in its pure state is the bliss energy body but in its impure state it is a low energy body which has energy mixed with passionate and stupefying subtle force.

September 4, 2603

Nityananda

He said, "You must be attentive. Send everything through memory including the pains of asana postures. The stupor force rules otherwise."

Yogeshwarananda

He asked, "What was that instruction?"

I explained what Nityananda said above. He responded, "Yes, memory control. That is part of Patanjali's yoga course."

Remark:

When doing asana postures and breath-infusion, one should make the effort to send all pain energies to the memory. Nothing should be ignored. One should be attentive. Whatever is sent to the imagination orb, goes into the memory. This is why one can recall incidences. Sometimes the memory impressions travel deep into the causal body. Some impressions in a parallel format are sent into the sushumna nadi. These affected the kundalini chakras and form as instincts in the subtle body. Usually the memory and the imagination faculty work automatically based on impulses from the passionate and stupefying forces.

Each yogin has to study how this operates. It should not be ignored. One should not feel that this is irrelevant nor that one may not have to know this. It must be studied in detail. Faith in God is alright, but if such faith cannot give one the insight, then what is its value?

October 5, 2003

Memory reform posture

This was inspired to give control over the information that enters the memory. The memory chamber has a mouth which is usually at the top of the chest, as one looks down into the subtle body. This memory like an eating-digesting mechanism, eats whatever it acquires from the sensuality. These eaten tit-bits enter the mouth of the memory in an impression form, as a digital marking. It is then packed into the memory in layers. Deeper layers which were packed in previous existences, exist in the lower part of the memory chamber which is called the subconscious. It is sub or below conscious retrieval except by special supernatural means.

A yogin should train the memory to eat and digest a new type of sensual information which comes from transcendence experience. This is first done by digesting the naad sound and any flashes of light which manage to penetrate into the cloudy normal consciousness in the subtle head.

The posture below helps with memory control. In this, the genital organs are kept in the back. One pulls hormonal fluids up the front of the body, while pushing down fresh air into the subtle body from the front. This is a masterful posture for celibacy.

By purifying the subtle body of its sexual tendencies, one causes a change in the appetite of the memory, which allows one to better appreciate the naad sound, otherwise that sound will be boring and uninteresting to the yogi.

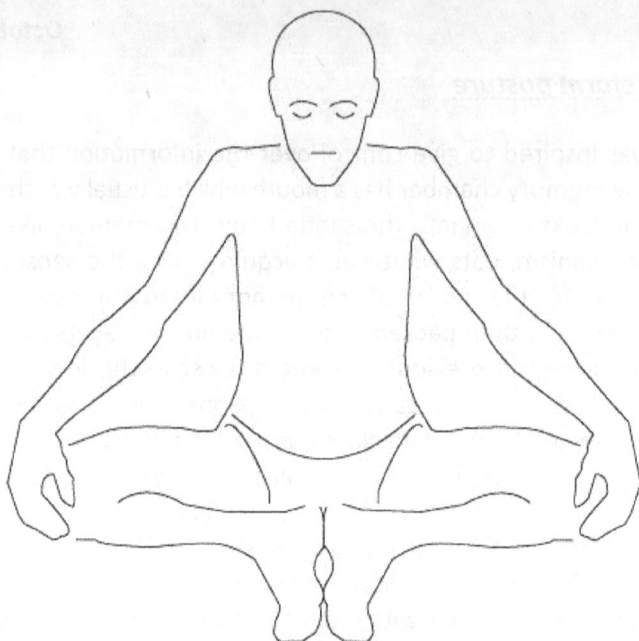

October 5, 2003

Charged prana affecting memory

During breath-infusion sessions, a yogi should direct charged subtle energy into his memory pouch. This is not always possible but whenever it may be done, one should push the energy into the memory chamber. This will cause a purification of the memory and a cancelation of certain bothersome impressions which disturb meditation. There is also a tendency in the memory to link with the imagination orb, to disrupt a yogi. If one pushes subtle energy into the memory, one can gradually eliminate that tendency.

One must first locate the memory. One must also locate the digesting mouth of it. Sometimes the memory may move but it does have a general location. The yogin should meditate silently and find that place. He should work on cleansing bad energies from the memory chamber. Each yogin must do this work for himself. It is stupid to feel that these cleansing actions will be done by God or by the spiritual teacher, or by chanting the name of God or any such process. One must directly do this in mystic yoga. What Is the problem since God provides so many details of these cleansing processes through this writer and others?

October 6, 2003

A parallel world experience

I was in a parallel world with a renunciant (sannyasi) from this world. During the experience, I realized that we transferred out of this world. The renunciants did not realize that he was in another existence, but his subtle body had the same attitude towards mine which it usually had in this world.

As I considered this, I become aware of Ramana Maharshi. He said, "That is what I meant by the question, *who am I?*"

He said further, "There are many social identities which we assume. Which one will persists? Are all factual? Are all fallacious? Why should any sane person continue with these schizophrenic attitudes? Is it not better to stop and realize the core person?

In consideration, I saw that it is the kundalini lifeforce which causes these bizarre relationships in the numerous dimensions or worlds. One should control this kundalini. It should be brought into pristine purity or into its sublime state. Only then would one know what is primal and basic.

October 6, 2003

Rama Bharati

He showed a deliberate transcendence focus. In this one focuses on the naad sound but one remains in the memory chamber having the imagination orb quieted there. Since the sense of identity has a resistance to moving from its central position in the subtle head, this is a difficult practice. These methods help to free the yogin from impulsive attraction to the intellect.

October 7, 2003

Fruma

Fruma is a yogini who took training from Rama Bharati. She lost her body when it was around fifty years of age. For a time, she lived in the astral world as a wandering ghost. Even though she did not commit suicide, still because the energy in her subtle body was not expended sufficiently through her last form, she was unable to immediately assume an embryo.

On this date, I worked on subduing the thinking tool, the analytical part of the intellect. Each yogin should struggle with this himself or herself. It cannot be achieved for anyone by anyone else besides the very same person.

One begins by curtailing thinking energy. In meditation, one should observe the trigger mechanisms which causes thinking to be indulged impulsively.

The link between the memory and the imagination orb must be discovered by the yogi. He must also see how the analytical orb takes orders from the sensual energy and memory. The transfer of information between these parts of the psyche must be curtailed and eventually stopped or one will never enter into deep absorption or consistently be able to pierce through to the chit akasha, the spiritual energy environment.

It is a big joke to feel that one will go on and on with life, without making these endeavors nor achieving what I describe, and then to feel that one day, suddenly, God will, all of a sudden, make it happen, so that from then on, one will see into the spiritual environment. This is a nonsensical and completely illogical and impractical idea. In the Bhagavad Gita there is a verse.

तेषामेवानुकम्पार्थम्
अहमज्ञानजं तमः ।
नाशयाम्यात्मभावस्थो
ज्ञानदीपेन भास्वता ॥१०.११॥

tesāmevānukampārtham
ahamajñānajaṁ tamaḥ
nāśayāmyātmabhāvastho
jñānadīpena bhāsvatā (10.11)

teṣām — of them; evānukampārtham = eva — indeed + anukampā — assistance + artham — interest; aham — I; ajñānajam — ignorance produced; tamaḥ — stupifying influence of material nature; nāśayāmy = nāśayāmi — I caused to be banished; ātmabhāvastho = ātmabhāvasthaḥ — situated in the self; jñānadīpena = jñāna — knowledge, realized + dīpena — with light, with insight (jñānadīpena — with realized insight); bhāsvatā — clear, shining, clarity of consciousness

In the interest of assisting them, I who am situated within their beings, cause the ignorance produced by the stupefying influence of material nature, to be banished by their clear realized insight. (Bhagavad Gita 10.11)

One must read such verses carefully without squeezing out of them what one intends to derive. One should not create an easy path of religion by oneself without carefully reading what God said. This verse is not a verse by itself, the three verses before it are connected. One should carefully read each to for knowing the qualifications which would qualify one for the action of Krishna which is described in this verse.

On this date Rama Bharati entered into my subtle head in a miniature form. He showed a method for forcing new infused breath energy into the memory. This helps to get the memory under control and to break its alliance with the imagination orb and analytical faculty in the intellect. The memory must be retrained. That is like working with a mischievous strong-will child.

The memory has to be re-trained in what to recall and what to ignore, what to present to the imagination orb and what to leave as an unrevealed impression in the subconscious. It must be re-trained in what to take from the sensuality and what to grab from the outer world with the help of the sensual orbs.

October 9, 2003

Atmananda Vaishnava Yogi

This yogi was the main guru of Yogeshwarananda. He entered my subtle head and ask if I knew whom he was. He looked around inside the subtle head and left. He make made no remark nor gave any practice.

October 9, 2003

Rama Bharati

He stated that proper rest and austerity are required. Austerities alone will not suffice. This is why one has to greatly curtail cultural activities. A person who is unable to curtail social involvement cannot succeed in yoga. As such his or her spiritual life will be for the most part superficial. But that does not mean that one may stop cultural life at the snap of one's finger.

Tongue roll back procedure

This method, where the tongue is lifted, curled back and pushed back into the mouth to reach the soft palate, may on occasion during meditation, cause the imagination orb to be separated from the memory. Such experiences allows the yogin to see what happens when the various parts of the psyche do not have their natural linkage. What is read in books or heard of from yogins, even from myself, must be experienced directly by students.

Ramana Maharshi

He stated, "I found mantras to be quite useless. One has to go inside and confront, as well as sort, the parts of the psyche which operate automatically. What is the use of other disciplines, if the psychic organs remain disordered, impulsive and impure?"

October 11, 2003

Ramana Maharshi

He entered my subtle head and then went down into the chest of it, going into my memory chamber. He picked up some details of my life when I first went to New York City in 1967. He saw an impression of my body being dressed in Western-type suits. I explained to him the Western attire. He wondered why yogins go to a place like that. He asked me to beam down a path of light from my subtle intellect into the memory chamber where he was located. I did that. He checked about nine or ten of my past lives when I practiced yoga before. I went into the memory but could not open the information from those lives. It all remained compressed but he was opening everything and assessing it for himself.

After that, He said to me, "In my past life as Ramana Maharshi, I did transcendence absorption yoga without doing breath-infusion on a consistent basis, but I overlooked the fact that others cannot achieve that. I used to advice others but many were unable to follow my path successfully because they needed the advantage of doing breath-infusion. In your memory from past life, I see that you did much breath-infusion. Now if someone did not have such an ascetic background, then he or she cannot at all succeed merely by meditation. It is good that you are setting this example by doing the austerities that are required for others."

October 12, 2003

Ramana Maharshi

He stated "Persons use advanced techniques in the lower stage of yoga and get no result, because those techniques only yield a benefit at the higher level of practice."

Remark:

He said this after observing my use of the tongue curl-back technique for letting pranic energy pass between the imagination orb and the memory.

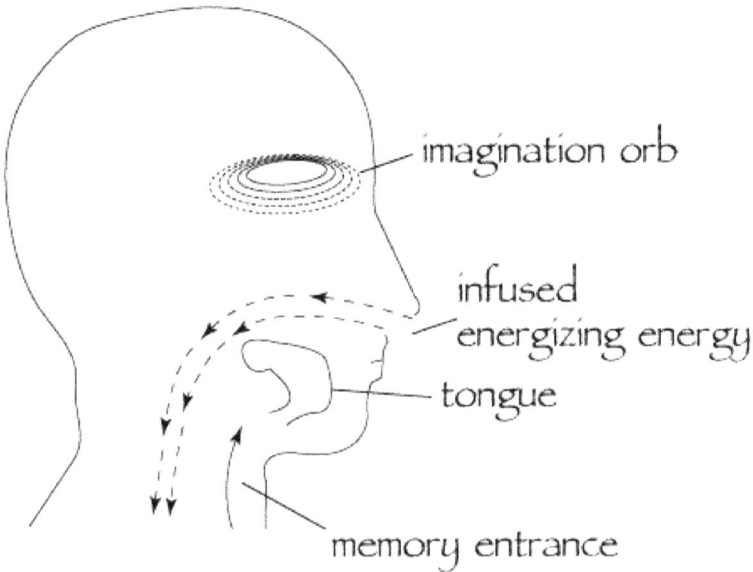

imagination orb

infused

energizing energy

tongue

memory entrance

October 14, 2003

Kundalini Shakti Ma

I had an encounter with her in the subtle world. She was preparing meals just as if he she was my wife. She had a rip in her anus region. She began tearing the skin from her buttocks.

The significance of this was not realized by me at the time, but in November of 2005, I got the insight about this. At the time my meals were greatly curbed but on occasion by force of providence, I used to increase food intake when it was not necessary, thus breaking a law of nature. It is found that in yoga practice, one is sometimes force to do things which contravene practice. This comes on by enforced destinies which are against the yoga habit.

If one does that there will be an irritation. From that, there will be another irritation. One will find oneself doing things which are self-destructive. If one over-eats for whatever reason, regardless of whether one is forced to do so or not, the anus will have to process more food than necessary. It will be strained. That strain will cause an irritation, which would result in a harmful action, such as her tearing the skin from the buttocks.

It is for this reason that it becomes necessary for students to get a waiver from the Universal Form, so as to be exempt from cultural activities. But even if one gets such a waiver, one will be threatened by providence for its removal. And from time to time, one will find that one is dragged back into suicidal cultural life. Actually this happens repeatedly in the life of a yogin.

On November 2, 2005, there was the annual Diwali celebration in Guyana. This is a big event for many Hindus. I was forced by social convention to eat at various homes on that Diwali evening. As a result I suffered terribly that night. I lost time for meditation practice and had to indulge in silly activities in the astral world with some friends in the neighborhood where my body lived.

When I relocated to Guyana, I intended to be far away from these Hindus for the very same reason of wanting to greatly reduce if not eliminate altogether these cultural involvements, but as destiny would have it, I was unable to get a safe location which was more isolated. One can see that in some cases, one will be forced to perform a certain quota of cultural contacts regardless of whether one likes it or not, or regardless of whether it disrupts yoga practice or not.

On this same day, I met an energy in the subtle world. It was of a message sent by a sister of a friend. The subtle energy, when it hit my intellect organ, translated into a message for my meeting the woman. I immediately avoided the energy and causes it to subside in the mental atmosphere around my intellect. Such contact with such messages is a subtle violation of celibacy. It is very subtle indeed, but if a yogi cannot avoid contacting such energy, he will be drawn into such association at a later date, and then in the current or in some future life, he will have a sexual relationship with the said female. This all means that he will be held accountable for the sexual energy.

October 15, 2003

Ramana Maharshi

In his presence, I realized that the mind is attached to the rajaguna passionate force. Thus one goes on thinking of ways to create activities in this world. For instance at the end of a hard day's work, a man usually thinks of his next day' occupation. Even though there is really no shortage of work in this world, still human beings are compelled by their passionate nature to think on and on and on about working, just as if they were mindless scatter-brained animals. This is all being done under the influence of the passionate energy.

I realized that when there are cramps during meditation, one may ease out of a posture gently without disturbing the focus of the meditation, otherwise one can endure the cramps if one find that one can use the energy which emanates from the cramp to assist in the meditation focus. This must be determined by the yogin himself.

A kundalini force

I experienced a kundalini force which was unusual. It cut through under the middle rib sternum area. Then it cut upwards on the right side as shown by the line in the diagram. I used a white light body at the time.

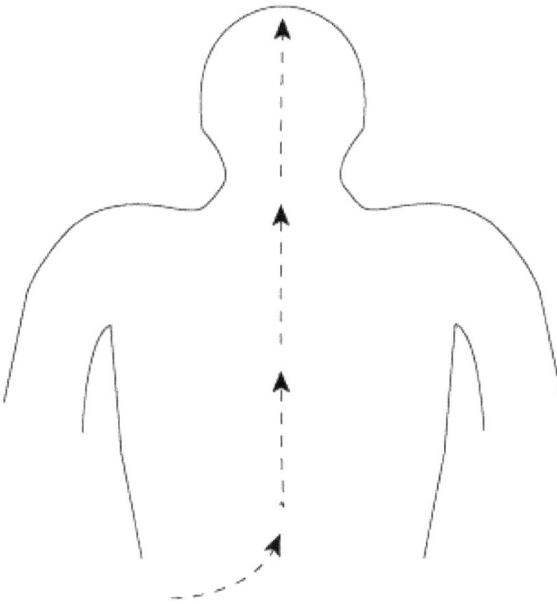

The experience of different subtle bodies and other types of supernatural forms is part of the course of yoga. The yogi should know of these forms before he finally leaves the physical body. This enables him to better understand the various areas of manifestation which would be available once he is evicted from the body.

On this day I had a vision of Kundalini Shakti. She showed a woman's breasts hanging on the inside of a low cut bodice. Both breasts were plump but small. They hung down like two fat eggplants. The woman was white-skinned and about thirty-eight years of age.

Such an exposure shown by Kundalini Ma is an invitation for the yogin to consider having children. Even if one already produced children, and even if they reached maturity, one will be propositioned by providence for taking more responsibility. This is because there is always a constant pressure for new bodies for those departed souls who would require physical life. Thus unless one is eager about celibacy, one may give in and begin family life all over again, a second or even a third time.

On this day I had the realization that kundalini yoga must be done to completion. If one does it partially, one will not be successful at higher levels of practice. The kundalini lifeforce is contrary. Unless it is fed sufficient subtle energy, it will disturb the meditator in one way or the other. One must be careful about kundalini to get its system of energy distribution purified and filled with higher pranic force. Kundalini is a nuisance that sponsors this creature existence, but one must still deal with it by doing breath-infusion, and by adopting a simple lifestyle.

October 19, 2003

Muktananda

He instructed, "Hold it. Do not let it get away. Stay close to it."

Remark:

The irritating imagination orb which produces images and sounds which contravene yoga, must be kept track of. As soon as it reveals anything, one should confront it. It takes impressions from the senses or from the memory. It operates a photo studio, video program and stereo sound production. One should always confront it and put it in its place, where it does not produce images or sounds during meditation.

Muktananda made an observation. He said, "The kundalini lifeforce is represented in each body as the kundalini-individualized force. It completes the gross and subtle interactions. Detach from it."

October 21, 2003

Nityananda

He said, "Patanjali is for brahma-yogins. He will direct them. Instruct that kundalini yoga should be completed first. Brahma yoga is more advanced. Watch this. This is unwarranted. *(He pointed to food in the lower intestines at 2 am.)* Send air and fresh subtle energy to the merge points where thoughts break out in the psyche. Meet it in that way. There should be no response. Hammer the thoughts with fresh subtle energy."

Remark:

The practice of brahma yoga is so advanced that it cannot be done in fact until one masters kundalini yoga. Many persons take the brahma yoga meditation and feel that they can sit down and meditate on the core-self and on the paramatma, the Supreme Soul who supervises His little friend the core-self. Unless one's subtle body is purified of negative energies, the attempts at brahma yoga will bear no results. One may of course come to realize that one makes no progress by mere meditation without the purificatory action of kundalini yoga, but most persons who attempt brahma yoga, go on trying to meditate year after year in the hope that somehow by the mercy of God, by the mercy of a guru or by their divine right, they will succeed at it. Most of this is a hoax.

October 22, 2003

Nityananda

He instructed, "Sit up. Do it. Notice what can be done with a pre-session of breath-infusion."

On the same day, Yogesh said to me that in his years of practice, other great yogins did breath-infusion. He then asked me, "Where is the infused breath energy? How is it directed? By whom?"

On this day I realized that the same passionate energy creates thoughts and causes the attention to be enthralled by ideas and schemes. This energy continually surrounds the self as the self is centralized in the mind. One must practice breath-infusion to displace that energy from the subtle head. One must be properly rested, having left aside much cultural involvement in the gross and subtle environments.

The passionate energy is not only present as lust, envy or greed. It is in the mind space as the energy which converts into images, pictures and sounds. A yogin should realize this and then take a cleansing action to remove this subtle influence which thwarts the efforts for liberation.

It is important to understand what one's spiritual mission will be once one is purified. This is relevant because unless one takes the position of a student at the feet of the really great yogins, one will be misled and will be inspired in the wrong way. Ask yourself the following questions:

Will I become a spiritual teacher like Buddha or Jesus Christ, once I become purified? Or will I remain as a student of great teachers?

One must realize that the imagination orb uses the passionate subtle influence to create pictures in the mind. This is sponsored and urged by the memory and the baser feelings. This causes a wastage of that passionate force. For success in brahma yoga, one should stop the passionate energy from being converted into ideas.

October 23, 2003

Rama Bharati

He explained that he traced Sombari Yogi to me. He said that I was either that yogin reborn or that yogi's energies passed through my body when that yogi made entry into a hidden dimension to avoid others. Rama Bharati said, "Except that you associate with women, your postures and practice are similar to his. He was a total isolated celibate."

Sombari Yogi

September 24, 2003

Nityananda

He discussed that a yogin should check for the residual effects of the practice. The chief method for this checking was shown to me some years ago by Shivananda, who instructed that one should rest early and have a stress-free life. Shivananda advised that the yogin should get up early during the night. He should check the contents of mind very carefully to see how the psyche was affected or was not affected by yoga practice. If one notices incremental or very small advancement, that is alright but if there is none,

one should be concerned and should realize that the austerities are not as intended. Every so often, during the day and during the night, one should make efforts to meditate. Then one should check to see how the mind performs. One should do this without doing breath-infusion and also after doing breath-infusion. In that way one can assess for oneself the effects of breath-infusion.

In his last body, Nityananda was a master of isolation, so much so that even if there was a crowd about him, it was just as if he was alone, an island in the middle of the ocean. Unless one has isolation, one cannot be immune to the influential social activities which exude from others. If there is no isolation, the mind will be charged for activity in this world, thus contravening yoga.

October 25, 2003

Muktananda / Zipruana

These two yogins went to check on a student named Balyogi, who lived in Berbice, Guyana. When returning from that visit, Zipruana said, "They should do kundalini yoga justice. They should not short cut it or think that they can advance without its full practice. Nityananda's process is brahma yoga but they cannot do that unless they complete kundalini yoga practice. That is their friend to award purification. Brahma yoga is not for beginners. They may imagine that they practice it but unless there is purify in reference to kundalini, brahma yoga is a farce."

After saying this, he raised his hands in disgust. Then he said, "It is the weather in there. *(He pointed to my head.)* Who cares what happens outside physically? It is the modes of nature in there. Teach them that."

Soon after this Yogesh arrived. He challenged Zipruana. He said to him, "You do not know anything. When you had a human body, you were known as a lunatic. Get away from my disciple."

In this way, the two great yogins were joking with each other.

Then Zipruana showed some hand-holds of the head. These are done in the advanced stage of kundalini yoga to cause the kundalini chakra to remain stabilized in the head. This causes one to advance into brahma yoga practice.

Yogiraj Zipruana said to Yogesh, "What sort of friend were you? You did not even mention me in your books."

Yogesh replied, "I certainly did but I did not mention your name. Why should I tell people about a person who was known as a lunatic."

Zipruana pointed to Muktananda and said, "Well he did. So I got some fame."

Yogesh remarked, "Yes, you are a fame-seeking yogi. That is all. Better go away. Leave my disciple. He does not need your confusing advice."

After this they laughed. Then they went away.

Ma Lakshmi·

She transmitted a message that she would not offer me coins again, but offered a blessing for success in yoga and for being able to go with the siddhas. She said, "Let it be according to your determination to be with the siddhas."

Remark:

Some of the supernatural boon givers may approach a yogin for the fulfillment of desires. There is no danger in this, since if a yogin is motivated for benefits, he will be eased and will be freed from anxiety by the attainment of his wishes. However on the other hand, a yogin may have benefits coming to him which accrued from past lives. Even though in the past he wanted these things, now he no longer regards them as desirable because he is in a different place and a different time with different needs, after having many other experiences which cause such aspects to be undesirable. Still however, since he applied a desire pressure, and released a need energy into the creation, a supernatural boon giver may offer the results of those desires to him. Their idea is to release such pent-up force from the cosmic pool of reward energies.

What should such a yogi do? What should the supernatural boon givers do with that energy? Should they give those boons to others? We see in the case of advanced yogins like Dhruva, that they were unable to stop the God of the world from giving them what they formerly desired. This also happened to Prahlad. Thus in some cases, a yogi cannot side-step the boon fulfillments and must accept whatever is due in history.

It is a technical part of a yogi's life, since he has to be careful with both good returns and bad reactions which come to him based on past social involvements in previous lives. Any reaction can forestall yoga practice and cause him to be thrown back into the social world of conditioned existence which is devoid of spiritual advancement. For a time in this life and in some previous one, I refused money from the Goddess, running as it was from what good returns were due to me. Now she permitted that I may sidestep this energy. It may go to others as a free contribution from me. That does not mean that I am magnanimous, because even the good returns which are due to me, are fraught with hazards. Anyone who would be awarded such returns would be in a danger just as much as I myself would be imperiled if I misused such energy or if that energy influenced me to accelerate a vice or to exploit a needy person.

The kundalini lifeforce

In a parallel world, I found myself with a donkey-sized penis. With force I pissed a large stream of clear urine into a toilet. Ma Kundalini, the lifeforce personified, sat on the commode looking. After the fluid ended, the organ remained aroused.

The kundalini lifeforce then came for me to kiss the nipples of her breasts. She was nude. I had gone to bed early that evening, at the later part of the afternoon. She woke me at fifteen minutes before midnight. She said she was rested and that I should awaken the physical body for doing exercises.

Remark:

Some of these experiences with Ma Kundalini may seem to be quite weird but these are normal for those yogins who do kundalini yoga in earnest. The sexual nature of these experiences is also normal, because Kundalini energy is mostly a sexual force. The relationship between the core-self using a subtle body and that subtle form itself, is something like the relationship between a man and his lover. It is for the most part a sexual relationship. Thus it is quite fitting that there be experiences of this sort when one begins to purify the kundalini force.

Nityananda

On this day he instructed that I check on meditation before doing exercises. He wanted me to remove thoughts which were in the background of consciousness. He said, "Use the naad sound only as mental support."

Remark:

This remark concerns checking to see if the psyche is responding in a progressive way to the exercises of kundalini yoga and the other austerities. After all, if the psyche will not retain the advances it makes while doing the exercises, then the conclusion is that ultimately the exercises are a waste of time. This is exactly what some non-yogis feel. A yogi should not be bigoted about the practice. He should check to see how the psyche retains the benefits. It should accumulate progress no matter how incremental.

Apart from general consciousness, one has a background consciousness which is mostly control by urges and subliminal needs. In higher yoga, one must confront that background of consciousness and flush any undesirable energies which lurk there. Such energies do not run away from a beginner. In fact they defeat him. But if he tries to confront them repeatedly and if he takes advice from superior yogins, he will ultimately remove them from the mind chamber. It will not happen overnight. When Arjuna asked Krishna about the removal of such impurities which are embedded in the mind of a yogin, Bhagavan Krishna said they may be eliminated by consistent practice.

October 31, 2003

Swaminarayan

In a whisper he said, "Train the mind to think of mandatory physical work only at certain times, never during the time allotted to meditation. If something persistent occurs stop the practice. Record it in writing. Deal with it, or it will repeatedly disturb you."

November 1, 2003

Nityananda

He said, "After resting, check the residual effects of practice by meditating early before practice. Check to see if thoughts are absent and how the mind responds to the meditation habit. The feelings-energy and intellect are like a woman and man respectively. They should be kept apart. The unrestricted proximity of these ruin the chance for success in meditation."

November 2, 2003·

On this date I had the realization that sexual intercourse and other forms of social involvement are actually the kundalini lifeforce energy being involved with itself in different aspects. This can be realized when a yogi is proficient in tracking subtle energy.

Nityananda

He advised, "Pray to her to allow you to explore higher aims, up in the crown chakra, leaving aside her lower objectives. Let her switch the mission. She worked on Adi Shankara for a superior understanding of her lower objectives. This happened when he took the king's body for sexual experiences."

Remark:

This concerns Kundalini Ma, but it may be applied to demigoddess Ma Durga.

Kali and Dwapara supernatural beings

I met these two persons in a parallel world. They were rough looking tribal chiefs. They killed two wild cows who looked old and crippled. They had a weird race of aborigines following them. They looked like hordes of wild tribal people.

In that parallel world, as I watched them, I had a few women and some children in my care. I then saw the kundalini lifeforce in feminine human form, looking at me for affection and sexual petting. She said that she introduced my Bhagavad Gita commentary and some of my other ideas to others.

Remark:

Kali (pronounced kul-lee) and Dwapara are supposed to be in control of the hearts and minds of most human being in our time. These supernatural persons are not interested in spiritual advancement. Their main objective is promote the vices which usher in a sure and certain degradation. The two wild cows which they killed represent the two traditional religious methods of the Eastern and Western cultures. These systems are being wiped out by television and internet. In fact the modern media uses the two wild cows in a mocking way, just as a cattle rancher raises livestock and then kills and eats the creatures, which he so lovingly cared for.

The weird race of aborigines are the modern generations of human beings, people who rejected the old religious traditions. They come out from wombs and decimate the old cultures. For instance, even though a human being can only take birth through sexual intercourse and can only attain an infant body by parental care, still modern human beings do not regard sexual intercourse as anything but a source of pleasure. They are reluctant to raise families. As soon as children are born, they put them into day care centers, just as a greedy farmer would take away a calf from its mother, starve the calf and drink or sell the milk.

Kundalini Ma appeared in that dream as one of the females I cared for, but her objective was sexual love and affection. She had no idea about spiritual life. This meant that essentially human life is animal life. One has to raise the self from that level by purifying Kundalini Ma.

On this day I had some insight into the varied aspects of sexual intercourse. It occurs in the subtle world, even during gross sexual activities.

But this is not normally perceived. It does explain why sexual attraction is such a stubborn tendency to give up.

More or less an ascetic should learn to leave aside sexual indulgence. Sexual life will always be here in the material world as a potential activity and as a functional act. Still, one should leave it aside. It is by leaving that aside that one progresses to higher yoga and realizes that one can live without the sexual expressions.

During sexual indulgence, in one level of the subtle body one experiences strong and very acute touching sensations. These are sensations in the sexual organs. One also experiences tasting sensations, through the organ itself. I do not mean oral sexual acts like licking the organ of the partner or sucking on the partner's sexual part, or drinking of the sexual fluids of the partner. I mean that without that, the sexual organs themselves have tasting organs through which they taste from the organ of the partner. This occurs in a certain phase of the subtle body. On the physical level this is interpreted as pleasure in the spinal nerves of the human being.

During intercourse, there are bright flashes of golden light. These are the clashing interplay of the emotional energy of the partners. There is activation of smelling senses at the organ itself, where each organ smells the sexual part of the other. This occurs besides the normal smelling which occurs through the noses of the partners. There is also hearing of the sounds of the organs of each partner, done at the organs themselves. For instance, when the male has the sexual arousal, there is clashing sounds. A flourishing energy rushes into his organ to arouse the cells within it, and to cause them to become attentive and stand ready for the thrusting the organ into the female passage. These clashing sounds are heard by the female organ. The cells of the female organ react to this subtle noise by becoming firm, by secreting sexual fluids and by getting ready to squeeze and further motivate the activity. They get ready to drink fluids which they anticipate will come out of the male organ.

This and more occurs in a certain phase of the subtle body during sexual intercourse. An interest in this is gradually lost by a yogi. It may be opined that a yogi is foolish for giving up such pleasure, but that is something that he must do if he is to advance further. In some higher dimensions, persons use subtle bodies which allow them to perceive these sensual features of sexual intercourse. But a yogi works hard to skip such realms in the hereafter.

Essentially there are two types of persons who advance in higher yoga. One is the yogi who feels that he can ultimately transcend sex. This one feels that he is above sexual intercourse and that he will reach a level of advancement where he will never have to be attracted to it again. This person feels that he is a core-self and not a body. His idea is that as a core-self he has nothing to do with sex.

The other type of yogi is the one who realizes that sex is eternal. Gender is eternal and cannot be eliminated. This yogi aspires to skip it, to leave it aside. He does not have confidence that he can transcend it except by avoiding it. He also knows that he is a core-self but he thinks that the core-selves are eternally polarized for one sex or the other and that ultimately, since he is a minute self his likelihood to be overcome by a more powerful other self who is polarized with the opposite sex or gender, is always a possibility. Thus he aspires for avoidance. He has no hope that ultimately he will be free from sexual assault because he is not the ultimate controller.

We should always remember how afraid Laksman was of seeing the beauty of goddess Sita. He was so afraid that he never looked at her form and only saw her ankles. He never set his eyes on her complete beauty. Even when Laksman was instructed to take Goddess Sita to Yogiraj Valmiki's ashram and abandon her, Laksman refused to look on at her form, when she declared to him that she had missed a period of her menstrual cycle and was definitely pregnant.

Supreme Rama also, protected His dear brother Laksman by sometimes instructing that he should walk ahead of Sita anytime they would travel through the forest, a place in which they were obliged to stay for some thirteen years. In this way Laksman did not have to walk behind Sita and be plagued by her beauty.

We should remember how one of the Shivas lost semen after seeing goddess Mohini, and how King Pururava strayed from his course of existence by following the beautiful celestial nymph Urvashi, He did this for thousands of years, following that woman through many gross and subtle dimensions, just for her sexual company.

Only the Supreme Being can afford to be careless with women, or to boast that He is not attracted by feminine beauty. Others who make such boasts will definitely be ruined.

Two tantric yogis of note are Ramakrishna and Bamakhepa. These were condemned by some of our Vaishnava gurus, but nevertheless they were accredited by yogis of worth because of their research into the length and breadth of sexuality. Their example is not to be followed but nevertheless they gave us a peep into the matter of the limits of sexuality.

November 4, 2003

Lahiri

He was in my subtle head. He said, "Use sound, then focus upwards."

Remark:

This refers to the naad sound. After one anchors into it, one should attempt to lift the will power, the attention energy and the intellect. If these are heavy, it means that one should do breath-infusion, since the energy is of a lower nature. Breath-infusion may cause the lower energy to be flushed from the subtle head.

November 5, 2003

Nityananda

He explained that the discrimination vanishing point, or the dissolution of objectivity, occurs naturally, especially in a mind which is full of stress. The frequency of the vanishing point occurrence is reduced if one adopts a simpler lifestyle. Whenever the mind enters into that dissolution of objectivity, one becomes objectively aware again only after the attention becomes linked to images and sounds which developed in the imagination orb. These images and sounds are caused by impressions which hit the orb from the senses and memory.

Basically speaking, there is nothing anyone can do about that mental process, except to simplify the lifestyle and surcharge the subtle body with a higher grade of subtle energy.

November 10, 2003

Kundalini Ma

I met her again in a parallel world. She had a black very sexually-attractive, irresistible body. I bought her some romantic gifts. She was shy and chaste like a nineteen year old maiden who lacked carnal experience.

After that encounter I returned to this side of existence at about midnight. I did breath-infusion. I realized that Kundalini Ma in that black body was death personified, a black lady, a goddess with red lips. She wears red garments. She has red eyes, red palms and red soles. She is a sexual tease if one sees her but she is celibate, a woman brimming with sexual energy but with it absolutely contained.

Yogeshwarananda

He said, "I practiced that when the bear was burnt. I spend hours doing that. You should dedicate more time to that."

Remark:

He commented on naad meditation. A beginner will grasp its significance when he realizes that mantras have little effect. Naad sound, the Eeeeee sound which comes into the right side of the subtle head does not have to be said aurally or mentally. It is free of charge. The yogi should use it as an anchor to develop dharana deliberate linkage of the attention to higher concentration forces.

There are many subtle dimensions and parallel worlds which exist side by side. These are mostly a waste of time for the yogi. However he will have to experience them as part of the course. Beyond these places there is the sky of consciousness. Naad focus puts one on the footing to reach that chit akasha, the spiritual environment.

Nityananda always thought that we wasted our time with subtle worlds. His view is that the subtle existence which splintered as parallel worlds are merely different types of confinement.

Yogeshwarananda

He said, "That sound is used by the prajapatis and rishis. Before there was any of these creations they existed in it for thousands of years in bodiless forms.

Yogesh commented on the touch sensation, stating that it may extend to cosmic proportions even though that rarely happens. He said that some yogis who attained bodiless status, may reside in the cosmic sense of touch, and live there for thousands of years. In that state they feel as if they are gigantic in proportions.

When this body was nine years of age, I entered into the cosmic sense of touch. I felt as if I was cosmic. Sometimes it would be so gigantic that the psyche would become afraid of the vastness. This happens when a yogi's energies are linked into the cosmic sense of touch.

November 12, 2003

On this day I made a notation, about naad sound. The imagination orb is disagreeable to it. The orb will not cooperate at all times. It will try to move the attention away from naad. There will be stress energies in the psyche regarding one's day to day activities as well as energies which come from bad association. These interfere with naad focus.

I made a notation about brahma yoga practice. In truth, one cannot proceed with that unless the kundalini lifeforce is purified. The proficiency does not happen in a flash. Those who want results overnight will be frustrated.

After completing kundalini yoga, one should endeavor to cause kundalini to remain in the head of the subtle body. At that time, any elementary practice of kundalini yoga is done but not as frequently. One then flushes the subtle head, and causes the kundalini lifeforce to keep the neck cleared so that kundalini can always radiate into the subtle head.

This means that initially in kundalini practice, one should clear the lower part of the body which is below the navel. Once that is done, one works on the chest area below the neck·and then one works on the neck and finally on the subtle head. It takes time, depending on the amount of contamination one has in the gross and subtle bodies. Each yogin must patiently work to flush the psyche. There is no set time for this. It depends on the amount of contamination one absorbed and on the steadiness of practice.

At the end of kundalini yoga practice, when the yogi gets a foothold on brahma yoga, he should clear the head of the subtle form, so that the intellect is separated from the memory. The parts of the intellect organ should be segregated from each other. The intellect has a pick-up arm which acquires subtle impressions which ooze out of the memory chamber. This pick-up mechanism should be curbed. In addition the memory has an enticing feature which prompts the intellect to link with it. One has to squelch this feature. This and more must be done within the psyche.

November 14, 2003

Lahiri

He said, "Use the dynamic energy in the silence force to find a hollow in the frontal dynamic energy."

Remark:

From in the naad Eeeeee sound, a yogin may use any remnant of dynamic moving energy-feelings to find a void opening in the troublesome frontal energy which is active with memory and sensual impressions. The silence force is the naad sound resonance. It is not silent. It is saturated with sublime transcendental vibration. The materialistic intellect finds the naad sound to be boring and undesirable. But that same materialistic intellect must be oriented to transcendence energy. One will not be awarded a new intellect. One will have to upgrade that same troublesome intellect.

The process of purification becomes operative as soon as a yogin realizes that he is stuck with the psyche as it is. The God will not take away one's impure psyche. That will not happen. One will have to purify what one has. If God does not purify the psyche right now as one has faith in God, then when will God do that? The answer is that God will not do it, either now or in the future. He will give instructions on how it should be done. The quicker one can inspire oneself for purification, the better off one will be, and the more one will be able to utilize the ever-present grace of the Supreme Being. Otherwise one will be stalled forever with hopes and expectations unfulfilled.

November 15, 2003

Lahiri

He said, "The real wife is in the mind. It is that thing."

Remark:

He spoke of the imagination orb which is a portion of the intellect complex organ. It is ever occupied keeping the core-self enthralled.

November 17, 2003

Lahiri

He said, "The attachment is the consideration itself. The thing has the attachment-need which is like an arm it uses to grasp expressions for consuming."

Remark:

This is advice for the yogin to study the mental system of consideration. When one considers anything, one becomes drawn into images which are created by the imagination orb. The part of the intellect which considers, is itself a force of attachment. Once a yogi settles down in meditation practice, he may observe this in detail. This will not be done for him by others. He must do this himself.

November 22, 2003

Lahiri

He said, "Rest is necessary. There must be removal of any type of anxiety-association. The covering mental darkness must be understood.

"Use naad. Take it to the thoughts. After you find your attention in stupor energy patiently train it to go to the naad. Eventually the training will persist. The mind will obey after much training."

Remark:

Anxiety-association means persons who have a yogically-hostile lifestyle. When one associates with such persons, one picks up numerous anxieties. Beginner yogis are usually attached to being concerned about numerous things. This is a bad habit. In time though, they realize the fault of this and take steps to distance themselves from bad association. Each person must work with himself or herself on this. Beginners may feel deprived if the teacher restricts them. Thus it is up to them to develop a value for isolation.

The covering mental darkness is there in the head of the subtle form. One must endeavor to get rid of it, otherwise one will never get spiritual insight and will never see into the chit akash. It is not a matter of going here or there or anywhere in the gross or subtle existence. It is simply this: One is already very near to the spiritual sky but being surrounded by mental darkness one cannot peer into that transcendental atmosphere.

Each yogin should struggle to get out of this mental darkness. It is an individual accomplishment. Some feel that God will remove it. But they are wrong. Ask yourself a good question: What will God gain by removing it? God allowed that mental darkness to prevail over the limited selves for some millions and billions of years and now suddenly why should he remove it? The whole proposal that God will remove it by His grace and that the devotee has to do nothing but serve God is totally unacceptable and absurd. It is a very ridiculous proposal. God will do no such thing. You must work to remove it, just as you work to reinforce it in materialistic life.

November 24, 2003

Lahiri

He said, "The helper energy hides in reserve. Use it to help."

Remark:

This helper energy is the one used in parallel worlds, when one is found in such a world without one's developed discrimination. If one is transferred to a subtle world, a parallel world, then if one has not got the developed discrimination, one will do foolish acts. In other words, one will become responsible for socially-hostile acts. Thus when one is transferred, one may find sometimes that even though the developed discrimination was left behind in this dimension, a certain helper energy becomes manifest as an instinct for doing what is righteous.

In any world, one is transferred into, there will be an environment as well as a social order. One will be made to fit in. Thus one must help in discriminating right from wrong.

November 30, 2003

I had a realization that the imagination orb is the main cause of the lack of focus for dharana practice, the 6th stage of yoga, that of deliberate focusing on a higher concentration force. The imagination orb also causes stalling in the 5th stage, that of the pratyahar sensual energy withdrawal. This is because the imagination orb has an attachment to thoughts and memory images. This attachment must be broken by the yogi himself by hard endeavor in meditation.

December 3, 2003

Lahiri

He said, "Lifting the eyes mean moving the attention to the stillness and naad sound in the back. So long as the attention is focused impulsively and/or deliberately through the active mind in the front, nothing transcendental is achieved."

December 4, 2003

Lahiri

He stated, "The various actively-charged energy, or orbits of charged energy, must be retracted. That is part of pratyahar. The individual must himself do it for himself by realizing his vices acquired. He should shut down the sensual orbs in so far as they related to this world."

December 4, 2003

Lahiri with Yogeshwarananda looking from a distance.

Lahiri said, "Use the vacuum here. That is kutastha. You call it imagination orb. Get it to its vacuous center. Keep the attention there. That is kriya number 2. Kriya number 1 is the naad sound focus. Being stationed in the first one, do the second. Always sit early in the morning like this. I will meet you here.

"The top is sound from the subtle atmosphere. Then next is the sense of touch sensation from the air. This is that touching. It may be sensed in the vacuous space in the imagination orb. Keep holding the vacuous space. That is the place for the visualization."

December 6, 2003

Lahiri

He instructed for pulling the dynamic energy in the mind through the center of the imagination orb. That central place is where images or thoughts may appear suddenly in the mind space. There should be a holding on to the naad sound on the right side. Then one should pull back the energy in a centralized way.

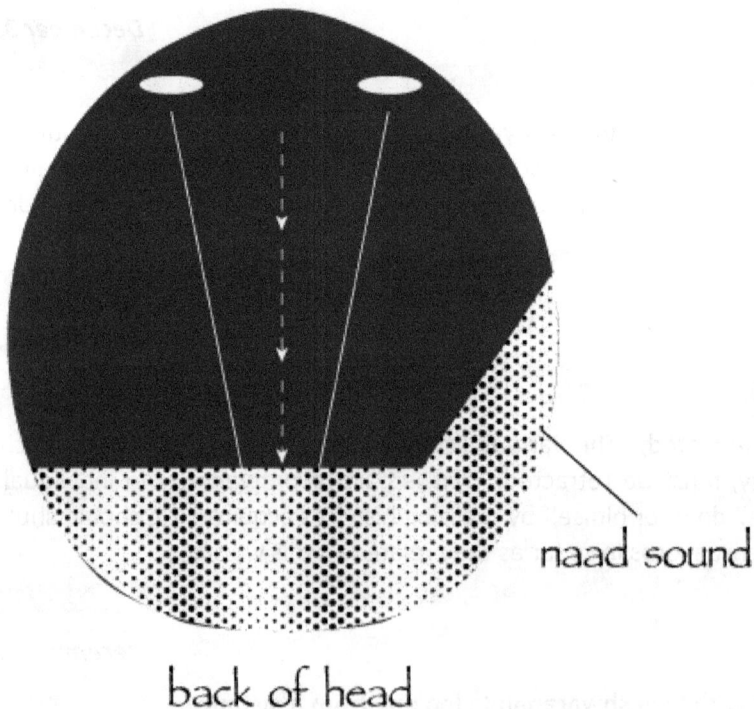

naad sound

back of head

Lahiri showed that attachment is created in the sensual energy flow which passes back and forth from remembered objects and from real objects to the attention. This sensual energy flow has an emotion, which becomes surcharged or colored with the energy from the said imagined or real object.

Such matter must be research thoroughly by a yogin.

December 7, 2003

Lahiri

He explained that the mobility orb in the foot does not come out until the sex orb is completely curbed. One walks, for instance, before he develops sexual impulse in a body. The mobility orb is established first. It is retracted last.

Vachaspati

He gave diagrams. These are advanced procedures which are done by will power. These only work for those yogis who curbed and purified the kundalini lifeforce.

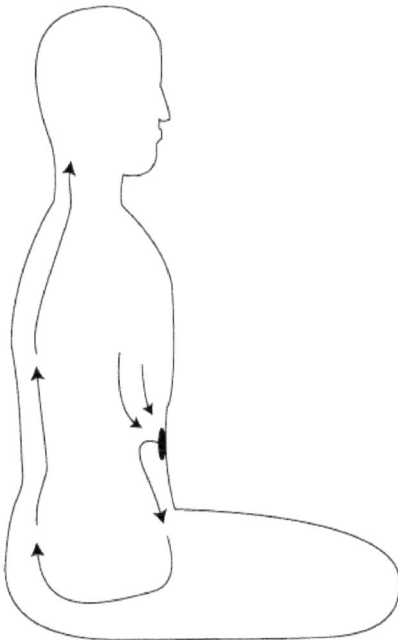

preliminary kundalini clearance   reversed advanced clearance

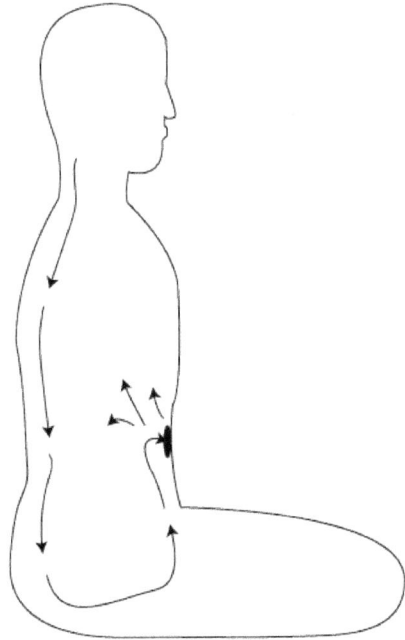

Part 7

Vachaspati

He discussed the exposure of the lower kinetic mind or intellect thinking-analyzing organ to the naad sound from the bottom of its tongue-like vagina-like opening.

Remark:

When the intellect is seen from the bottom, it appears like the hatch-opening at the bottom of a cargo aircraft.

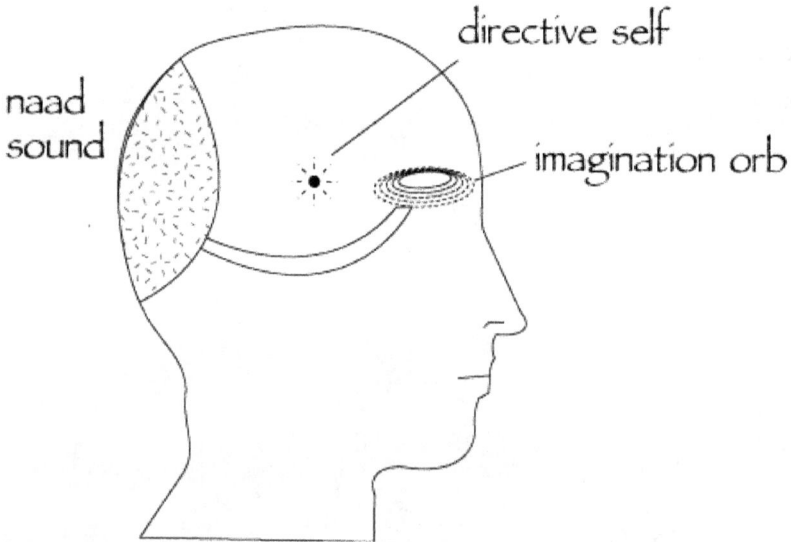

December 9, 2003

Vachaspati

We discussed causing the imagination orb and the sensual reporting apparatus to develop an attachment to naad sound. To attain this, a yogin must do dharana repeatedly by linking those organs and their related subtle equipment to the naad. If the yogi fails to practice he will get nowhere. A sit-down-and-wait attitude is non-productive.

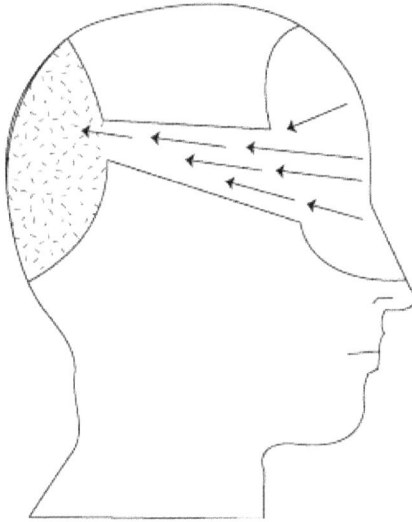

December 12, 2003

A cross-world

I was transited to a cross-world which had persons who passed on from their bodies after contracting the HIV disease. There were children and adults with children. There was one white-bodied lady with her black-bodied child. They went into a dark bungalow, which had no electricity or technology. The water was in gutters and streams. It disappeared from time to time. Another lady had a beige complexion. She complained of the conditions. She compared the situation to the physical environment,

The subtle bodies they used were like physical forms. It felt to them that they were in another physical world, except that they could remember what life was like on this planet.

Everyone there was spooked and had sexual intercourse in the back of their minds but they had a deadly fear of it. They suffered terribly from the HIV disease. A friend was there. He had a severe abdomen sensitivity which caused vomiting.

Later in the year 2005, he was released from that place. His subtle body began overcoming the disease. He wandered here and there, trying to get a body on this planet.

December 12, 2003

Vachaspati

He stated, "Brahma yoga begins where kundalini yoga ends, with the permanent clearing of the sushumna passage by intense bhastrika for 3 years of celibacy while knowing how to practice.

December 13, 2003

Vachaspati

He gave a new meaning for conquering sleep. He said, "One should reach a stage where one no longer pays attention even to occurrences which happen in the subtle world. The psyche should instead become attracted to naad sound. He explained that Lahiri did higher meditation for going to chit akash sky of consciousness. That was a hint, that other aspects are preliminary.

He explained that whenever it imagine, one may move a stream of naad energy into the imagination orb. One should note the location of the imagination and then feed the naad sound into that empty space.

So long as one is addicted to images and pictures in the mind, the imagination orb is difficult to locate. In fact Krishna discouraged the search for it when He told Arjuna this:

क्लेशोऽधिकतरस्तेषाम्
अव्यक्तासक्तचेतसाम् ।
अव्यक्ता हि गतिर्दुःखं
देहवद्भिरवाप्यते ॥१२.५॥

kleśo'dhikatarastesām
avyaktāsaktacetasām
avyaktā hi gatirduḥkhaṁ
dehavadbhiravāpyate (12.5)

kleśo — kleśaḥ — exertion; 'dhikataraḥ = adhikataraḥ — greater; tesam — of them; avyaktāsaktacetasām — avyakta — invisible existence + āsakta — attached + cetasām — of minds; avyaktā — invisible reality; hi — truly; gatiḥ — goal; duḥkhaṁ — difficult; dehavadbhiḥ — by the human beings; avāpyate — is attained

The mental exertion of those whose minds are attached to the invisible existence is greater. The goal of reaching that invisible reality is attained with difficulty by the human beings. (Bhagavad Gita 12.5)

The abstract existence of anything, whether it be in the psyche of the yogi, or beyond his individualized compartmentalized environment, is difficult to attain. But there is no other method of reaching these realities besides higher yoga. This begins with intellect yoga, which the same Krishna gave Arjuna in Chapter 2 and 3 of Bhagavad Gita. It is certainly a difficult lesson. It is painstaking, but its results cannot come in any other way.

For the time being we may stall the practice of abstract yoga but sticking to sanctified material forms like the forms of the deity of Krishna, but sooner or later we must practice the higher yoga and deal with what is abstract directly.

On this date, I made a notation about dreams. If one meets someone in a parallel world, and if that person is from this location, he may not recall the relationship with oneself. This is due to his leaving behind his cultural orientation and discrimination. In other words, part of the mind-emotions apparatus was left behind near the gross body which sleeps in this world. One should remember this when meeting others in dreams.

However the person would have a liking or disliking predisposition and would function in a relationship with oneself on that basis.

Lahiri

He said, "Do not be afraid. Pursue it. Confine it. Confront it. Do not let it hold you at a distance to keep you entertained by images and sounds."

Remark:

This refers to the imagination orb.

After this he descended into my memory. He pulled up an impression and had it rendered into a picture. It was a headless chicken. He said to me, "What is this?

I replied, "That was from my childhood."

He said, "Do not worry of it. The parents are responsible. It is their mistake but it is your fault now, your memory blemish. Send down some naad sound to scour these memories."

He explained that when one loses objectivity, it is due to actions of the imagination orb, which focuses and unfocuses time and time again. The attention follows this focusing and unfocusing and passes through a blank period between the two.

After this Lahiri called Yogiraj Vachaspati. They discussed the removal of the tendency for subtle activities. Lahiri wanted advanced yogis to remove subtle activities and instead spend time focusing on the naad sound vibration. He said that would anchor them into the chit akasha, the spiritual atmosphere, more firmly.

December 16, 2003

Lahiri

He advised that the imagination-orb be force-fed the naad sound, even when the orb is resistant to it. Each yogi should endeavor on his own to conquer the psyche.

December 23, 2003

Dharana / Dhyana considerations

Dharana may be the effort to link the attention to a concentration force such as naad or even to a strong infused energy current which developed while doing breath-infusion. Or dharana may be the effort to link a strong force or naad energy to the attention or the imagination orb.

If the yogi is observant, he will sense if there is a flow of energy from a concentration force. If the force does not have an outward bound flow from itself; the yogi has to link his attention to that force. He must be observant to know which practice applies on a certain day.

Dhyana practice is when the yogin finds that there is an automatic or spontaneous linkage of his attention to a concentration force, or when he observes that a concentration force comes into his psyche and strikes his attention or imagination orb of its own accord. He merely has to observe the linkage and keep himself in it for as long as it may last. Sometimes a farmer must flood fields with water. But at other times, nature itself does this for him. Flooding the fields may be compared to dharana, while nature's action of flooding them is compared to dhyana.

On this day I made notations about the subtle effects of liquid food. Some yogins feel that all solid foods should be abandoned. This is substantiated in the Puranas, where we read of successful ascetics who ceased eating solid foods and subsisted on liquids and then on air alone.

One should check the benefits and disadvantages of various types of foods. Each yogin must rate himself to see how his gross and subtle bodies operate efficiently or inefficiently according to the type of food intake.

December 26, 2003

Experience-seeking orb

On this day I saw an experience-seeking orb. This one pursued and hankered for subtle experiences in parallel worlds and dream states. This is a dangerous orb. If this orb is allowed free rein, the yogi will never be liberated. This is a subtler orb. I saw it near the nose. I made efforts to retract it but it slipped into invisibility.

Lahiri advised me to eliminate this orb, but he gave no details of a specific method. Orbs are discovered as one becomes more and more detached from so many varied experiences. But such detachment comes when one went to the subtle worlds and saw their lures for oneself. One person who had the resistance to the orbs was Mudgala, a yogin who reject the offer to go to the heavenly cities of Indra.

On this day I had a notation about sexual life withdrawal. This is a part of pratyahar sensual energy withdrawal practice but it is attained during the practice of dharana deliberate transcendence focus. Even though pratyahar is the 5th stage of yoga, it cannot be completed until one mastered the 6th and 7th stages of dharana deliberate focus and dhyana spontaneous focus. As one progresses, one finds that one regresses repeatedly to complete some phase of a previous practice.

When one mastered celibacy by virtue of an aggressive kundalini and celibacy yoga practice, one reaches a stage where the sexual fluids in the gross body begin avoiding the lower tube.

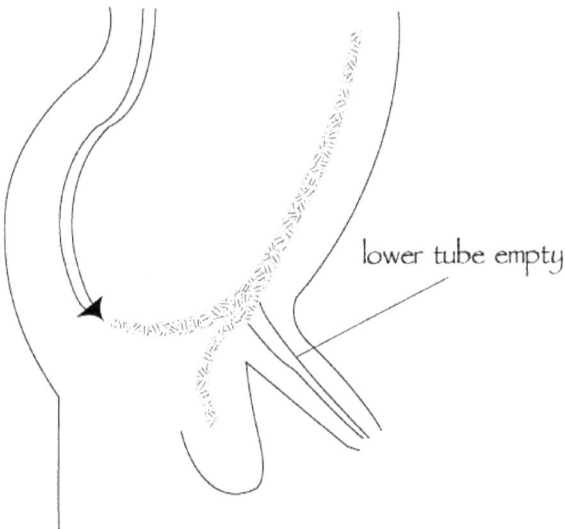

lower tube empty

Instead of coursing through the lower tube, the fluids just go around the loop and move upwards. One gets experience of this, when one meets females, either physically or in the subtle world and then one finds that even though there is a strong sexual attraction by virtue of destiny, still the sexual fluids do not go down the lower tube. In some cases, when one links sexually with a female in the subtle world, one finds that her fluids enter the lower tube and come into the loop but one's fluids do not descend as previously.

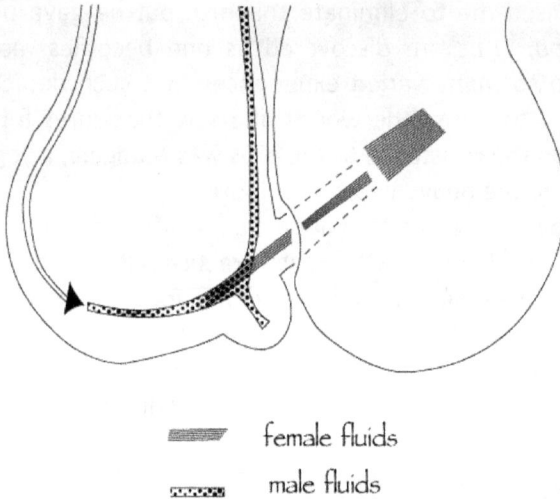

female fluids
male fluids

In hatha yoga practice, this is called vajroli. After a body changes so that it no longer uses the lower tube for seminal fluids, there comes a stage where one regains boyhood innocence regarding sexual information. One forgets sexual pleasure and its related feelings.

Shivananda

He advised that the imagination orb and memory contents be moved into the void energy in the mind and into the naad sound. He said that if there was an active type of subtle energy in the mind, one should find a way to use that, otherwise it will act on its own to ruin meditation. In dharana, an effort is made for meditative focus but in dhyana there is no exertion.

January 1, 2004

Vachaspati

He said, "Naad solves the mantra repetition problem. It frees one from having to produce a sound on this side of existence. Use naad constantly.

"*Om namah Shivaya* is the only mantra that glides you from the front to the back of the head into the naad sound. Try other mantras. If any mantra moves you forward into the frontal lobe in any way, even incrementally, it will not serve the purpose."

Remark:

This is his view. One does not have to accept this. That was his experience. If one can use some other mantra and get success that would be fine. Yogesh did not mentioned *Om Namah Shivaya*. He vouched for the savitur gayatri mantra. Each yogin should discover what gives progress.

January 3, 2004

Inner sound / speckled darkness

Sometimes in meditation practice there seems to be a competition between the inner sounds and the speckled darkness in the space of the subtle head. At other times, each seem to be complimentary to the other and to aid the focus, all depending on the objective of the yogi during the session.

Sometimes the speckled darkness is stronger. It attracts the attention more. At other times the inner sounds are compelling and hold the attention, making meditation easy during the session.

January 7, 2004

Yogeshwarananda

He said, "Use naad as the first procedure. Add sight, but when that is a stable, add touch, which should be the second mystic action. Start with pain in the feet, which is reflected in the brain. Then there is a pyramid type pushing force upward. That is touch. Work on that with naad. Then go back to sight. This is how you establish dharana deliberate focusing practice.

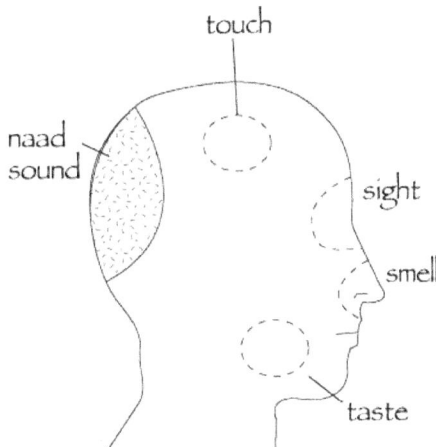

January 9. 2004

Yogeshwarananda

He asked about celibacy, regarding its possibility for modern people.

I said, "It is part of pratyahar practice for Western people and for those who are similar to Westerners. They let that sense be expressed too much. Hence the need to make so much effort to retract it. The animalistic humans may work hard to retract that impulse, otherwise they cannot be free of it."

January 14, 2004

Buddha

I said to him, "There are no techniques in your history."

He replied, "That was not my mission. When you meditate, hold the attention in the imagination orb. It is there that takes place. Capture that in steady focus. Stop the enchantment."

On this day I realized that naad sound helps to detach from the enchantment of the images and sounds created by the imagination orb. Once the detachment is gained, one may challenge the orb, confronting it, forcing it to stop the impulsive creations. This practice has to be done by each yogi for a time, to gain control over the memory, the sensual energy and the imagination faculty.

Buddha advised me to bring forward the naad sound into the imagination orb. This he said if done regularly for sufficient time, will cause the nature of the orb to be adjusted, so that it helps in yoga success, rather than contravene progress.

January 25, 2004

Lahiri

He commented, "The problem is the attention. Why like a slave does it go to the imagination orb? It has no independence. Notice how it is charmed by the orb. The attention is the same as the will power. It has to be separated from the imagination faculty by lifting it up with eyes upturned."

Lahiri

He gave a procedure for pulling the attention away from the front part of the subtle brain

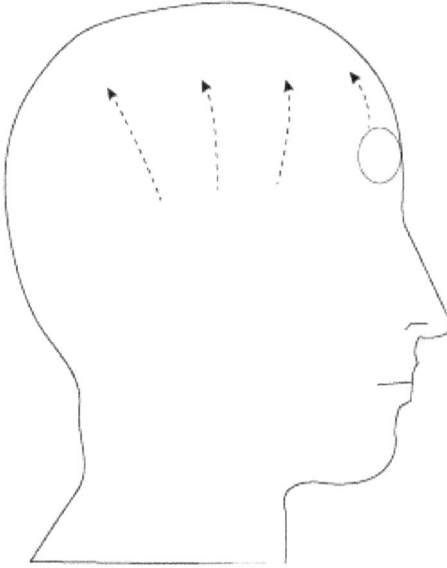

On this day I had a realization, that eating foods which have a strong after-taste is a mistake, since it makes the mouth desire more. A yogi should stick to basic ordinary food taste and should stay away from foods which are spicy or very sweet. Eating without discipline is a sure way to stagnate in spiritual life.

Naad grace force

Sometimes naad sound comes into the right side of the subtle head, and then it splits off or spreads into various directions. Whenever this occurs it is a grace energy for the yogin and serves to put him into transcendence focus. Here is one example of how that may occur by a spreading of the sound upwards.

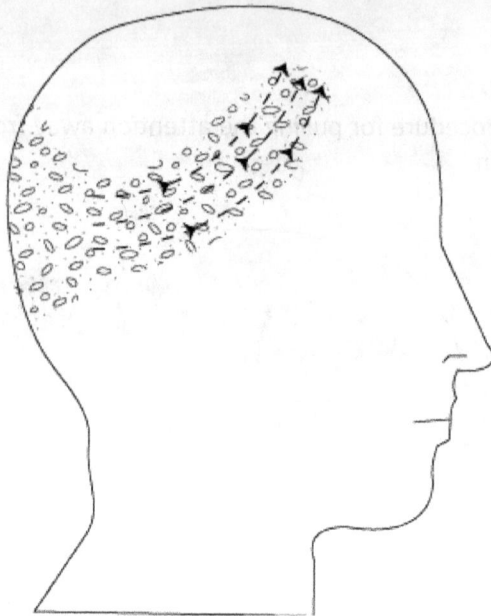

January 28, 2004

Lahiri

He gave a kriya for subtle energy breathing through the mind. To do this, one should with breath-infusion surcharge the subtle body and then the subtle head specifically. Thereafter, one should sit for meditation. One may notice an energy concentration moving into and out of the head, just as we notice air moving in and out of the body through the nostrils. Sometimes this observation is made through the visual sense. At other times it is made through the sense of feeling, the touch sense.

Once perceived, if one follows the energy in and then out, one does not lose objectivity. This subtle energy intake and expiration does not coordinate with the physical breathing system but sometimes it seems as if they are synchronize. It does coordinate with the disc that is sometimes seen moving in and out of the brow chakra or moving to the right and then to the left of center.

February 4, 2004

Patanjali

He advised, "Move back to the center of the sense of identity. Stay secluded from the intellect. Instead lean on the naad sound."

Remark:

This is how one switches one's vision from this existence to the chit akasha, the sky of consciousness.

February 5, 2003

Lahiri

He advised that the entire frontal lobe be lifted. Since this area of the psyche will be heavy with anxieties, this is a strenuous exercise for those who are still involved in cultural affairs. If one is fortunate enough to have a simply lifestyle and to be away from cultural involvements, this frontal lobe will be light weight, otherwise it will feel as if one strains mental, and even physical muscles in the head, to lift it.

February 6, 2004

Vachaspati

He explained that longevity depends on a lack of disciples. "From disciples," he said, "comes retardation of a yogi's practice."

He stated that longevity is directly related to lack of stress and a lack of healthy self-attentiveness. Other aspects which affect that are bad habits like over-eating, unnecessarily starving the body, lack of exercise or too much strenuous endeavor.

February 7, 2004

Krishna

He gave these objectives:
- Naad sound
- Focus on tip top of the nose bridge between eyes. Use a mild focus only. There should be no thoughts. Keep with the naad sound.

He instructed that I stop helping others, so as to develop detachment. But I may give some serious students ideas of how they may develop the practice. He said, "Do not foolishly sacrifice your development. All you will get for it is responsibility. With that responsibility, always consider this, "Can you free yourself and another as well through execution of such responsibilities?"

Remark:

One must be anchored in naad sound without activity by the imagination orb in its impulsive creation of sounds and pictures. If one finds that these activities cannot stop, one should find a method to terminate them.

February 8, 2004

Pulling force

One may pull in at the center of the eyebrows, the high point on the nose ridge. If one finds that focusing there is a losing battle with thoughts and pictures, one may pull in the energy instead. On some days, this pulling action will be effective.

A consistent problem will be lost of focus and discovering oneself looking at thoughts or hearing sounds and seeing pictures in the imagination orb. This is similar to a person who became so intoxicated, that he is not aware of his actions. He finds himself in a theatre looking at a play. He then asked himself, "Why am I here? How did I get here?"

February 11, 2004

Buddha

He instructed, "Use naad only. Get into that. After a time, vision will develop. There must be stability, dhirah, first. Stick to that. Let everything else develop from that. Go backwards into the sound. Retreat there."

Remark:

This method of staying in the back of the head in the naad sound seems to be the best way to prepare the self for seeing into the chit akasha. There is a mantra that may be used in that sound. It is *Om Namo Bhagavate Vasudevaya*. However the chanting requires too much attention as a separate endeavor, and it is useless if it is done superficially or only as a prop or if the mind is jumpy.

Location is the factor that works. Mantra, though highly advertised, is a disturbance. To keep a location is not easy, because the locations which should be kept are unnatural for the mind. For instance the attention is usually focused in a forward direction towards the face of the body. Now if the location is in the back of the head, that seems unnatural and the sense of attention will resist doing that. Thus location as a method of focus requires endeavor, at least until the mind becomes accustomed to it.

One should test to see if a forward location, which is more natural, will facilitate. After all the forward locations are the usual places for the focus since most of the senses are oriented to the face area of the body. Thus when the attention moves in a forward position, it becomes victimized by the memory, the sensual activity and the imagination faculty. These aspects enthrall the core-self and keep the attention spell bound in nonsense activities. Thus the sound in the back of the head, particularly in the right back side is the best place for transcendence focus practice.

February 14, 2004

Lahiri

He said, "Keep that body by that body. There is no need for it to go elsewhere."

Remark:

He spoke of the subtle body. He advised that it should stay by the physical form. He felt there was no need for astral projections or for going to various subtle worlds.

When trying to go backward, one has to figure if one will go back with the intellect or not. It is best for beginners to leave the intellect in the front and just go back with the observing-self only. This means that one goes back with the sense of initiative.

What is this sense of initiative?

It is an energy which surrounds the core. The intellect may be perceived as a surrounding power but it is mostly functioning in the front of the head. Thus it is easy to recognize the sense of initiative which in comparison surrounds the self spherically. Look at these diagrams.

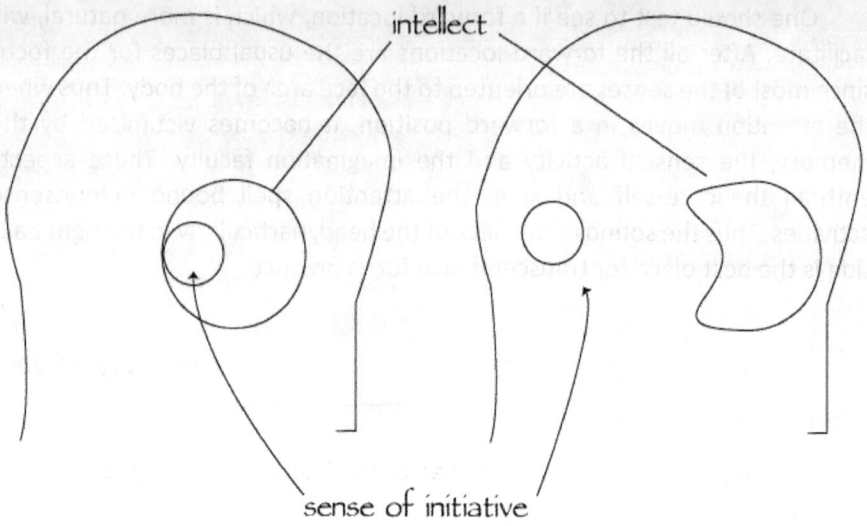

intellect

sense of initiative

In the second diagram, when the self moves to the back of the head, the intellect the splits off because it is resistant to going to the back, but the sense of initiative remains with the self.

Look at these diagrams.

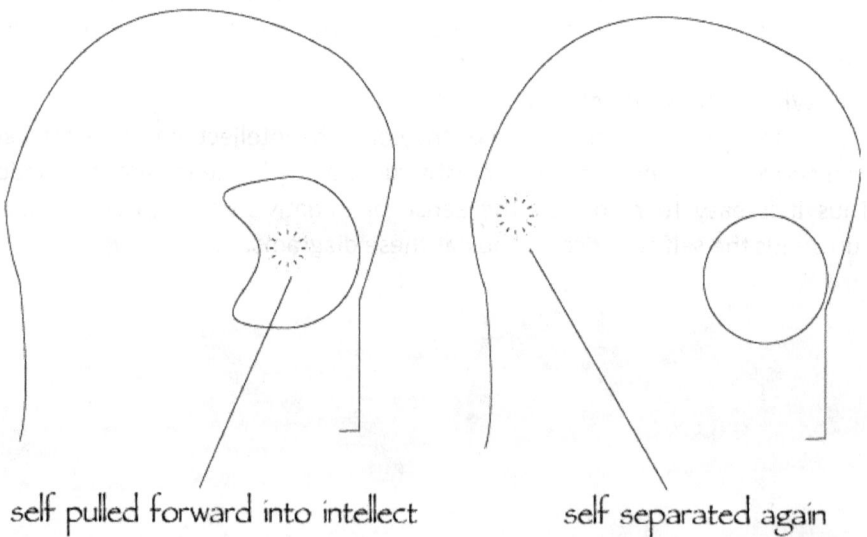

self pulled forward into intellect   self separated again

One must practice repeatedly to understand what I illustrated. At first when one practices, it may seem as if none of these things are separate objects but with continued practice, one will begin to see the segregation.

When one makes the effort to go to the back of the head, one will find that even if one is successful, still one finds the self to be back in the front behind the intellect looking at its pictures against one's will. This will happen repeatedly. Do not be discouraged. This only proves that in the conditioned state, the self is ruled by the intellect. However, that predominance can be reduced.

Once one attains a clear separation between the sense of initiative and the intellect analyzing picturing organ, one should figure if there is a difference between the attention and the sense of initiative. The fact is that there is no difference, except that the attention is a pointing force which comes out of the sense of initiative. It is something like a wave and the ocean. The ocean is the entire mass of water; while the wave is a protrusion of the very same water. When there is no need to focus, when the attention is not tense, there is an all-surrounding sense of initiative. As soon as there is tension then there is a pointed energy force out of the initiative. That is the attention.

There is a lot of misinformation about the core-self and the paramatma, such that some people say that God is within you, or that within the core-self there is the paramatma inside of it. Some say that the two may merge together. This is absurd. The core-self and the paramatma are nicely described in the Upanishads, where there is a statement to the effect that the two of them like two birds on the same tree. They live in the same psyche. Now if you feel that you are your psyche, then of course you will think that God lives in you. The fact is that the psyche is a housing compartment. Both God and the limited spirit reside in that enclosure. It is not that God lives in the core-self. That is misinformation.

The other point is this. God's being there is not helping anybody in the conditioned life. If God is really there, then what is his value? After all, if for millions of years, I reside in individual psyche, and God is there for that time, what has he done to help me? Therefore once you can answer that question, you will realize that his presence there is not the issue. The issue is my endeavor to improve the psyche. He is there but he does nothing to improve the psyche. This is because he does not reside there in the same filthy disorganized impulsive level where I function. He is not bothered by my condition. If he was stressed, he would have changed it a long time ago. It is my headache. If I am satisfied with the psychological conditions of your existence there, then that is fine with the God. I must be self-motivated to improve my condition.

One has to get a clear understanding by mystic actions, of the attention and the sense of initiative. One should rotate the attention around the sense of initiative, which is located in a spherical way or circular way around the core self. Just as a wave may move about the surface of an ocean, so the attention may move around the surface of the sense of initiative. See these diagrams.

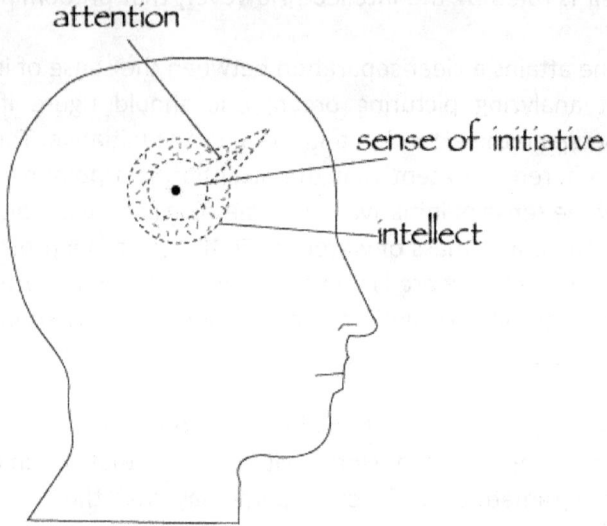

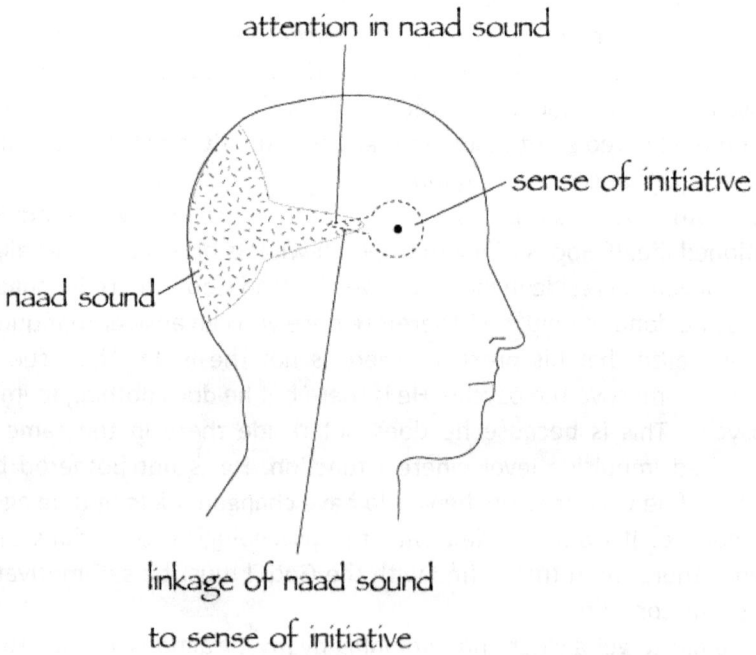

attention

sense of initiative

intellect

attention in naad sound

sense of initiative

naad sound

linkage of naad sound

to sense of initiative

Krishna

He said, "Kaivalyam means aloneness not one-ness. It means that the core-self is separated from its psychic equipment. It means that the core is alone psychically. It is detached or disconnected from the intellect. It is not subjected to the intellect's operations. Since it needs a prop, it adheres to the ghosham naad sound.

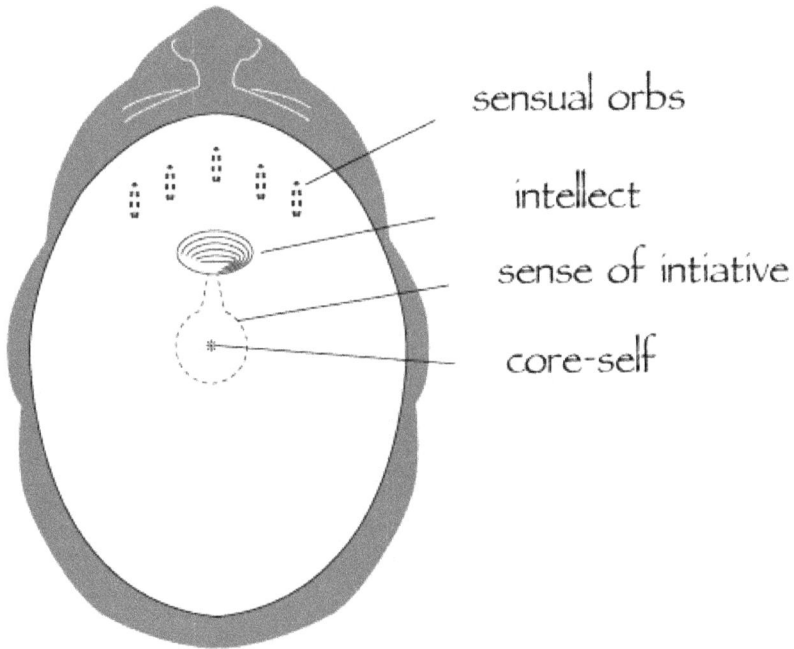

sensual orbs

intellect

sense of intiative

core-self

normal focus through intellect

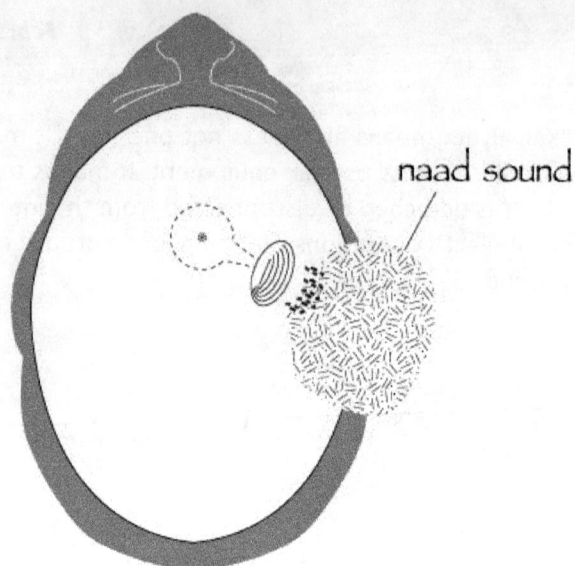

naad sound

focus on naad using intellect

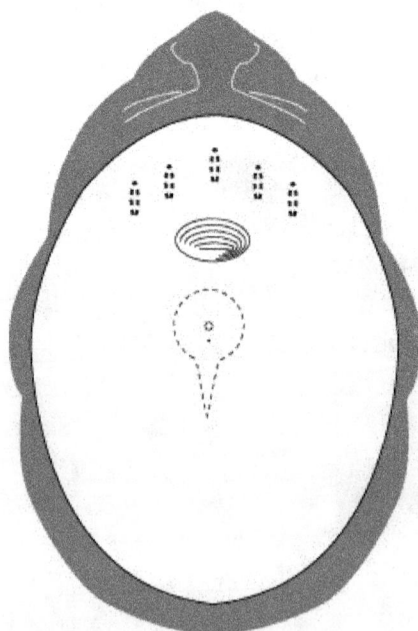

aloneness without naad

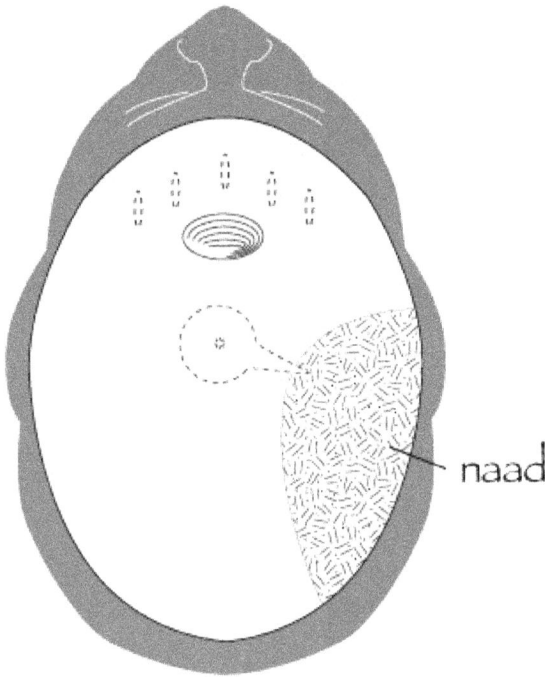

aloneness with naad

Lahiri feels that at first a yogin should try to get the core-self away from the intellect. When there is a clear separation between the two and when the core can effectively discipline the intellect, that core may be gentle with it. Otherwise attempts to curb it will result in the core being controlled by it.

February 20, 2004

Feet in dreams

If the feet are wearied and painful in dreams or in parallel world transfers, it means that the astral body transferred too much energy to the gross body. Due to that loss of power in the subtle body, it is unable to operate its feet. Usually if one finds oneself in a parallel world or in an astral dimension and finds that one can hardly move any of the limbs, it means that energy from the astral body was transferred to the physical form. Due to a low power supply, the astral body is temporarily incapacitated.

Babaji

He said, "Do not look on this side. Search and make contact through the chit akasha using the naad entrance."

This was an instruction for me to stop using call prayers to reach him. He felt I could reach him on the spiritual side by going through naad sound into chit akasha. He stated this, "You could also reach Krishna in four or two-handed forms or Shiva or Yogeshwarananda in chit akasha. Why continue trying to reach anybody in the mundane gross or subtle worlds?"

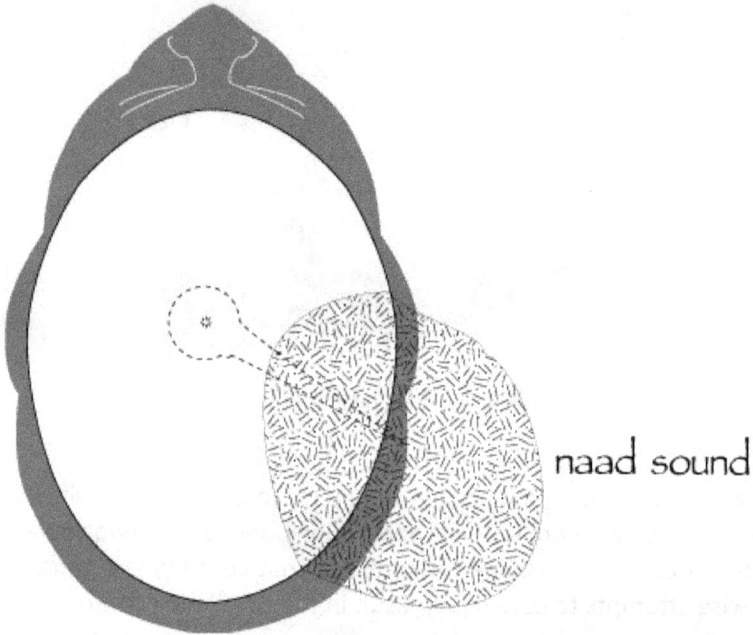

naad sound

Reaching someone in the chit akasha is not easy. For one thing, the yogin must have a clear connection with the spiritual presence of that person. This spiritual presence is not the same as the cultural identity of the person, or the cultural identity the person used in his or her last material manifestation. Chit akasha is like no-man's land to a yogin who lacks spiritual sight. This is why many spiritual leaders stay away from it and force themselves to accept materially-formed deities as the all in all.

Naad sound gives the intellect a detachment ability, where it can resist the sensual influence and ignore the memory translation impulses. However at first the intellect does not like naad and stays away from it. When the yogin spent enough time placing his attention in naad, then after a while he finds that the intellect gains an interest in naad. At that time, he finds it easy to take the intellect into naad. After doing that for a time, he feels that the intellect develops a resistance to the sensual energies and their pursuits, and to the memory signals as well.

A yogin may sometimes use naad sound as a mantra. What he does is this. On some days naad sound seems to be much louder than usual and more forceful. Instead of staying in the right side back of the head, it moves into the left side, middle or front. Then the intellect is hit by it. The intellect is stabilized by it. A stream of energy from naad may not only strike the surface of the intellect but enter the intellect to strike the imagination orb. Then it acts like a mantra, one which is not uttered by the yogi.

March 5, 2005

Nityananda

He said, "The senses must be protected from elongation. Their elongation is the bane of yoga. The presence of certain objects may cause such elongation. Hence the need for avoidance."

On this day I saw the entertainment orb. This is a small orb. It stays near the attention beam to the left of it. It acts like a gyroscope to always move the attention to worldly interest. It acts quietly like a secret guard. It is totally dedicated to illusory pursuits, the sensual affairs of this world.

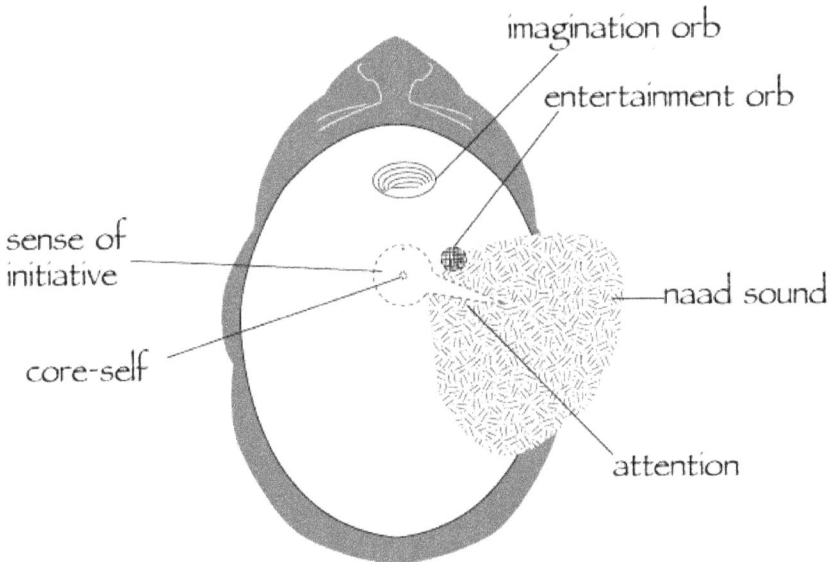

This entertainment orb acts as a chaperon for the attention to see sights in the memory, imagination orb or subtle and gross sensual realms.

Lahiri explained that whatever elongates the senses or causes them to inquire and to protrude, is against introspection. It bars one from deep absorption. He said, "The senses become elongated in the subtle body just as the sexual organ becomes enlarged upon arousal, or just as an entity who enters a pig's uterus, will be born with a snout, or just as an elephant has a trunk. The elongations are due to uncontrolled sensual inquiry.

I discovered an escort orb. When it takes a concentration force to the intellect organ or when it takes the intellect to a concentration force, this orb may assist meditation. On this day, the escort orb took a stream of naad energy to the imagination orb and to the memory orb. One should note that the escort orb is not always within reach. It is not always in visible form. When it is available it acts on its own to aid meditation.

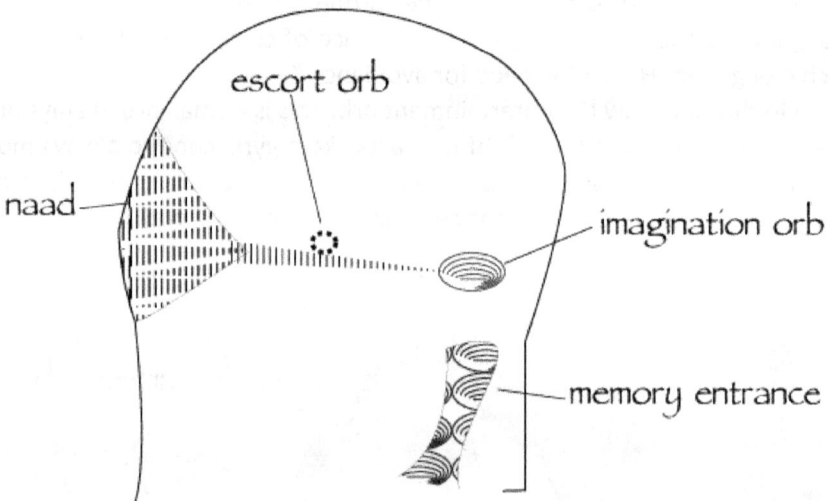

I found the discrimination orb. This orb may be obstructive to a yogi. It also functions as the sense of conscience for judging good or bad, right or wrong. It uses memories to make judgements.

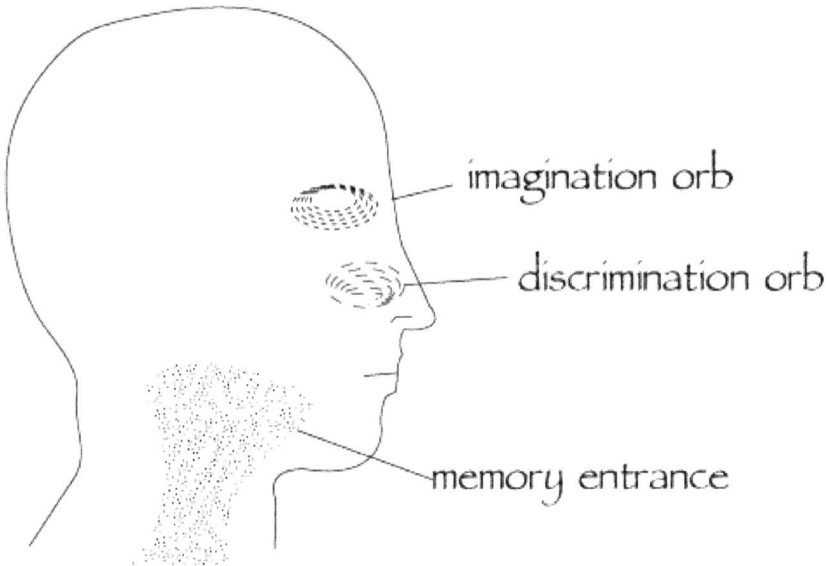

imagination orb

discrimination orb

memory entrance

Lahiri

He instructed, "Give up the subtle world. Take to naad. Stop subtle encounters in dreams. It will be the same after death of the present body. Renounce it now. Join the mahayogins at naad. Note that the daily intake of impressions which are not related to yoga, destroy and retard the practice."

Shivananda

He gave an information, stating that the female forms are made of subtle feeling energy, the same energy which is in every psyche except that in the female forms there is a greater percentage of it.

March 24, 2004

Yogeshwarananda

He instructed for a focus on the middle of the light in the front brain. This is a mild focus, using naad as the base. One should send the attention in a loop form. See this diagram.

speckled light

naad

loop of
attention

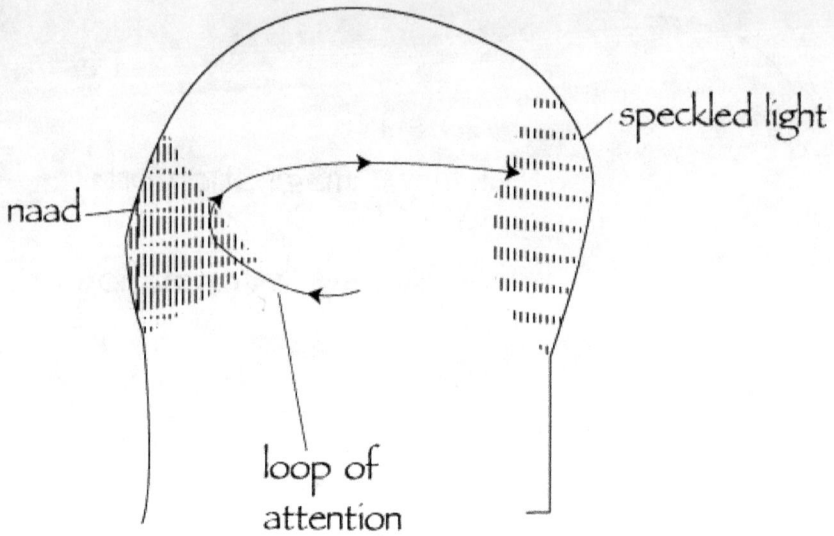

In Bhagavad Gita, especially in chapter 2, the term *dhirah* is used by Krishna. This terms applies to a yogi who has steady attention. One method for this is focus on naad.

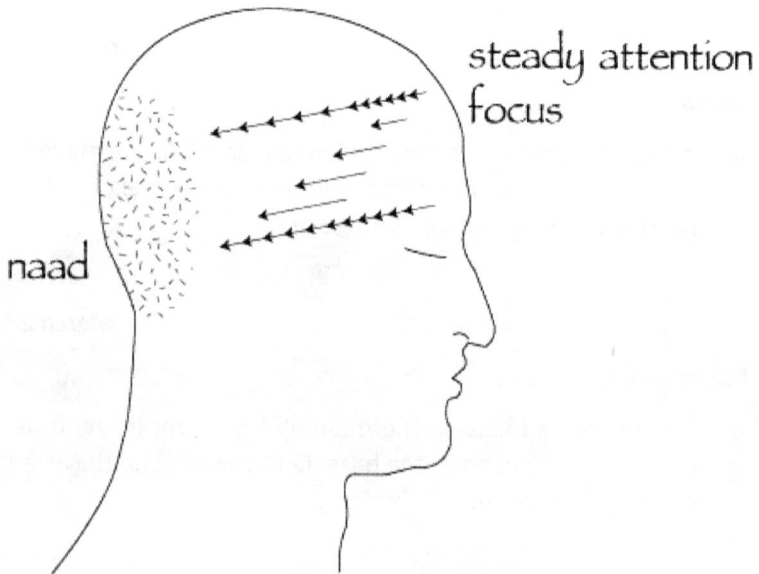

steady attention
focus

naad

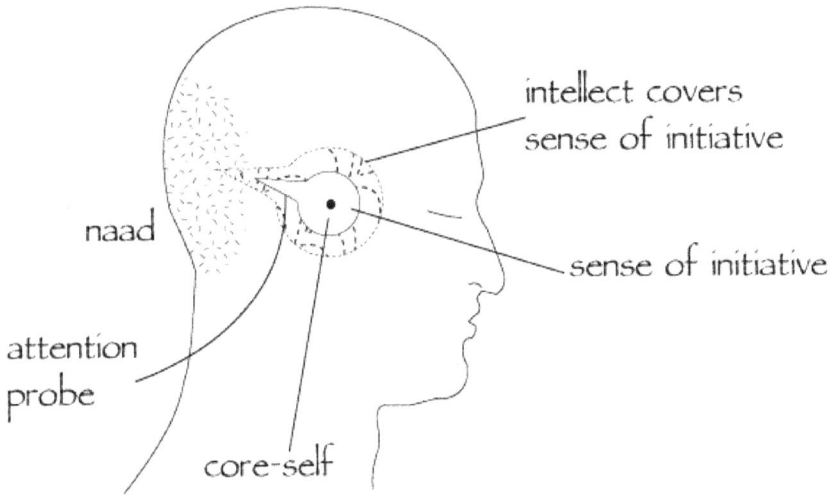

intellect covers
sense of initiative

naad

sense of initiative

attention
probe

core-self

March 25, 2004

Nityananda

He said, "Use naad. Do not bother with the vision part. Orient the intellect to naad. It requires hours of practice. There is no substitute for it."

April 1, 2004

Satyeswarananda

He was sent by Babaji to check my practice. I asked him, "Why, it was a long time since I saw you Swami."

He replied, "In each case, it is different. Keep the practice constant. It is something individual. Keep with naad but used naad as a sight tool by putting the vision energy on it. Sometimes the front sight field has the same vibration. Control that. (He pointed to the escort orb)."

He added, "With my disciples, I find that it is the same struggle due to different admixtures of the external distracting forces."

He then left. I asked him if I should make an effort to see him physically. He replied, "No. What good is that? Everyone wants to meet physically. It has no value. This is better. If need be, I will check. You are Babaji's agent. Call me. I will hear."

Hariharananda

He said that brow chakra focus means naad first, then the entire intellect in naad, then intellect pulls back into naad by its own force, then intellect focuses forward and up on its own. This happens after long consistent practice.

April 3, 2004

I got an inspiration to move into naad, to test to see if intellect would pull back into it. In this method one moves back in a slant pull. If there is resistance by the intellect, one leaves it to itself. One moves back with the sense of initiative only.

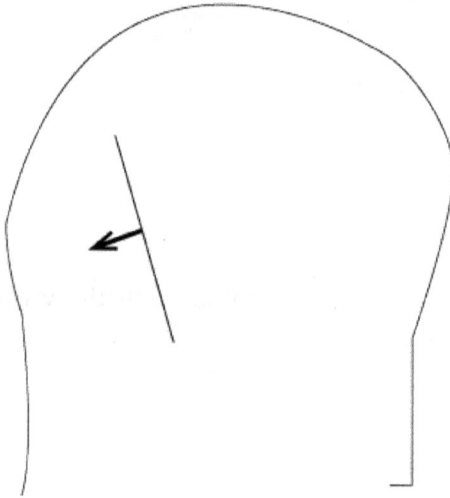

On this day there was a realization that these higher yoga practices, which are called *samyama* by Patanjali, cannot be done if one has much human interaction. The reason is this. Human association usually causes much mental interaction with names and forms of this world. The result of that is a regression in meditation. One then endeavors again for situating the mind in pratyahar sensual energy withdrawal. In addition, the most costly aspect is that one loses the association of great yogins. Much hashing over in the mind of names and forms of this world, deforms the senses, thus bringing an end, for the time being, of whatever progress one achieved.

As far as naad sound is concerned. It is essential to hear it. One should train the intellect to become habituated to naad. The mind must have a prop. The support for it is naad. Some feel that the prop is God or love of God or the holy name of God, but they are wrong. The psyche is designed to provide the naad vibration free of charge, as an entrance point into the chit akasha. However this does not mean instant results. One must patiently listen to naad for a time. Ultimately all focusing on this side of existence, for holy or unholy reasons, is a sheer distraction from the focus into the spiritual atmosphere.

On this day I attended a Hindu function. There was a lady who wrote a bright outfit. Suddenly I realized that Rama Bharati (my grhasta sannyasa guru) was present in my body and was looking at the woman through my eyes. Later on, at the same place, I happened to stumble over the lady's shawl. This was because Rama Bharati controlled my body. When I questioned him about his desire to see the lady and the effort to go near her, he said that there was a need for him. I said, "Okay, Do as you desire with this body."

After some time, we discussed the naad kriya. He recommended going straight back into it, rather than going back to the right side only. He said that was balanced and it would work. I then asked about his books. I stated that in his books there were hardly any techniques and that it was not laid out in a clear and consistent way. He said that in his time, most yogis in India did not take notes while doing austerities. They do not usually anticipate that they would have to teach. He concluded that in any case, no matter what is written down, each ascetic must struggle for self-purity.

April 7, 2004

Naad sound research

I tried the advice of Rama Bharati but I found that if one goes straight back, it usually causes one to lose touch with naad and/or finds the core self staring into the imagination to see pictures, images sounds and the like in the front of the head. Of course Rama Bharati cannot be incorrect. This means that if the mind is not already purified of the impressions, one will have to go back to naad by going to the right and then after some time, one may use his advice.

Once the yogin has success with the naad and he is not moved forward by the force of the imagination orb, memory and sensual energy, he will see in front of him some bunches of light. He should look at these ahead of him but one should remain in naad. If these seem stable, he may attempt to move to the center of the head and if after moving there, one still remains stable with naad, one may continue peering forward. Otherwise if one finds that one loses focus and is again pulled forward to view pictures and images in the imagination orb, one should retreat into naad and remain there.

April 8, 2004

On this day I saw the elongation of the senses. What happens is this. When one sees an object the prospective sense reaches out to grasp it. If the object is desired, then the sense extends itself. For instance in the case of sexually-appealing forms of the opposite sex, the sight of it, causes the vision sense to become elongated. Once extended from the psyche, that sense is unable to retract itself immediately. It hangs out for a time. Gradually it is retracted.

This may be understood by studying male dogs. In the mating seasons, male dogs become sexually aroused. They pursue females. Sometimes the penis become extended from their bodies. They pass semen in a fit. At some times, if one dog finds a female dog which is in heat, he will mount that animal, jerk his body back and forth and in a fit pass semen. When he tries to pull his limp organ out, it does not come out of the female's body. Then the female moves around pulling the male animal backwards. All the while, the male organ remains limp but is extended out of its body. After a while by nature's system, that male organ will reduce in size and slip out of the female opening but then, still then, the male organ will hang outside its body for a time, until by nature's system it is withdrawn into its body. Something like this happens on the subtle plane to each of our senses when either of them makes contact with a desired object.

On this day I made a notation about memory. This special and most convenient organ in the subtle body is a nuisance in higher yoga. Patanjali listed it as one of the five disturbances. This memory is like a mental abdomen, which regurgitates and digest ideas and images which are sent to it by the senses and by the imagination faculty. All yogis, were warned of it by Krishna in a statement to Arjuna:

कर्मेन्द्रियाणि संयम्य
य आस्ते मनसा स्मरन् ।
इन्द्रियार्थान्विमूढात्मा
मिथ्याचारः स उच्यते ॥३.६॥

karmendriyāṇi saṁyamya
ya āste manasā smaran
indriyārthānvimūḍhātmā
mithyācāraḥ sa ucyate (3.6)

karmendriyāṇi — bodily limbs; saṁyamya — restraining; ya = yaḥ — who; āste — sits; manasā — by the mind; smaran — remembering; indriyārthān — attractive objects; vimūḍhātmā = vimūḍha — deluded + ātmā — self; mithyācāraḥ — deceiver; sa — he; ucyate — it is declared

A person who while restraining his bodily limbs sits, with the mind remembering attractive objects, is a deceiver. So it is declared. (Bhagavad Gita 3.6)

It is because of the memory, that a yogin may spend years practicing without substantial progress. Memory is very resistant to yoga.

On this day, Rama Bharati asked about my practice of naad sound. He said that I should increase the time of practice. I told him that I was his disciple and thus it should be easier for me to gain success. Both of us laughed for we knew that each yogi has to practice on his own.

April 9, 2004

A set back

On this day I had a setback in practice. This is because I had to work with some persons who had no interest in yoga. One will find that association may hurt practice. It depends on how much one interacts with others.

A woman who went to temple functions wanted to see me in the astral world. She used to see me at religious functions. Somehow she developed this idea for me to fondle her breasts. Since she was supposed to be morally-inclined, she did not approach me in public but her desire was strong. It remained on the subtle level. It activated her subtle body to find mine. I saw her in another dimension and avoided her but I could see that her breasts itched her. In her mind, she felt that if I fondled them, the itching would go away.

April 11, 2004

Discouragement due to thoughts

There may come a time when a student yogi becomes discouraged because of thoughts and memories. These two aspects, the thoughts and memories, haunt a yogi whenever he tries to achieve higher yoga. These aspects stops him dead in his tracks on the move upwards to acquire divine vision. If the yogin becomes discouraged, he may give up the practice. He may use meditation to relieve stress and become a non-entity among yogins. This can certainly happen to anyone who has not reached the high end of yoga.

We should take lessons from the Bhagavad Gita. Krishna chided Arjuna about killing or being killed, about fighting the righteous war (dharmyaṁ saṁgrāmaṁ, Bhagavad Gita. 2.33). This means that unless we completed our duties in the social world, we will have no peace of mind or stress-free mental outlook and with that there will be no success.

If one finds that one cannot get the success, one should meditate on the Universal Form of Krishna, to be inspired about the duties one must execute on his behalf. Arjuna also had an idea to do higher yoga, but he could not complete it before the battle of Kurukshetra. He did not have the approval of the Universal Form.

Imagination orb strays off

It is the nature of the imagination orb to stray away and to lure the attention. As soon as the imagination strays away, it comes under the influence of the senses and the memory. Then it lures the attention, while the core self struggles alone as if it has no choice. This process must be arrested by steady day to day practice. Even though in these books and in those of other yogins, there are detailed description of the yoga process, still each ascetic must study the workings of the psyche to see what one must do to conquer it.

On this day I made a notation, that trying to be a know-it-all, a spokesman for God, trying to explain everything to help others, to correct all and adjust all; these are impediments to transcendence absorption. One has to forego all this to achieve success This of course does not mean that one should not or will not have to explain to others, but that should not be one's ambition or objective.

Passion energy all-surrounding

A yogin must note how the core self is surrounded by certain zones of energy. These zones cause it not to see into the sky of consciousness. It is essential to realize that the sky of consciousness is here already. There are zones of blocking energy around the core-self. What we see in our minds, the atmosphere in the mind and the emotions are mostly a passionate force. It is like a cloud in which one hovers.

Part 8

Yogeshwarananda

He said, "The others do not know the details. They are not attentive. Naad is the higher gayatri."

He gave some mystic practices for freeing the core-self so that it could eliminate the intellect's influence and it could absorb naad instead. These practices will help if one finds that one cannot get free of the thinking, analyzing, and imagining organ in the subtle head.

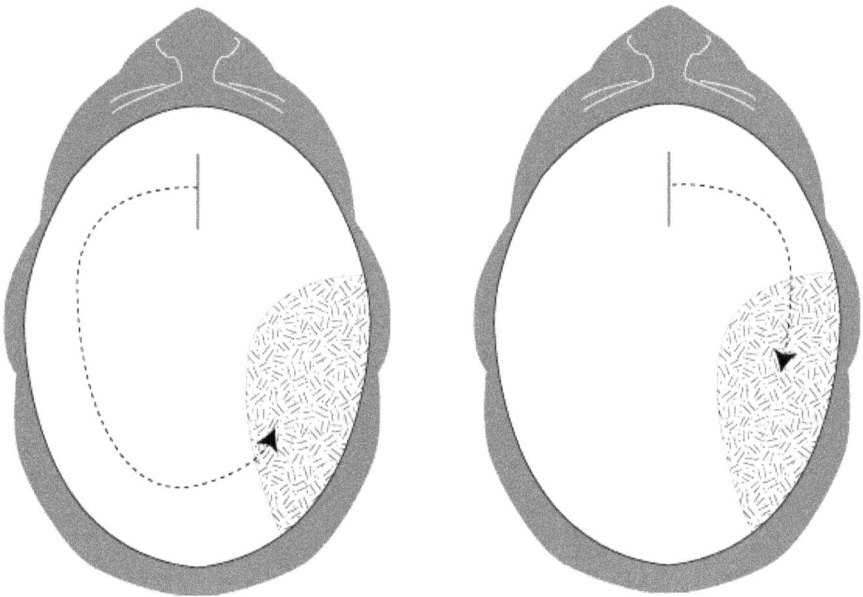

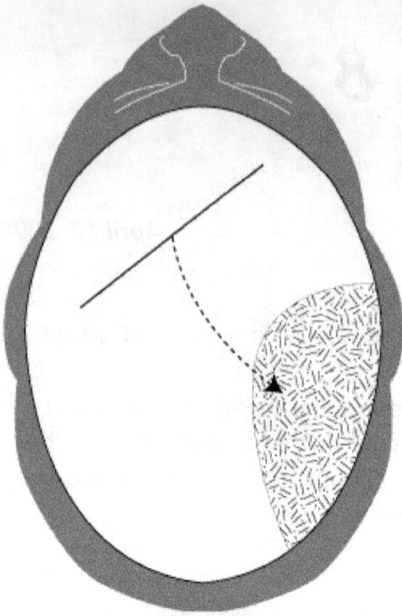

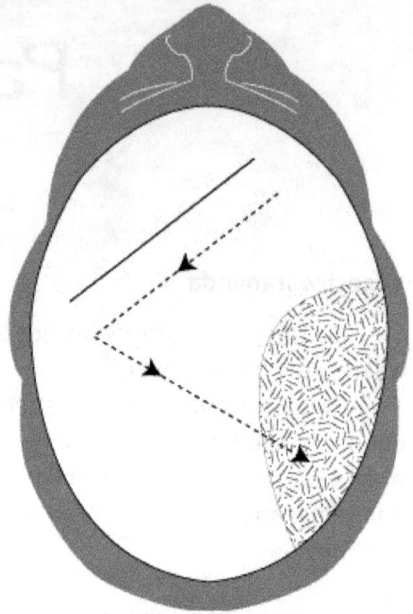

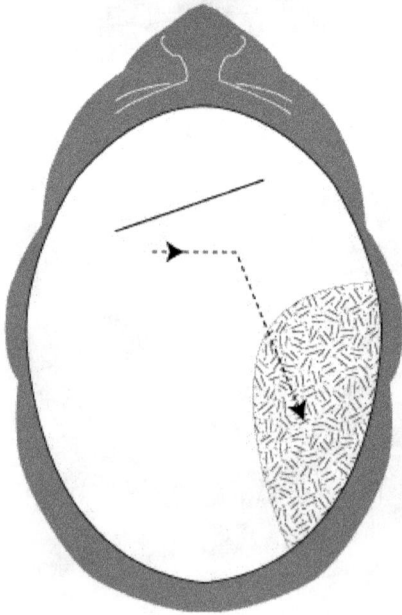

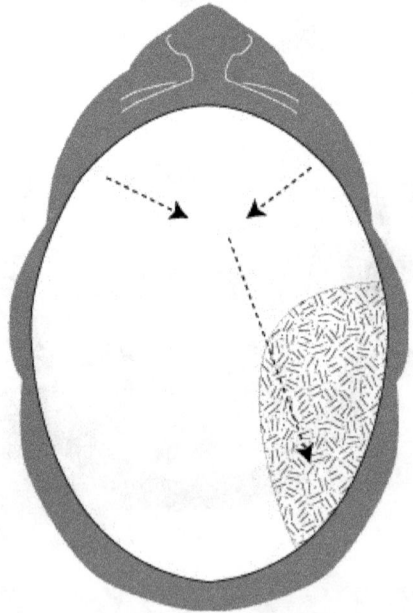

On the next day, he explained that when the core-self is settled in naad, a diffused intense light may appear. That is seen though the darkness which is usually in the subtle head.

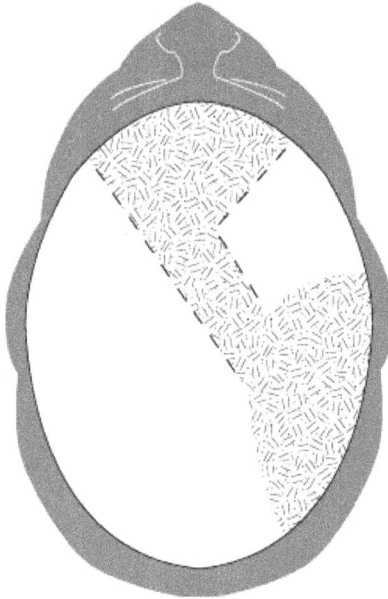

Yogesh said that when he was meditating in caves in the Himalayan region, he spoke to many yogis. In the conversations he learned that they struggled with meditation, trying to get the mind to cease the distractions.

April 21, 2004

Kirpal Singh

He said, "Turning away from this world to enter the naad current cannot be told to everyone. It is a secret process. It is private. Even if you got a loud speaker and told people about it, they would ignore you. You should do it and not tell others. Do not waste time."

April 23, 2004

Lahiri

He said, "The pictures in the mind should be turned into voidal energy. These pictures are of the rajaguna passionate nature, while the voidal energy is of sattvaguna insightful nature. However, this sattvaguna is a lower type of sattvaguna. It is not the sattvaguna that will give freedom. Still it is better than the picture energy. When the picture energy inspires the body to act, that is tamaguna stupefying influence."

He advised, "Use *Om Namah Shivaya japa* when you have to be in the association of others. That will help to send your attention to naad. But you should chant that as *ajapa*, as being without making any external sound. The frontal lobe in the brain is dangerous because it leads the self back to the external world.

He made some other remarks as follows, "*Chitta nirodhah* means to stop the natural operation of the mental and emotional energies which are usually converted into ideas. Force those to revert into quiescence. The subtle energy should convert into light only, otherwise it is an impediment.

"In assisting others be careful that they do not disrupt the practice. You help others up to the point where they do not destroy the practice. Stop the reasoning tendency. That usually operates automatically upon impulse from the senses and memory. Break its connection with those organs. Quiet it. Do less reasoning since too much of it empowers the memory to disturb meditation."

April 26, 2004

Yogananda

He spoke about second initiation. Knowing that some teachers differ on the definition of this, I asked him what it was. He said, "When they focus on light from the naad absorption that is the second initiation."

I asked about the third initiation. He said, "It develops automatically from the second. Just as the second develops automatically from the first. But the difficulty is to complete each. Usually kriyabans are unable to complete due to the distractions in the mind. He said that thoughts and images which arise must be confronted and be forced back into quiescence.

April 27, 2004

Yogananda

We discussed the absorption of thoughts from others. Thoughts enter the mental area which functions like a sponge. These thoughts penetrate that energy like a bullet entering the flesh of an animal's body. It can be flushed but only by yogic technique. One should guard the formation of relationships with others, since that is the main problem. When relationships are formed, thoughts of the persons involved, develop rights to interfere with advancement. Yogananda said that kriya practitioners must struggle with such thoughts. Each student must acquire resistance to this by practice.

April 29, 2004

On this day I made a notation. Thoughts from others do pierce through and penetrate the mental and emotional energy. These explode in the imagination orb as sounds and pictures. One has to develop the power to stop this from occurring. Thoughts do force the self to turn away from naad. They do this repeatedly. Thus one has to stop this power of the thoughts.

Naad sound absorption is the key to success with this. Naad is available, free of charge in the psyche. One should tie the attention and the core-self to it. Over a time, the intellect will take to it kindly.

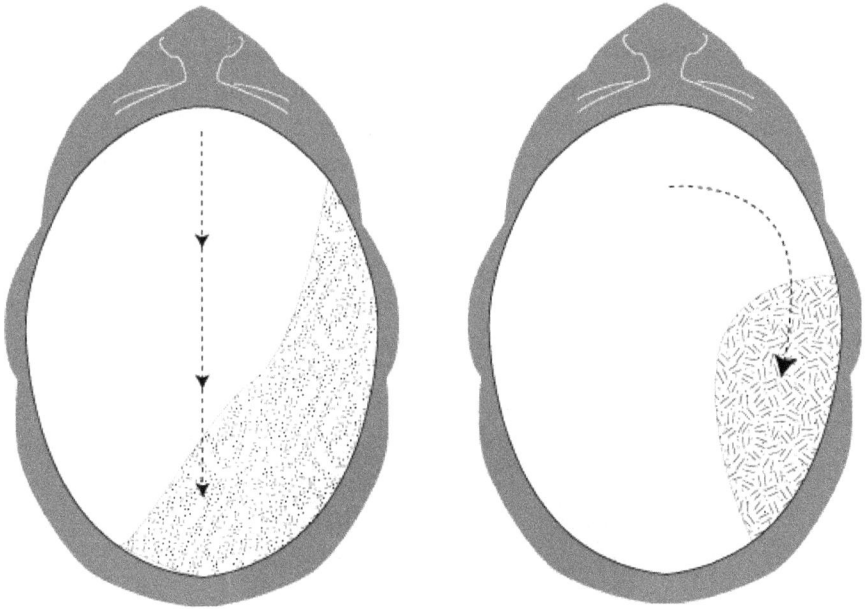

Naad sound may also be perceived as light, but rarely. Usually one perceives it as sound in a vibrating consistency. It is steady and continuous and maintains itself by itself. After settling in naad, the yogin may look ahead to the front of the subtle head. He may perceive a golden-glow of light. He should look at this mildly, making sure that he remains in the naad sound and does not come out of it to chase the light.

May 1, 2004

On this date, I made a notation about three types of supernatural vision
- through the imagination orb in the mind
- perception within the mind itself or faculties in the mind
- vision through the mind apparatus as one-seeing organ.

Vision through the mind apparatus as one seeing organ is the lowest type of vision. In this one has no idea of the various parts of the mind. One feels that the mind is one organ only and cannot differentiate various faculties and their particular functions.

May 2, 2004

Response to thoughts

When a yogin replies to the thoughts of others who are not genuine yogis, he hurts himself. In fact such replies are a violation of Patanjali's Yoga Sutras. When a thought penetrates the psyche, that itself is a disruption to yoga. Now if the yogi replies, he by that action, disrupts yoga even further. The incoming thought ruptures the inner silence, destroying insight potential and down-grading the mental energy. The reply thought attacks the energy of the incoming thoughts. It explodes near that thought as soon as it contacts the surface of it. Both thoughts damage the insight potential.

If a yogi cannot stop incoming thoughts from penetrating the psyche, he should at least not respond to them. A response causes double damage.

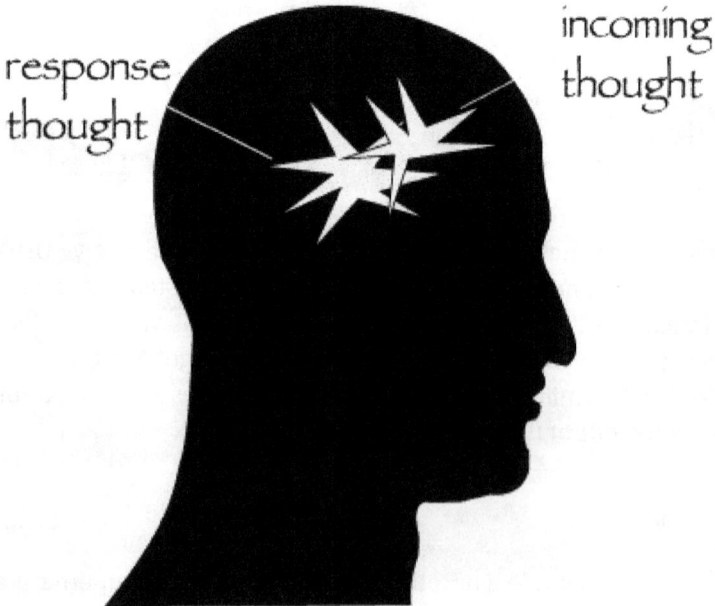

response thought   incoming thought

Lahiri

He stated that lack of attachment to naad sound, causes the feelings in the form of mental and emotional energy to serve the idea sequences. He said that the feelings should develop an attachment to naad sound. In addition he stated, "Wanting heavenly visions is also destructive to higher meditation. Such heavenly places are part of this mundane existence, even though they are subtler than the earthly environment. The automatic application of the mind, of the yogi's sense of interest, to this side of existence is a mistake. Both constructive interest in this world, as well as destructive concerns for it, are mistakes."

May 7, 2004

Isolation necessary

Other types of association, even the ones we must endure in the line of social duty are destructive towards yoga. Only association of genuine yogis have value in the progress of a yogin. Other types of association bring with them dynamic energies for materialistic concerns. Once these are lodged in the mind and emotions, one is force to expend them by materialistic actions, regardless of whether one is willing or not. Thus there is a need for isolation and simplification of desires.

May 8, 2004

Vachaspati

He said, "People, places and objects which stimulate thinking on this side of existence, and which cancel out the tendency to listen to naad, should be scrupulously avoided."

May 9, 2004

Memory

In a parallel world, when one's discrimination is left behind in the subtle energy which is left with the physical body, the memory recording device is taken along, or there would be no recall of the encounter. The memory accompanies the spirit like a photographer who takes pictures automatically.

May 17, 2004

Mental thought touching

When one touches the minds of another, one destroys the voidal focus during naad sound contact. This causes associative thoughts to burst into one's mind from the other person's transmittance of thought energy or response thought energy. These responses burst open in the mind screen, the imagination orb.

One must associate with naad to reach the dhira steady state.

May 18, 2004

Lahiri

He gave this practice for linking naad to sushumna nadi. This works after sushumna nadi is cleared by virtue of a steady kundalini practice.

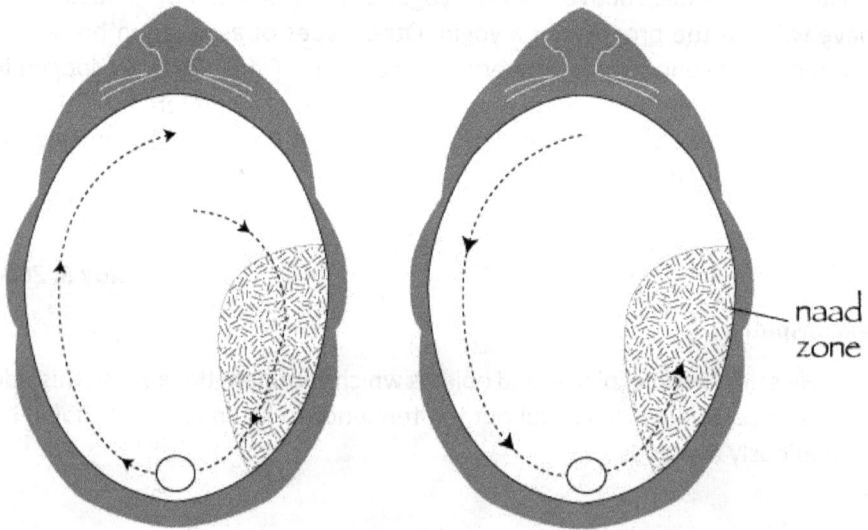

naad zone

sushumna nadi subtle passage
back of head through spine

A notation was made about austerity and its effects:

Austerity performed in this dimension which is not transferred out of it, must be used here, either by the yogin or by someone who is awarded the effects. When others use it, they may misuse it for boosting vices like sexual intercourse or the exercise of political influence.

Such energy from austerities may be transferred out of this dimension. A yogin may project it through naad sound or into some other dimension. Otherwise he may donate it to the universal pool of austerity-energy in this dimension.

June 6, 2004

Nityananda

He stated, "Total detachment from criticalness to others is required. Even the impulse to correct others or to become irritated by their opinion or idiosyncrasies, must be subdued. The part of the psyche which acts to such responses must be squelched.

On this day there was a realization that the imagination orb cannot be forced to conceive the spiritual dimension. However, by keeping the orb in the interval between conceptions, it develops the supernatural and divine visions. The interval between conceptions was discussed by Patanjali. This is the blank state of the imagination orb. One has to train it to remain in that blank condition.

June 14, 2004

Buddha

He advised, "Do not allow arising ideas to jump to another location in the mind space, nor to reach full display. Instead develop the habit of suppressing it, pushing it back into its location, as soon as it is recognized. Cause the considerations part of the intellect not to act on an incoming thought. Without such action, the thoughts must subside.

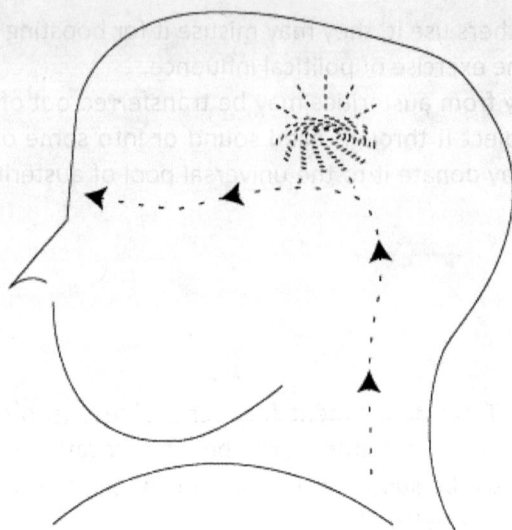

kundalini force
to brow chakra

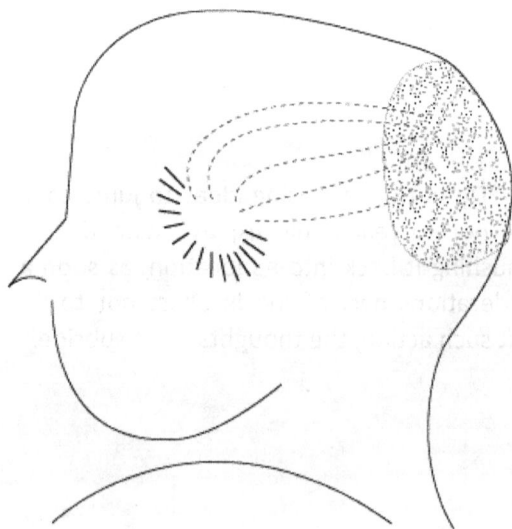

dharana to naad
attention rays linked to naad

Even before emerging ideas manifest visibly or intelligibly in the imagination orb, the attention is pulled by the ideas,. Thus the attention does not perceive what it is being pulled into, until the ideas burst into inner sounds and pictures. For example, if the attention is tied to naad, it finds itself pulled away and focused on an idea as the idea becomes visible, not before that. But in the advanced stages due to increased sensitivity, one perceives these energies before they manifest.

The self or its initiative is tied to the attention and so it is pulled along but it relies on the attention for the objectivity and sensing. In that it is helplessly dependent.

July 16, 2004

Ramakrishna

He stated, "Fame causes neglect of practice. It did so for me. Resist fame further. Do your work perfectly. Vivekananda too, was caught in the fame fever after his speech in Chicago."

Naad sound current

In this the sound current may avoid the intellect. It will hit the attention zone which surrounds the ahankar sense of initiative.

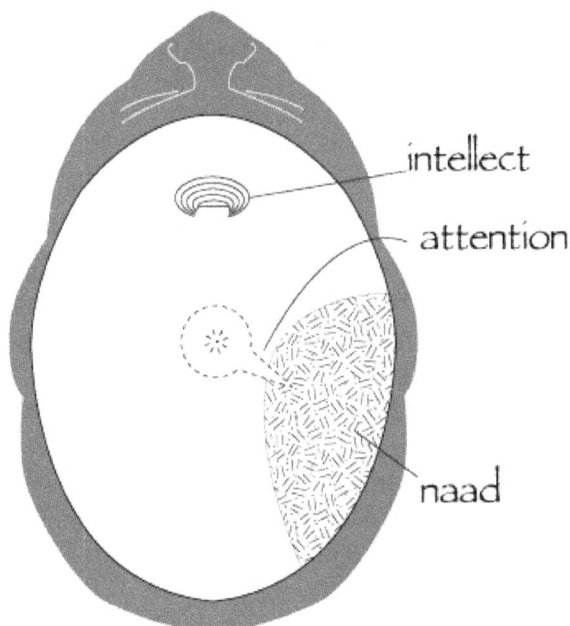

July 17, 2004

Intellect's compulsive usage

The cause of the seemingly seamless unity of the self with the intellect is the impulsive usage of the intellect. As soon as one begins to not let it be used, to reject its compulsions and to restrict its access to the emotions, one gets some detachment from it. It appears as a separate object in the head of the subtle body. Beginners will perceive it as a subtle or invisible object, but they can understand that it is separate. It appears and disappears according to expression of ideas.

July 19, 2004

Linkage of attention to sensual energy

The linkage of that attachment force to the sensual energy, memory or to the imagination orb, means the development of attachment to whatever is displayed in the mind or felt in the emotions. This is spontaneous. The attachment force should be linked to the naad sound as an alternative. That is the first step for creating genuine detachment. After gaining a footing in the naad sound, one should wait there for the development of light from the supernatural environment. A yogin may notice that while he waits, the attention may be lured by the sensual energy or by a memory or by creations in the imagination orb. He should train himself to ignore this.

July 27, 2004

Influences

The memory influences the imagination orb. The orb influences the attention beam. That in turn, influences the sense of identity, which in turn influences the core-self. This is the systematic connection process which a yogin must control. Running here and running there will not help to subdue this. One should sit in meditation dally and study the psyche to get an understanding of how it operates. The yogin must do this. If he has no time for this, he cannot be successful.

If the memory is restricted to naad, the other components may become attached to naad. Such attachment if done consistently will lead to spiritual perception.

July 28, 2004

Yogeshwarananda

He stated, "The no-response practice is done by mentally not responding to ideas, circumstances and thoughts, as well as by not correcting and adjusting others. One must notice how one talks within the head, as if one talks to someone or a group of persons who reside in one's head. This mental chatter must cease. Most of it is responses to vibrations which come into the subtle head and convert into sounds and images. One should curb this by not responding to these incoming vibrations. At first one must catch oneself hearing messages which come into the head. Even though after hearing one automatically responds and sends back a signal as a reply to the incoming messages, usually one hears, responses and does not realize it.

"Train the self to hear and to silently decide not to respond to the numerous in-coming communications. These vibrations flare out in the imagination orb as desires, suggestions and urges to act. One should not interfere with them, but should be disinterested in a way which does not elicit a response from the person who sent the message. Since their psyche operates impulsively without their willing consent, those who sent the message may not be consciously aware of it.

"One should not send an indication as to whether one is responsive or not. One should be completely neutral, since that is the only way to stop the energy from reacting.

"Usually people are so involved with multiple ideas, that if one does not respond to one of these, it does not interfere with their involvements. They have many ideas which are in production. If one or two yield no results, it is of no importance to them. A merchant who cannot get a particular product will not worry, if he has other items which are in demand.

"A yogin has to develop a no-interfere-with-the-world attitude. When this is firmly established, he will be free to study his psyche and get it controlled. Once the psyche is studied, one will see its different parts distinctly. If there are any other living entities living in one's mind or in one's emotion, one will perceive such persons and can make agreements with them for yoga progress. Those who cooperate will stay in the psyche. Those who are against yoga, will be told to go away. Of course the yogin has to develop that authority over his nature, over his mental and emotional energy."

Babaji

He advised that there be no exhibition of knowledge or even of accurate foreknowledge. He said, "Do not use the imagination orb. Cease its varied functions and activities."

July 30, 2004

Detailed thinking

Detailed thinking should stop during normal social life when not meditating. The mind should be habituated to not executing detailed analysis of anything. This is the advice given by Patanjali in the Yoga Sutras.

It is by detailed thinking that one comes to take up yoga practice in the first place. But afterwards, one should cease the same thorough analysis

August 4, 2004

Babaji

He explained that the portions of the attention which go to ideas during naad meditations, should be identified as strayed rays of attention. These should be arrested and moved into naad. Sometimes the entire attention does not stray away, only a portion of it. That portion no matter how small, should be arrested and brought to join the major part which remains attentive.

If there is a sour attitude in the psyche over this straying of the attention energy, one should get rid of that sour mood. One should do the practice with a neutral feeling.

August 5, 2004

Appropriation energy

The appropriation energy is troublesome. This is the energy which grabs many subtle aspects in the gross and subtle material world. Initially a yogin will find that this energy remains neutral to naad. It displays a clear disinterest in naad. It may be silent in the mind but as soon as there is any hint of anything from the memory or sensual energy, it will encourage displays in the imagination orb. This appropriation force should be controlled. Due to its indifference to naad sound, there seems to be a dislike for naad in the psyche. This dislike may convert into a sense of feeling bored or disliking of naad. One must therefore stick to the yoga practice and not rely on the opinions or moods which come out from the appropriation energy.

Yogeshwarananda

He said, "It can only form if the attention is calmed and no longer seeks to appropriate such things. It will gather under the proper circumstances only. Be patient. Practice. It cannot be forced to gather. There must be right lifestyle, right practice and sincerity."

August 15, 2004

Identity pointer

Naad absorption is important. One should keep the will-power tamed. Willpower functions as a pointer for the identity energy which surrounds the core-self but when light appears ahead one should keep the willpower in the naad energy and not activate it impulsively. If it is activated and it chases after the light, that illumination will disappear. This disappearance is due to the lowering of energies; because of willpower agitation. Naad must be kept as the anchor point. The willpower should be habituated to staying in naad. It should stop pursuing sensations in the front of the subtle head.

Sometimes while being stationed in naad, one will realize that only part of the self energies are involved in that. Other parts will stray in search for sensations in the memory or sensual energies. One should make efforts to arrest these strayed portions.

August 20, 2004

Naad focus effects

Naad focus, if done repeatedly will in time, draw the psyche mechanism away from its pre-occupations with this world. But that will not happen overnight. In addition when one is forced to be in too much worldly association, there will be regressions, whereby one finds that one lost the taste for naad focus. Still the yogi should begin his meditation endeavors afresh and regain lost progression.

August 21, 2004

Appropriation

The appropriation energy is an aspect of the reasoning faculty. It functions as a tiny orb or active energy in the mind, as part of the intellect complex. After appropriating an impression, it gives that to the analytical part of the intellect. However these functions must be terminated by the yogi. It is their continued activation that bars the yogin from developing supernatural and spiritual perception.

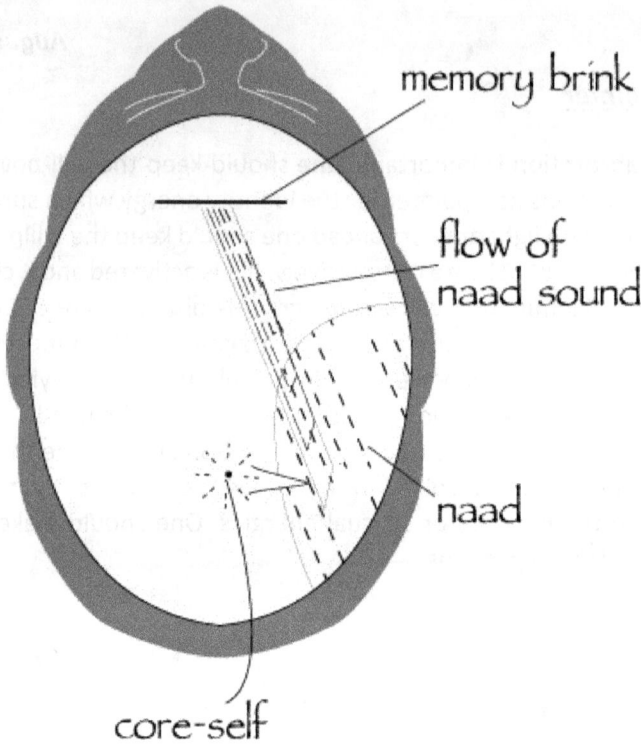

The diagram above was made on August 27, 2004. That shows the flow of impression from the naad sound to the memory brink edge. If this flow is allowed, then over a time, the memory will get a habit of wanting to accept naad sound for recording. It will hanker for pictures and may express disinterest and a feeling of boredom in relation to naad. However the yogi should ignore that and cause the naad impressions to flow to the memory.

When doing this practice, a yogin may see a bright moon to the right, just right of center. But this may be seen only momentarily. That bright moon is a light from the spiritual atmosphere. Lahiri used to record seeing such a moon light from the spiritual sky.

Naad focus is important as a preliminary practice through which one would see directly into the spiritual world. It is not an ordinary method. It is definite but it takes time to give results.

September 1, 2004

Naad pranavision

There is a pranavision in naad. A yogin does not see it on every occasion in naad meditation. When it is seen, it seems like billions of tiny colored dots of varied hue. Sometimes one sees little dashes of colored hue about this - size or smaller.

Even though the memory is troublesome for meditators, still it is the sense of appropriation which is the real culprit. If something is not retrieved from memory, the memory itself or any of its contents cannot affect the yogin.

September 3, 2004

Lifestyle

The lifestyle of a yogi has some effect on his failure or success in yoga. If his lifestyle is not simple, then even if he practices he will only get so far. Some ancient ascetics went into isolation. Social involvement deters yoga. It slows down a yogin and deprives him of certain benefits.

If for instance one does not go to bed early, one may miss the early wake up call. This is because the lifeforce will need more rest. Of course a modern yogin has the advantage of alarm clocks. But even when using such aids, there will be a lack of full success until the time comes when one can have a stress-free life where no alarm clocks are necessary.

One should not feel that one can cheat yoga. If one cannot help but to have a stressful lifestyle one should still endeavor and use aids like alarm clocks, knowing fully well that one will only get partial success.

There are some yogis who are attached to modern conveniences. Some are attached to large modern cities like Amsterdam, London, Tokyo and New York. By these attachments, they convince themselves that it is necessary to live in these places. But such life will cause a certain inefficiency in practice.

An all-out effort.

Initially a yogin may feel that he can make an all-out effort to reform the psyche in one sweep, regarding it all as one entity or as one personality or energy. This is a good effort but it is made on the basis of ignorance. If we study Patanjali's *Yoga Sutras,* we will find that he recommended *kaivalyam,* or aloneness, in two ways. The first is the separation of the core-self from its psychic perceiving tools. The second is the core self in conjunction with the purified perceiving tools. Thus if one feels that one can begin at the end, in terms of regarding the core self and the perceiving tools, one is going at against the recommendation of Patanjali.

At first one should segregate the parts of the psyche. It is a conglomeration of various psychic instruments and a core self. Regrettably one will not be able to purify the self and its psychic apparatus in one stroke. That is not possible. This is because each of the psychic adjuncts like senses, memory, imagination faculty, analysis and inner observational faculties, operate at a different frequency. Thus no one frequency will adjust them all. One has to work on them one by one. By retreating into naad sound vibration, one develops the objectivity, and partitioning required to deal with the psychic adjuncts one by one.

The help of a guru

A guru can certainly help but that does not mean that one will be free from having to endeavor. Even if a guru pitches in and gives assistance, still if one does not pitch in by steady endeavor in practice, the help from guru or from God will serve only as an impetus, which one either ignores or takes as impetus to practice.

We should realize that real help from a guru comes in the form of causing us to make the endeavor whereby we practice ardently and gain control of the psyche. It is not that the assistance of the guru makes us weak or makes it so that we do not have to endeavor. In fact, the guru's help is the very force that causes us to commit the austerities.

Yogeshwarananda

He made this equation:

identity with anything of this world =
responsibility for the said items =
loss of psychological energy =
opening of the closed loop of psychic power =
loss of transcendence absorption potential =

spiritual blindness

Naad compass

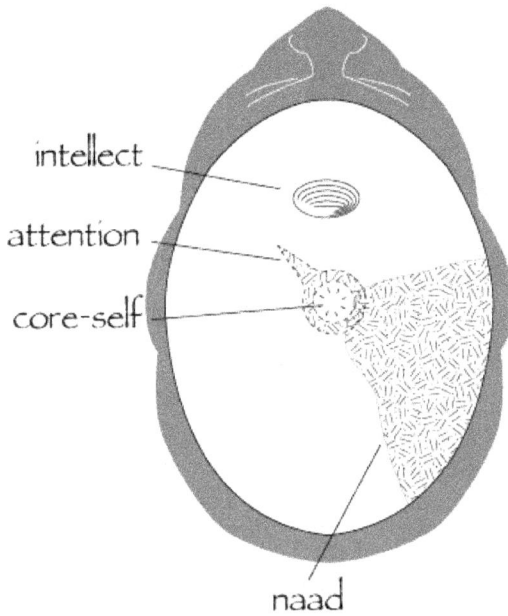

In that practice, the attention beam is pulled back into the naad sound. The core-self retreats there also.

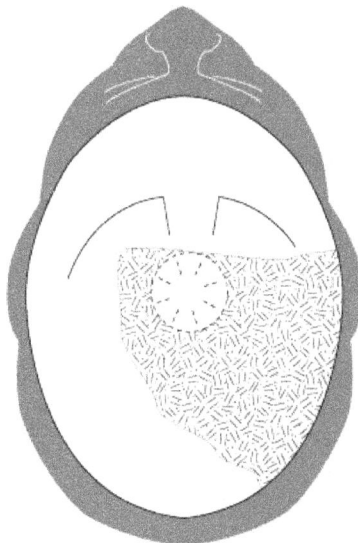

In that practice, one keeps the core-self attuned to naad sound. While stationed in naad one looks forward. If one sees light from the transcendental world, then one absorbs it in a funnel-shaped mystic receptor.

April 13, 2004

Observation about brahma yoga

Brahma yoga is a continuation of kundalini yoga, but some persons skip kundalini yoga and proceed with brahma practice. Usually a great guru emerges from deep transcendence practice and teaches brahma yoga just like that, without giving preliminary practice. Such gurus may cause even coarse materialistic persons to have divine experiences. However their effort to help ordinary persons to come up to brahma yoga practice usually turns out to be a farce. In the end, their missions become productive only to causing some moral reformation in the lives of the followers. In other words, the followers practice an imaginative brahma practice, while in fact improving their lives on the social plane by following the moral principles enunciated by the teacher.

Due to resistance for making endeavor at austerities, a great yogin may make his disciples do preliminary austerities. He will fall under their lazy influence and then will tell them that he will empower them with the necessary purity. This is a hoax. If a guru cannot make someone do the austerities, if he cannot empower someone to do these, then certainly a question arises about his influence?

September 17, 2004

Nityananda

I was in Sheffield England on this date. I considered that I may be set back since I could not do breath-infusion practice at the location. Nityananda came into my subtle bead and showed a mystic action. When this was done the thoughts, images and sounds decreased because the core self move into a cone-shaped energy above the back of the head.

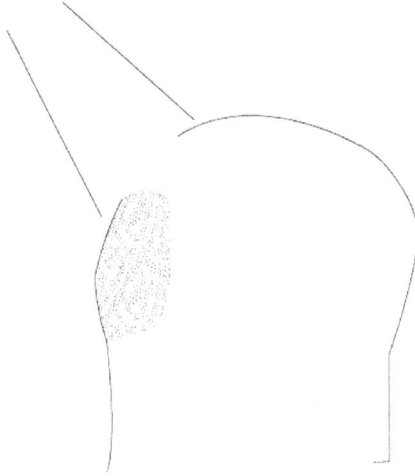

Nityananda discussed a fault of gurus where they force persons to serve them when such persons come forward for information, procedures of worship or techniques of practice. He said the forced service is wrong and that it decreases the potency of the guru. Some gurus charge money for initiations. Others charge in a way to make the disciple do menial services. All this is not part of spiritual life. If a person wants to give money or to serve, that is his concern. A guru should not set up hurdles nor pick the pockets of followers. This makes for a haphazard spiritual life for both the guru and the disciples.

Muktananda

He told me that sex is the mask of dharma, which is responsible lifestyle. After sex one must assume a responsible lifestyle, either in this life or in some other, willingly or unwillingly. He considered that it was a good system, this responsible lifestyle. He said that one should not begrudge it.

He explained that Nityananda taught him that the senses are reduced to the sense of touch or feeling. Everyone touches through audial contact, membrane contact, vision rays, tasting and smelling. These are forms of contact. To comply in higher yoga, one should cease the contacts, particularly not to touch or be touched by natural or supernatural means. The registration of the impressions of any contact is the cause of the slowness of progress in higher yoga. If one stops the registration system which involves the imagination, orb, the senses and memory, there would be conservation of psychic energy, which would lead to deep absorption.

If one could adhere to this one would master Patanjali's yoga system in a jiffy. This is the key to the rapid success in yoga practice, which was demonstrated by the supreme entities like Bhagavan Krishna, Bhagavan Balarama, or even Buddha Shakyamuni.

In this connection, I had a realization that the photo-copying ability of the mind and its delivery of impressions into the memory, is the main obstacle to transcendence absorption and insight yoga. It is the theft of impressions of odors, flavors, colors, surfaces, and sounds.

September 29, 2004

Not disturbing others

On this date I was in Sherborne, Nether Compton, England. This is South England. I realized that by controlling the appropriation instrument, one does not disturb others, even though one may suffer in their association. Materialistic persons have no idea that a saintly person, especially a yogin, suffers in their company. They feel that their selections are the very best that money and company can select. But when an advanced yogin surrenders to the conditions of their association, he does not lose anything, even though he suffers because of their ignorance and animal habits.

It is better for him to suffer under the circumstances, than to deal with their primitive resentments.

October 7, 2004

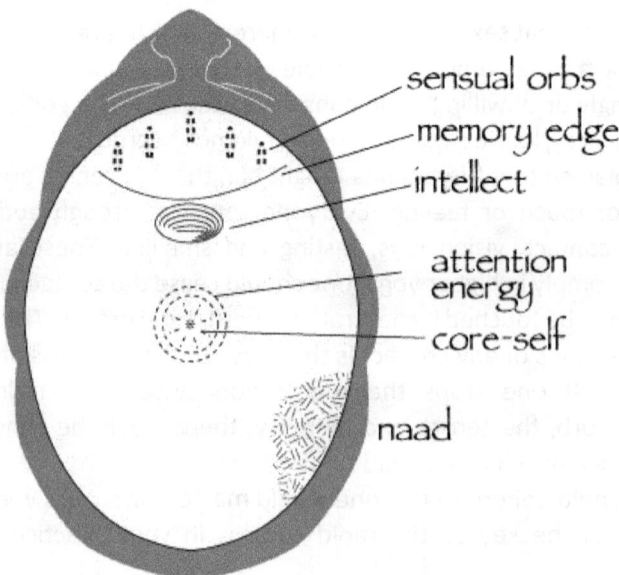

- sensual orbs
- memory edge
- intellect
- attention energy
- core-self
- naad

October 26, 2004

Parallel world

I had transferred into a parallel world, where a bright sun set behind me. There was a creation being formed of a residence for me. Suddenly a woman came who looked exactly like the wife of my current earthly life, but that person was someone else. The subtle energy in that world, formed such a body to accompany the psyche which I used when I entered that world.

Nityananda sent into my subtle head some details to remind me that my discriminating faculty was left behind near my gross body in this world. I was not able to use all the references from memory which I would have used if that experience took place in this dimension.

Due to the absence of the earthly memory, I was unable to use certain moralities which were formed this world in the current life and in other lives. This is evidence that the memory is different from the core, and so is the discrimination faculty. The idea that these aspects form one personality is incorrect. In fact what we usually term as the personality is a mock-up or a bundling of various aspects, like memory, sensual energy, discrimination, imagination, sense of identity and core self. Each of these are a separate aspect or object. If the person was the same as his memory, he would never be separate from it on any occasion. If he was the discrimination, it would not be possible for him to go to another dimension without that subtle tool. Thus one has to go this far in distinguishing the core.

October 20, 2004

Pratyahar retraction practice of intellect and senses

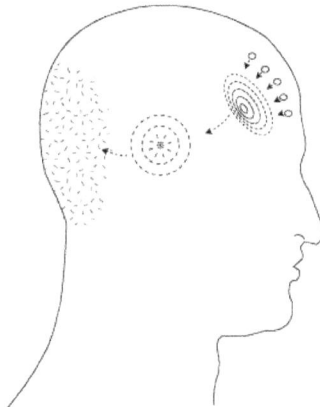

When going into parallel worlds, one usually goes with a relationship predisposition and nothing else. One does not carry the social identity from this world, nor tools like the memories of information from experiences here, nor the developed discrimination which was formed here. Of course this is easy to accept even if one has not experienced parallel worlds because when we appear through a mother's body in this world, we begin with very little discrimination. For instance, infants may eat dirt. Newborn babies will take the breast milk from any woman but later when they are sure to identify their mothers, they act in a prejudiced way to other women. It means that their presence here began with little or no discrimination.

One does however travel to different dimensions with a predisposition. Sometimes a baby cries as soon as a certain person picks up its body. This is done on the basis of an attitude towards that person which is inborn.

It is important for a yogin to study this, since he should prepare to transit from this world. Where will he be after death of his body? Whom will he be with? Into which world will he be transferred? Whom will be his friend there? Whom will be the enemy?

October 27, 2004

Nityananda

He said, "Hatha yoga as it is described by Gorakshnath is the mother of the brahma yoga practice. I recommend it."

November 2, 2004

Yogeshwarananda

We discussed the issue of the attainment of full transcendence absorption. The conclusion is that one cannot achieve it unless one has certain practices mastered. Rest and postures practice are absolutely necessary. Rest is a must. Retirement from cultural associations is a must, since responsibilities and resultant anxieties make the psyche incapable of going into full transcendence absorption. Desires must not be there, since even from a dormancy, they itch the psyche for fulfillments, causing subtle energy to remain active in the direction of this physical existence and its subtle counterpart.

November 7, 2004

Shiva's asana

On this day Babaji left the seat (asana) of Shiva. Then Nityananda took that seat.

Yogeshwarananda

He stated, "Just as naad sound has location and is heard through subtle hearing, so the jyoti light of intellect or rtambhara intellect, jnana chakshu, jnana dipa, has location and is seen through subtle vision. Naad is also intermittently perceived by some yogins. Some do not hear it, just as mental or emotional light is not seen by some.

"Supernatural sound and light are continuous but a yogin may not be in touch with either."

Yogesh said that a yogin should note how the attention energy is gathered in the naad sound. This observation may be used by the yogin to direct attention energy forward and upward into the subtle head to activate crown chakra and to find light from the spiritual sky. Sometimes a yogi remains in naad until the light from the sky of consciousness penetrates through the lower subtle energy which surrounds the core self.

November 6, 2004

Memory location

A yogin should find the location of the memory. At first he may do this by studying how the intellect contacts the memory to get images of past experiences. It will be noticed that the intellect either stays in its position or it goes forward or slightly forward and downwards, to contact the memory. Or the memory may rise and move back just a little to contact and goad the intellect, to impregnate it with impressions. This will show the yogi that memory is definitely not behind or above the intellect. In this way after such observation, a yogin can pin-point the location of the psychic faculties.

A yogin must admit also and he does this admittance by careful study in meditation, that his attention favors the intellect and memory. It does not favor naad sound. There is no sense in thinking that one's attention is so pure, so sublime, that it will favor naad, because this is not a fact; just as in this world, no matter how well respected a gentleman is, still his tendency is to favor sexual pleasure. Being cultured, he will not exhibit vulgar sexual behavior in public but that does not mean that in the final analysis he does not like sexual pleasure because the nature of his material and subtle body is to enjoy that. Similarly the memory, the sensual energy and the attention, along with the intellect, are mainly interested in working together to promote cultural involvements in this world or in a parallel world that is similar to this one. These psychic faculties may prefer a heavenly world, but still they are not interested in naad sound or in brahman as termed in the Upanishads.

November 23, 2004

Babaji

He sent a massage about raising the eyes in the head while doing naad practice. In this technique, the yogin goes back to naad sound. When he feels stabilized there he looks forward, raising the intellect energy into the top of the head. If he finds that the intellect energy is heavy, he should release it and return into naad and remain there for a longer period of time, before attempting to lift the intellect again.

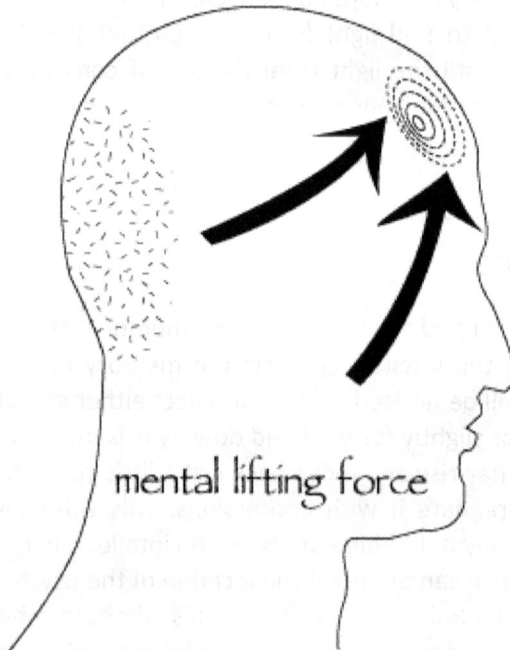

mental lifting force

The intellect does not favor naad. It prefers the memory, the senses and their gimmicks. Thus one has to stay in naad for long periods of time, in order to subdue the intellect. Otherwise if one tries to come forward in the subtle head, one will be defeated by the memory, senses and their operations.

Yogeshwarananda preferred if I meditated in a dark cave. However I use dark colored cotton fabric, which is wrapped around my head. This may be used to simulate the darkness one would get in a cave. One should be sure that the nostrils are not covered by the cloth. The idea is to cover the skull so that light does not enter into the head.

November 28, 2004

Naad

Naad sound is usually heard on the right back part of the head, just by the right ear. However it may be heard all around the head. Sometimes, one hears it on the left side or coming from the back. It may ascend the sushumna nadi subtle spine. It may manifest from the causal cove which is in the middle of the chest.

November 30, 2004

Naad / Memory

A yogin, once he gets used to listening to naad, and once he finds that his psyche is no longer adverse to it, may practice to bring the mouth of the memory to naad. This will cause the memory to become favorable to acceptance of the sound and energy of naad. At first the attention will transmit impressions from naad into the memory but the memory will act indifferently to this. It will not be eager for this even though it will be eager for anything imagined by the imagination orb. However noticing this bad attitude of the memory, a yogin should not be discouraged.

One should also try to encourage the vision energy in the subtle head to see naad energy. At first the vision energy will be indifferent but after a time, as it takes cues from the listening energy, the vision power will begin to see little slashes of color energy in naad. It will feel that these are not sufficient to hold its interest, but the yogin may still encourage the vision energy to focus into naad.

The question is that if the yogin does not practice to develop himself for entry into the spiritual atmosphere, then who will? Will the Guru or the God do this for him?

Please be reasonable with yourself. Practice to attain this. Do not fool yourself. Do not think that someone else will do these austerities and that you will benefit from the effort of another person.

After long practice, when the intellect is willing, it will move to the back into naad. At first it will resist moving back due to its attachment to the sensual energy and memory, but after a time, it will give up this attachment. Then it will move back into naad. When it does that it will appear to have shrunk in size and influence.

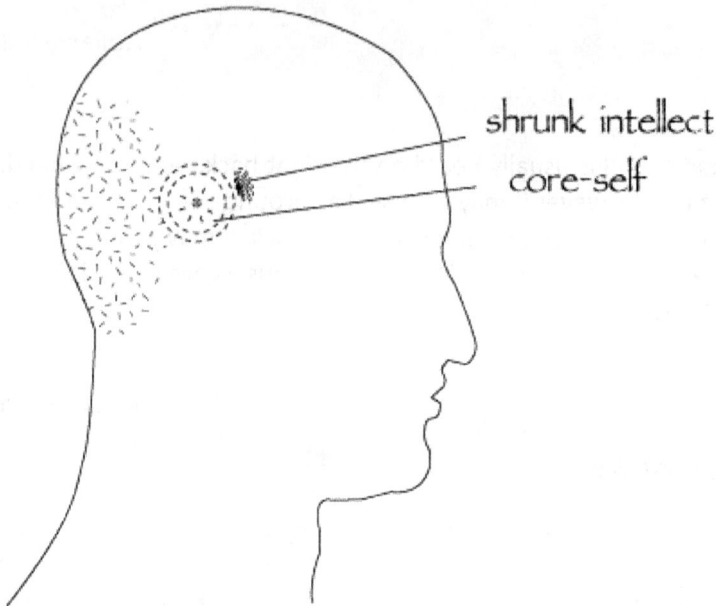

shrunk intellect
core-self

December, 4, 2004

Vice of intellect

A yogin has to admit that his intellect is attached to the memory, the sensual energies and the intellect's bad habits like imagining and impulsive analyzing. When the yogin tries to take the intellect to naad, it will resist. Sometimes he may be successful taking it there in the back right side of the head, but soon after he will find that it escaped silently without his being aware when it did. He will find himself looking at its imaginings in the forms of pictures and sounds. This will happen repeatedly but he should not cease yoga when he faces this.

If the intellect is a strong enemy, one should not desist from curbing it. Even if it takes many years to do so, one should assume the challenge to get it controlled.

December 11, 2004

Krpalvananda

This yogi said that the attention rays have the ability to lengthen or shorten, all depending on the objective being investigated. He said that the length of the rays is determined by what is to be contacted, either the memory, the sensual energy or an imagination. The rays go out and make contact according to the psychic distance to be traveled in reaching either of these faculties.

A yogin can stop the rays from reaching the memory or sensuality. Then he saves himself from exposure to non-yogic energies.

When the attention rays hit the sensual orb, there arises a desire for sensing externally. But there is also an interest which is developed in the memory, which serves as a reference for everything. Memories come up by the attention rays which hit the memory casement. There is thinking and analyzing when the attention rays hit the intellect.

If the attention is restrained, there will be less interference during meditation.

Krpalvananda feels that a yogin can train his attention to give up its addictive focus on the memory, sensual energy and imagination faculty. The yogin can retract his attention, keep its rays shortened and restrain it from contacting the intellect, memory and sensual energy which is outward-seeking.

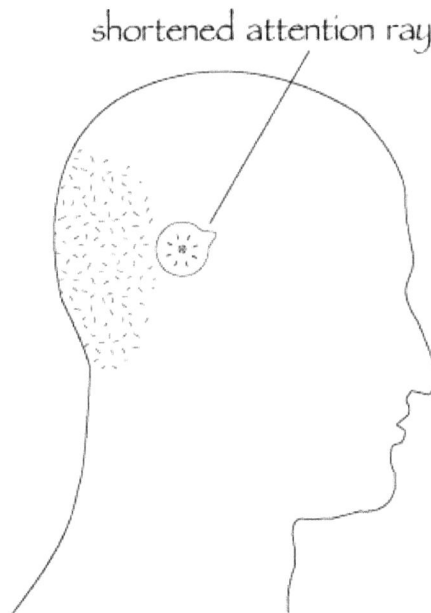

shortened attention ray

December 15, 2004

Krpalvananda

He said that the sleep influence can be curbed by proper rest, decrease of anxieties and not over-taxing the psychological and physical systems.

Yogesh gave a technique. In this the attention rays are like short stubs, such that the attention does not protrude far. They are focused upwards in the subtle head.

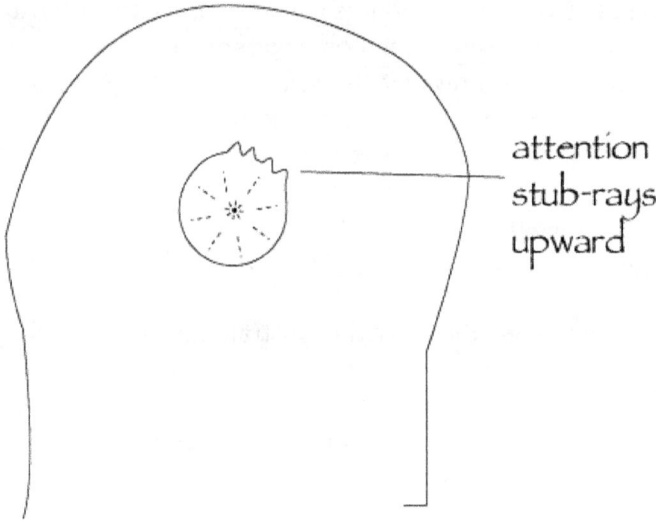

attention
stub-rays
upward

He explained that things going into the memory will resurface. A yogin must protect the memory chamber. He should not feel that he can transcend the images and impressions at a later date. It is not like that. Whatever he allowed into the memory will resurface to interfere with higher meditation. The memory entrance or mouth must be protected.

Index

E

F

G

H

About the Author

Michael Beloved (Yogi *Madhvāchārya*) took his current body in 1951 in Guyana. In 1965, while living in Trinidad, he instinctively began doing yoga postures and tried to make sense of the supernatural side of life.

Later in 1970, in the Philippines, he approached a Martial Arts Master named Arthur Beverford. He explained to the teacher that he was seeking a yoga instructor. Mr. Beverford identified himself as an advanced disciple of *Śrī* Rishi Singh Gherwal, an Ashtanga Yoga master.

Beverford taught the traditional Ashtanga Yoga with stress on postures, attentive breathing and brow chakra centering meditation. In 1972, Michael entered the Denver, Colorado Ashram of *kundalini* yoga Master *Śrī* Harbhajan Singh. There he took instruction in bhastrika pranayama and its application to yoga postures. He was supervised mostly by Yogi Bhajan's disciple named Prem Kaur.

In 1979 Michael formally entered the disciplic succession of the Brahmā - Madhava-Gaudiya Sampradaya through *Swāmī* Kirtanananda, who was a prominent sannyasi disciple of the Great Vaishnava Authority *Śrī Swāmī* Bhaktivedanta Prabhupada, the exponent of devotion to Sri Krishna.

However, yoga has a mystic side to it, thus Michael took training and teaching empowerment from several spiritual masters of different aspects of spiritual development. This is consistent with *Śrī* Krishna's advice to Arjuna in the *Bhagavad Gītā*:

Most of the instructions Michael received were given in the astral world. On that side of existence, his most prominent teachers were *Śrī Swāmī* Shivananda of Rishikesh, Yogiraj *Swāmī* Vishnudevananda, *Śrī Bābāji Mahasaya* - the master of the masters of *Kriyā* Yoga, *Śrīla* Yogeshwarananda of Gangotri - the master of the masters of *Rāj* Yoga (spiritual clarity), and Siddha *Swāmī* Nityananda the Brahmā Yoga authority.

The course for kundalini yoga using pranayama breath-infusion was detailed by Michael in the book *Kundalini Hatha Yoga Pradipika*. This current book was composed from meditation and breath-infusion notes which were originally shared in staple bound booklets as Yoga Journals.

Michael's preliminary books relating to this topic are *Meditation Pictorial*, *Meditation Expertise*, and *Meditation ~ Sense Faculty* (co-author). Every technique (kriya) mentioned was tested by him during pranayama breath-infusion and *samyama* deep meditation practice.

This is a result of over forty years of meditation practice with astute subtle observations intending to share the methods and experiences. The information is published freely with no intention of forming an institution or hogtying anyone as a disciple.

Publications

English Series

Bhagavad Gita English

Anu Gita English

Markandeya Samasya English

Yoga Sutras English

Hatha Yoga Pradipika English

Uddhava Gita English

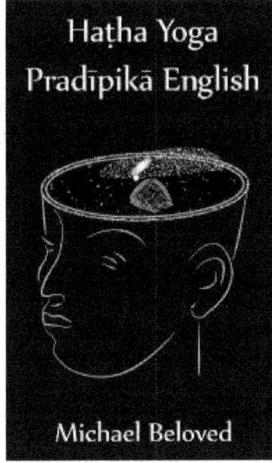

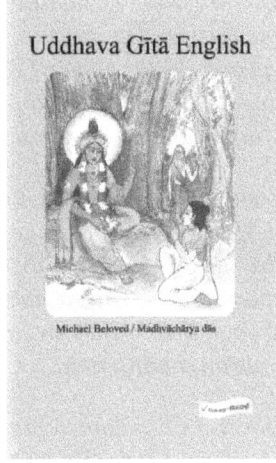

These are in 21ˢᵗ Century English, very precise and exacting. Many Sanskrit words which were considered untranslatable into a Western language are rendered in precise, expressive and modern English.

Three of these books are instructions from Krishna. **In Bhagavad Gita English** *and* **Anu Gita English**, *the instructions were for Arjuna. In the* **Uddhava Gita English,** *it was for Uddhava. Bhagavad Gita and Anu Gita are extracted from the Mahabharata. Uddhava Gita was extracted from the 11ᵗʰ Canto of the Srimad Bhagavatam (Bhagavata Purana). One of these books, the* **Markandeya Samasya English** *is about Krishna, as described by Yogi Markandeya, who survived the cosmic collapse and reached a divine child in whose transcendental body, the collapsed world was existing.*

Two of this series are the syllabus about yoga practice. The Yoga Sutras of Patanjali is elaboration about ashtanga yoga. Hatha Yoga Pradipika English, is the detailed information about asana postures, pranayama breath- infusion, energy compression, naad sound resonance and advanced meditation. The Sanskrit author is Swatmarama Mahayogin.

My suggestion is that you read **Bhagavad Gita English**, *the* **Anu Gita English, the Markandeya Samasya English**, *the* **Yoga Sutras English**, *the* **Hatha Yoga Pradipika** *and lastly the* **Uddhava Gita English**, *which is complicated and detailed.*

For each of these books we have at least one commentary, which is published separately. Thus your particular interest can be researched further in the commentaries.

The smallest of these commentaries and perhaps the simplest is the one for the Anu Gita. We published its commentary as the Anu Gita Explained. *The*

Bhagavad Gita explanations were published in three distinct targeted commentaries. The first is <u>Bhagavad Gita Explained</u>, which sheds lights on how people in the time of Krishna and Arjuna regarded the information and applied it. Bhagavad Gita is an exposition of the application of yoga practice to cultural activities, which is known in the Sanskrit language as karma yoga.

Interestingly, Bhagavad Gita was spoken on a battlefield just before one of the greatest battles in the ancient world. A warrior, Arjuna, lost his wits and had no idea that he could apply his training in yoga to political dealings. Krishna, his charioteer, lectured on the spur of the moment to give Arjuna the skill of using yoga proficiency in cultural dealings including how to deal with corrupt officials on a battlefield.

The second Gita commentary is the <u>Kriya Yoga Bhagavad Gita</u>. This clears the air about Krishna's information on the science of kriya yoga, showing that its techniques are clearly described for anyone who takes the time to read Bhagavad Gita. Kriya yoga concerns the battlefield which is the psyche of the living being. The internal war and the mental and emotional forces which are hostile to self-realization are dealt with in the kriya yoga practice.

The third commentary is the <u>Brahma Yoga Bhagavad Gita</u>. This shows what Krishna had to say outright and what he hinted about which concerns the brahma yoga practice, a mystic process for those who mastered kriya yoga.

*There is one commentary for the **Markandeya Samasya English**. The title of that publication is <u>Krishna Cosmic Body</u>.*

There are two commentaries to the Yoga Sutras. One is the <u>Yoga Sutras of Patanjali</u> and the other is the <u>Meditation Expertise</u>. These give detailed explanations of ashtanga Yoga.

The commentary of Hatha Yoga Pradipika is titled <u>Kundalini Hatha Yoga Pradipika</u>.

For the Uddhava Gita, we published the <u>Uddhava Gita Explained</u>. This is a large book and requires concentration and study for integration of the information. Of the books which deal with transcendental topics, my opinion is that the discourse between Krishna and Uddhava has the complete information about the realities in existence. This book is the one which removes massive existential ignorance.

Meditation Series

Meditation Pictorial

Meditation Expertise

Core-Self Discovery

Meditation Sense Faculty

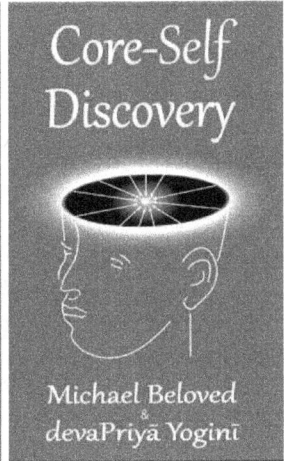

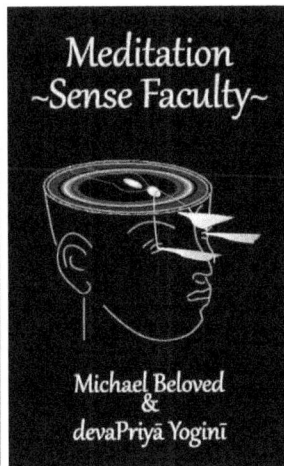

The specialty of these books is the mind diagrams which profusely illustrate what is written. This shows exactly what one has to do mentally to develop and then sustain a meditation practice.

*In the **Meditation Pictorial**, one is shown how to develop psychic insight, a feature without which meditation is imagination and visualization, without any mystic experience per se.*

*In the **Meditation Expertise**, one is shown how to corral one's practice to bring it in line with the classic syllabus of yoga which Patanjali lays out as the ashtanga yoga eight-staged practice.*

*In **Core-Self Discovery**, (co-authored with devaPriya Yogini) one is taken though the course of pratyahar sensual energy withdrawal which is the 5th stage of yoga in the Patanjali ashtanga eight-process complete system of yoga practice. These events lead to the discovery of a core-self which is surrounded by psychic organs in the head of the subtle body. This product has a DVD component.*

***Meditation ~ Sense Faculty** (co-authored with devaPriya Yogini) is a detailed tutorial with profuse diagrams showing what actions to take in the subtle body to investigate the senses faculties. The meditator must first establish the location and function of the observing self. That self must be screened from the thoughts and ideas which usually hypnotize it.*

These books are profusely illustrated with mind diagrams showing the components of psychic consciousness and the inner design of the subtle body.

Explained Series

Bhagavad Gita Explained

Uddhava Gita Explained

Anu Gita Explained

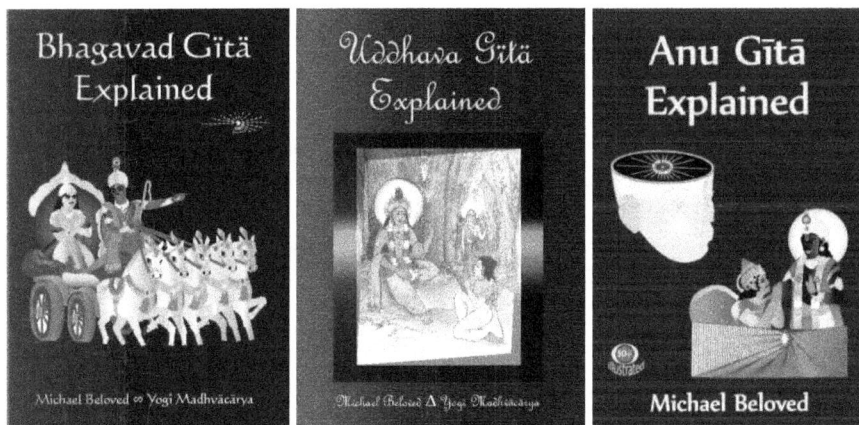

The specialty of these books is that they are free of missionary intentions, cult tactics and philosophical distortion. Instead of using these books to add credence to a philosophy, meditation process, belief or plea for followers, I spread the information out so that a reader can look through this literature and freely take or leave anything as desired.

When Krishna stressed himself as God, I stated that. When Krishna laid no claims for supremacy, I showed that. The reader is left to form an independent opinion about the validity of the information and the credibility of Krishna.

There is a difference in the discourse with Arjuna in the Bhagavad Gita and the one with Uddhava in the Uddhava Gita. In fact these two books may appear to contradict each other. In the Bhagavad Gita, Krishna pressured Arjuna to complete social duties. In the Uddhava Gita, Krishna insisted that Uddhava should abandon the same.

The Anu Gita is not as popular as the Bhagavad Gita but it is the conclusion of that text. Anu means what is to follow, what proceeds. In this discourse, an anxious Arjuna request that Krishna should repeat the Bhagavad Gita and again show His supernatural and divine forms.

However Krishna refuses to do so and chastises Arjuna for being a disappointment in forgetting what was revealed. Krishna then cited a celestial yogi, a near-perfected being, who explained the process of transmigration in vivid detail.

Commentaries

Yoga Sutras of Patanjali

Meditation Expertise

Krishna Cosmic Body

Anu Gita Explained

Bhagavad Gita Explained

Kriya Yoga Bhagavad Gita

Brahma Yoga Bhagavad Gita

Uddhava Gita Explained

Kundalini Hatha Yoga Pradipika

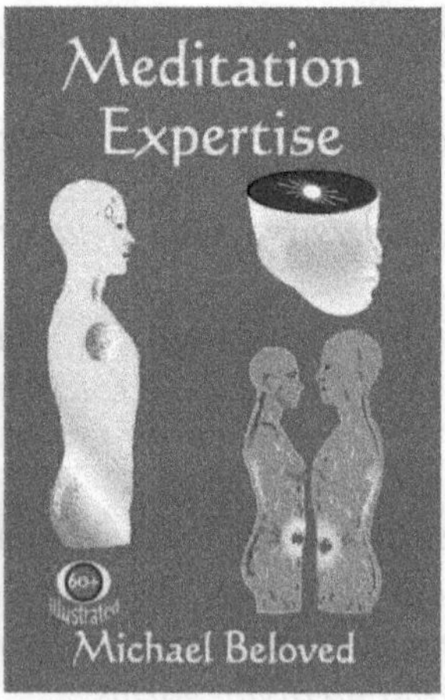

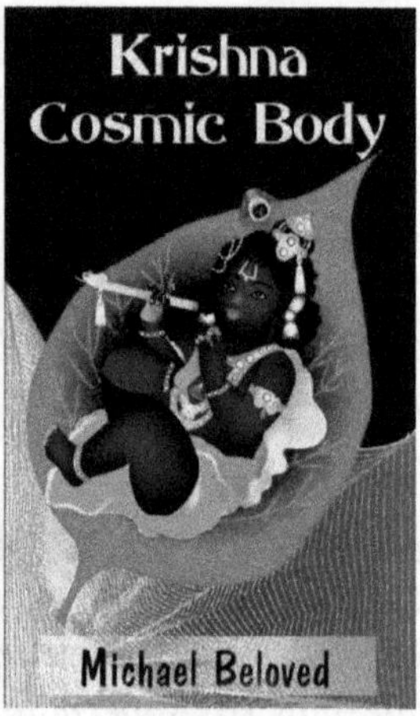

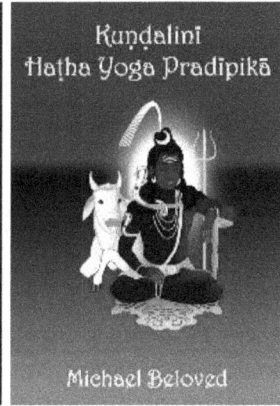

Yoga Sutras of Patanjali is the globally acclaimed text book of yoga. This has detailed expositions of yoga techniques. Many kriya techniques are vividly described in the commentary.

Meditation Expertise is an analysis and application of the Yoga Sutras. This book is loaded with illustrations and has detailed explanations of secretive advanced meditation techniques which are called kriyas in the Sanskrit language.

Krishna Cosmic Body is a narrative commentary on the Markandeya Samasya portion of the Aranyaka Parva of the Mahabharata. This is the detailed description of the dissolution of the world, as experienced by the great yogin Markandeya who transcended the cosmic deity, Brahma, and reached Brahma's source who is the divine infant, Krishna.

Anu Gita Explained is a detailed explanation of how we endure many material bodies in the course of transmigrating through various life-forms. This is a discourse between Krishna and Arjuna. Arjuna requested of Krishna a display of the Universal Form and a repeat narration of the Bhagavad Gita but Krishna declined and explained what a siddha perfected being told the Yadu family about the sequence of existences one endures and the systematic flow of those lives at the convenience of material nature.

Bhagavad Gita Explained *shows what was said in the Gita without religious overtones and sectarian biases.*

Kriya Yoga Bhagavad Gita *shows the instructions for those who are doing kriya yoga.*

Brahma Yoga Bhagavad Gita *shows the instructions for those who are doing brahma yoga.*

Uddhava Gita Explained *shows the instructions to Uddhava which are more advanced than the ones given to Arjuna.*

Bhagavad Gita is an instruction for applying the expertise of yoga in the cultural field. This is why the process taught to Arjuna is called karma yoga which means karma + yoga or cultural activities done with yogic insight.

Uddhava Gita is an instruction for apply the expertise of yoga to attaining spiritual status. This is why it is explains jnana yoga and bhakti yoga in detail. Jnana yoga is using mystic skill for knowing the spiritual part of existence. Bhakti yoga is for developing affectionate relationships with divine beings.

Karma yoga is for negotiating the social concerns in the material world. It is inferior to bhakti yoga which concerns negotiating the social concerns in the spiritual world.

This world has a social environment. The spiritual world has one too.

*Currently, Uddhava Gita is the most advanced and informative spiritual book on the planet. There is nothing anywhere which is superior to it or which goes into so much detail as it. It verified that historically Krishna is the most advanced human being to ever have left literary instructions on this planet. Even Patanjali Yoga Sutras which I translated and gave an application for in my book, **Meditation Expertise**, does not go as far as the Uddhava Gita.*

Some of the information of these two books is identical but while the Yoga Sutras are concerned with the personal spiritual emancipation (kaivalyam) of the individual spirits, the Uddhava Gita explains that and also explains the situations in the spiritual universes.

Bhagavad Gita is from the Mahabharata *which is the history of the Pandavas. Arjuna, the student of the Gita, is one of the Pandavas brothers. He was in a social hassle and did not know how to apply yoga expertise to solve it. On the battlefield, Krishna gave him a crash-course on yogic social interactions.*

Uddhava Gita is from the Srimad Bhagavatam (Bhagavata Purana), *which is a history of the incarnations of Krishna. Uddhava was a relative of Krishna. He was concerned about the situation of the deaths of many of his relatives but Krishna diverted Uddhava's attention to the practice of yoga for the purpose of successfully migrating to the spiritual environment.*

Kundalini Hatha Yoga Pradipika *is the commentary for the Hatha Yoga Pradipika of Swatmarama Mahayogin. This is the detailed process about asana posture, pranayama breath-infusion, complex compressions of energy, naad sound resonance intonement and advanced meditation practice.*

This is the singular book with all the techniques of how to reform and redesign the subtle body so that it does not have the tendency for physical life forms and for it to attain the status of a siddha.

These books are based on the author's experiences in meditation, yoga practice and participation in spiritual groups:

Specialty

Spiritual Master

sex you!

Sleep Paralysis

Astral Projection

Masturbation Psychic Details

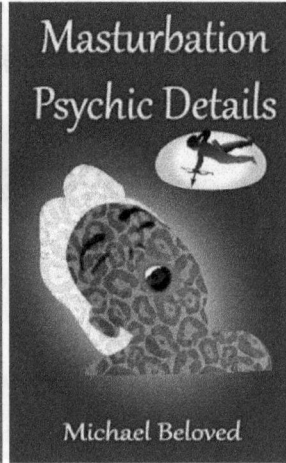

In **Spiritual Master**, *Michael draws from experience with gurus or with their senior students. His contact with astral gurus is rated. He walks you through the avenue of gurus showing what you should do and what you should not do, so as to gain proficiency in whatever area of spirituality the guru has proficiency.*

sex you! *is a masterpiece about the adventures of an individual spirit's passage through the parents' psyches. The conversion of a departed soul into a sexual urge is described. The transit from the afterlife to residency in the emotions of the parents is detailed. This is about sex and you. Learn about how much of you comprises the romantic energy of your would-be parents!*

Sleep Paralysis *clears misconceptions so that one can see what sleep paralysis is and what frightening astral experience occurs while the paralysis is being* *experienced. This disempowerment has great value in giving you confidence that you can and do exist even if you are unable to operate the physical body. The implication is that one can exist apart from and will survive the loss of the material form.*

Astral Projection *details experiences Michael had even in childhood, where he assumed incorrectly that everyone was astrally conversant. He discusses the life force psychic mechanism which operates the sleep-wake cycle of the physical form, and which budgets energy into the separated astral form which determines if the individual will have dream recall or no objective awareness during the projections. Astral travel happens on every occasion when the physical body sleeps. What is missing in awareness is the observer status while the astral body is separated.*

Masturbation Psychic Details *is a surprise presentation which relates what happens on the psychic plane during a masturbation event. This does not tackle moral issues or even addictions but shows the involvement of memory and the sure but hidden subconscious mind which operates many features of the psyche irrespective of the desire or approval of the self-conscious personality.*

inVision Series

Yoga inVision 1

Yoga inVision 2

Yoga inVision 3

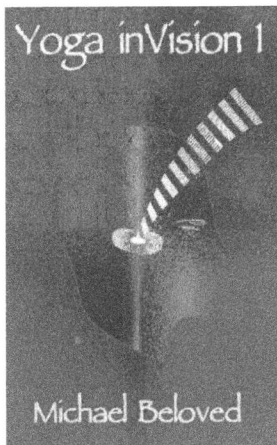

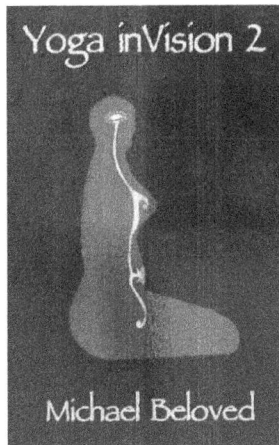

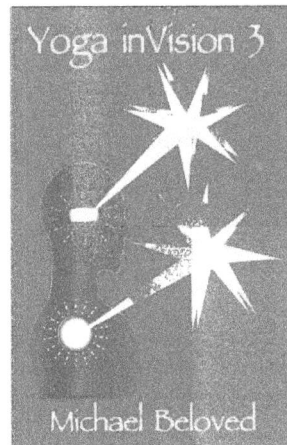

Yoga inVision 1, the first in this series, describes the breath-infusion and meditation practices during the years of 1998 and 1999. There are unique, once in a lifetime as well as recurring insights which are elaborated. inFocus during breath-infusion and the meditation which follows is an adventure for any yogi. This gives what happened to this particular ascetic.

Yoga inVision 2 reports on the author's experiences from 1999 to 2001. Each day the experience is unique, illustrating the vibrancy of practice. Many rare once-in-a-lifetime perceptions are described.

Yoga inVision 3 reports on the author's experiences from 2001 to 2003.

Online Resources

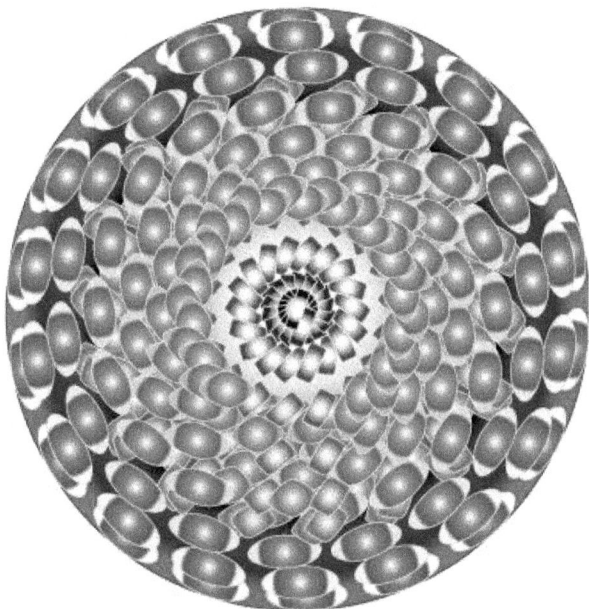

Email:	**michaelbelovedbooks@gmail.com**
	axisnexus@gmail.com
Website:	**michaelbeloved.com**
Forum:	**inselfyoga.com**
Posters:	**zazzle.com/inself**